A DREAMSPEAKER CRU

VOLUME 5

MW01000470

The Broughtons

AND VANCOUVER ISLAND— KELSEY BAY TO PORT HARDY

ANNE & LAURENCE YEADON-JONES

FINE EDGE

Nautical & Recreational Publishing

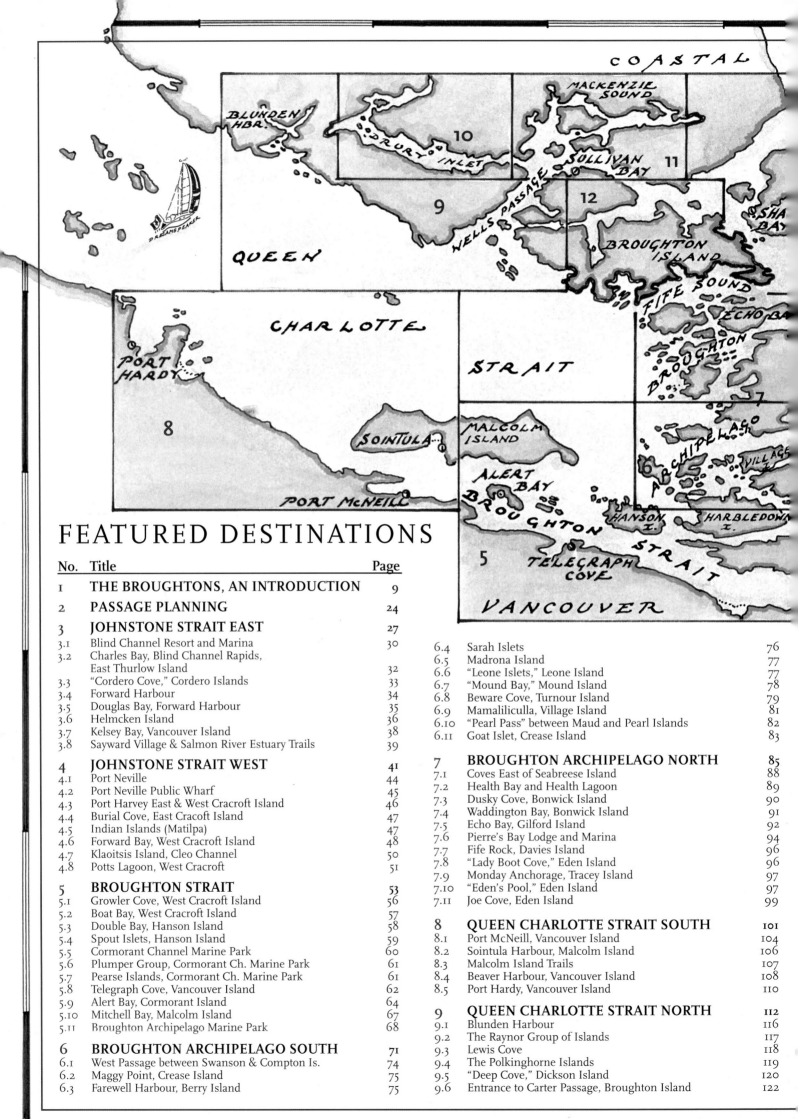

FEATURED DESTINATIONS

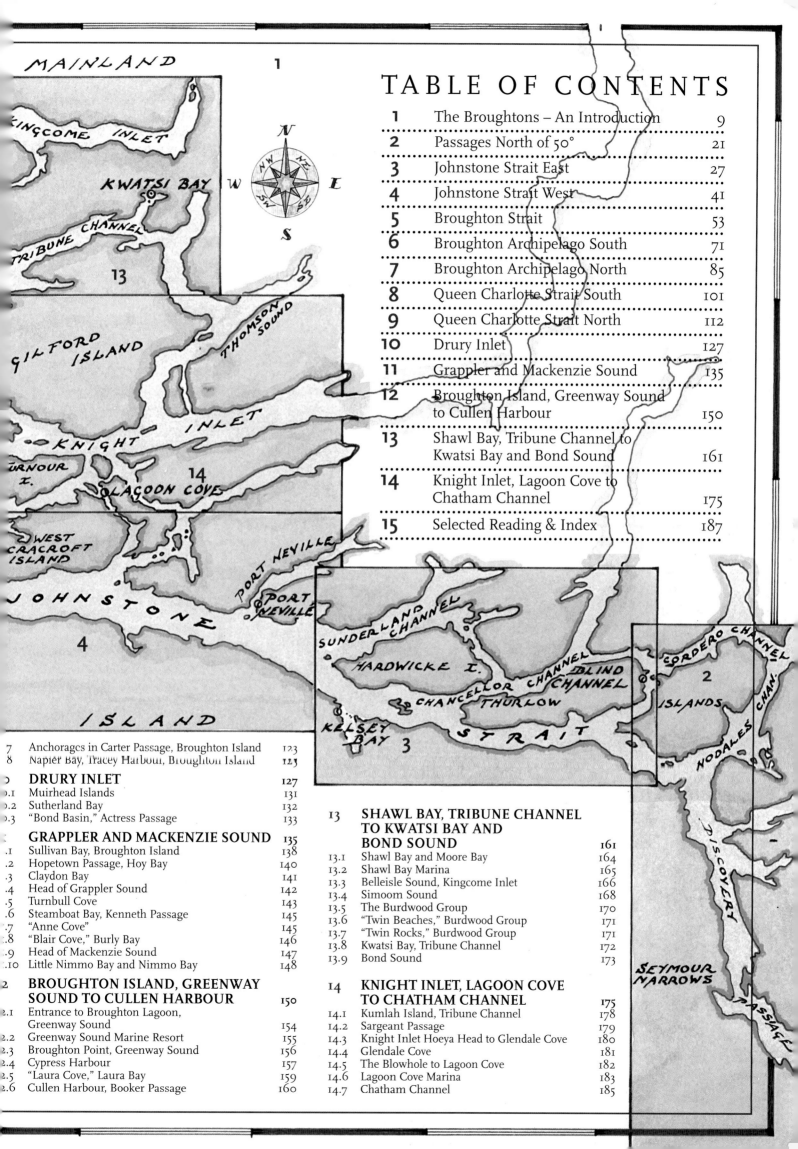

TABLE OF CONTENTS

Moored in Echo Bay back by the landmark rock bluff

Published in the U.S. by
FineEdge.com LLC
14004 Biz Point Lane
Anacortes, WA 98221
www.FineEdge.com

Edited by Mark and Leslie Bunzel
Copyedited by Pat Hillis
Composition by Melanie Haage

Address requests for permission to:
FineEdge.com LLC, 14004 Biz Point Lane, Anacortes, WA 98221
www.FineEdge.com

Printed in China.

Caution: This book is meant to provide experienced boaters with cruising information about the waters covered. The suggestions offered are not all-inclusive and, due to the possibility of differences of interpretation, oversights and factual errors, none of the information contained in this book is warranted to be accurate or appropriate for any purpose other than the pursuit of great adventuring and memorable voyages. *A Dreamspeaker Cruising Guide* should be viewed as a guide only and not as a substitute for official government charts, tide and current tables, coast pilots, sailing directions and local notices to boaters. Excerpts from charts are for passage planning only and are not to be used for navigation. Shoreline plans are not to scale and are not to be used for navigation. The publisher and authors cannot accept any responsibility for misadventure resulting from the use of this guide and can accept no liability for damages incurred.

Library of Congress Cataloging-in-Publication Data

Yeadon-Jones, Anne.
  The Broughtons and Vancouver Island : Kelsy Bay to Port Hardy
/ Anne and Laurence Yeadon-Jones.
    p. cm. -- (A Dreamspeaker cruising guide ; v. 5)
  Includes index.
  ISBN-13: 978-1-932310-17-7 (pbk.)
    1. Boats and boating--British Columbia--Broughton Strait--Guide-books. 2. Boats and boating--British Columbia--Vancouver Island --Guidebooks. 3. Pilot guides--British Columbia--Broughton Strait --Guidebooks. 4. Pilot guides--British Columbia--Vancouver Island --Guidebooks. 5. Broughton Strait (B.C.)--Guidebooks.
  6. Vancouver Island (B.C.)--Guidebooks. 7. Dreamspeaker (Yacht)
I. Yeadon-Jones, Laurence. II. Title.
GV776.B76Y43 2006
797.1'2409711--dc22

2006017402

FOREWORD

Dreaming of the Broughtons

The Broughton Islands comprise the vast cruising area of British Columbia that lies between the east coast of Vancouver Island and the mainland inlets. It stretches north from about Kelsey Bay to the top end of Queen Charlotte Strait. Except for the narrow, well-travelled thoroughfare of Johnstone Strait and Queen Charlotte Strait — part of the famed Inside Passage route — it is a remote section of the coast. Due to its distance from the major economic and population centres, it remains little touched by industry or settlement. It is an area of pristine beauty where cruising boats can have an anchorage all to themselves for as long as they like. It is an area so jam-packed with winding waterways and places to explore that one could spend a lifetime simply poking about. It's also home to some of B.C.'s more interesting destination marinas peopled by some of the province's true characters who will provide plenty of down-home hospitality and make your stay unforgettable. There is also a strong First Nations heritage, evidenced by the area's ancient pictographs, old and new villages and totems.

In this, the fifth *A Dreamspeaker Cruising Guide*, authors Anne and Laurence Yeadon-Jones have done an admirable job of trying to sort out this amazingly complex area and have done so in a way that makes it clear and accessible. This is no easy mission, and few other cruising guide authors have attempted such a daunting project. Not only have they tackled the Broughton Islands, they've also included cruising information to the east coast of Vancouver Island and the adjacent mainland inlets — a task that is almost as complex as the Broughtons.

As with their previous guides, the Yeadon-Joneses have a passion for the areas they write about and their text captures their enthusiasm and inspires the reader. The large format of the *Dreamspeaker* guides allows for numerous photos, plenty of text and Laurence's delightful and detailed hand-drawn maps. Together, the elements combine in a beautiful package that has a warm and inviting feel, but is also jam-packed with important cruising information.

Peter A. Robson
Editor, *Pacific Yachting Magazine*

The Authors, Dreamspeaker *and* Tink *in Sullivan Bay*

SPECIAL THANKS TO:

Broadband Express; Marine Wireless Broadband Network – who kept us well connected while researching this guide – www.bbxpress.net

Corilair – for their efficient floatplane service between Vancouver Island and 'The Broughtons' – www.corilair.com

GRATEFUL APPRECIATION TO OUR INDUSTRY SUPPORT:

HUB International TOS Limited; Specialist Marine Insurance Services – www.tos.ca

Canadian Hydrographic Service (CHS) – Charts and Nautical Publications

C-Tow, Vancouver; Pacific Marine Assistance Network – www.c-tow.ca

Canon Canada Ltd., Mississauga, Ontario; camera and lenses – www.canon.com

Henshaw Inflatables Ltd., Tinker Folding Rib, www.henshaw.co.uk

Mustang Survival Ltd., Vancouver; marine safety apparel – www.mustangsurvival.com

Nautical Data International, St. John's, Newfoundland; electronic charts – www.digitalocean.ca

Nobeltec, Portland, Oregon; navigational software – www.nobeltec.com

ACKNOWLEDGEMENTS

Marion and Rob, MY Office, for their steady support and quality service.

Rob Hare at Canadian Hydrographic Service (CHS), for his assistance.

Bruce Jackman, Port McNeill Marine, for his friendly assistance in locating aerial information.

The island and coastal people for their time and encouragement while researching this guide.

Peter Robson, Pacific Yachting, for his insightful foreword.

Dorene Gould and John Lopez, for technical assistance and friendship.

The team at Fine Edge, Mark and Leslie, Melanie, Pat and Don for their fine work.

The team at Harbour Publishing, Howard, Anna, Mary and Jenny for their fine work.

Our family and friends, for their conviction that we are still sailing in the right direction.

FOR THE BOUNDLESS SPLENDOUR OF THE BROUGHTONS

EXPLORE ITS DELICATE BEAUTY WITH RESPECT AND CARE

"*More boats are going north now, and I am hoping that an increased awareness of the beauty of our coast will bring concern for our environment everywhere.*"

—*John Chappell*, Cruising Beyond Desolation Sound, 1987.

THE BROUGHTONS—
AN INTRODUCTION

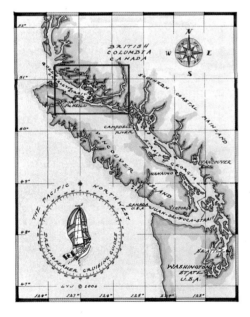

Chapter I
THE BROUGHTONS — AN INTRODUCTION

CUSTOMS

Call 1-888-226-7277 (8:30 a.m. – 3:40 p.m.) seven days a week. The ports of entry covered by this guide for recreational boaters entering Canadian waters are located in Campbell River at the Coast Marina, 250-287-7455 and Discovery Harbour Marina, 250-287-2614. Prince Rupert, on the Mainland, is the next customs port of entry.

HOLDING TANKS AND PUMP-OUT STATIONS

All craft should use their holding tanks while moored or at anchor. Pump-out stations available in Port McNeill and Port Hardy, or in deep water away from communities or aqua-culture installations.

A memorial totem pole in Alert Bay

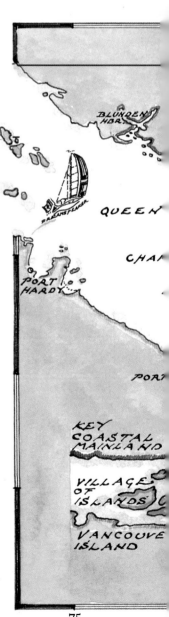

NOTE: All numbers on borders are distances in nautical miles. All depths indicated on illustrated charts are in metres.

In Canada's Pacific Northwest, mid-coast on British Columbia's vast and intricate coastline, lies a region known simply as The Broughtons – an area that hosts British Columbian and Washington State recreational boaters and is fast becoming internationally renowned for its spectacular beauty and abundant wildlife.

On a chart The Broughtons resemble a complex jigsaw puzzle, with the joints between pieces being navigable water. This puzzle is really quite simple and comprises three main components:

The Coastal Mainland anchors the region at 51° north and its backdrop of snow-capped mountains is deeply indented by sounds, channels and sinuous inlets.

"The Village of Islands" – the Broughton Archipelago – is a maze of islands and islets that creates a plethora of anchorages and one-boat hideaways. Family-run marinas offer fuelling, moorage and provisioning facilities, allowing boaters to intersperse their quiet explorations with a night or two of socializing with friends or new acquaintances, while enjoying the local trails, a hot shower, the convenience of laundry facilities, and the happy-hour gatherings and communal potluck suppers.

Northern Vancouver Island's mountainous backbone forms a rain shadow and natural breakwater from the Pacific Ocean, shielding The Broughtons and creating a gentle and temperate rain-coast paradise.

Cruising boaters will find that it's as much an adventure getting there as it is exploring the area's unspoilt wilderness and rich diversity of bird and wildlife. Take your time while cruising through The Broughtons to uncover the coast's 12,000-year history layered between the ancient white-shell midden beaches and clam gardens of the Kwakiutl First Nations to the first European settlers.

KEY DESTINATIONS—EAST TO WEST

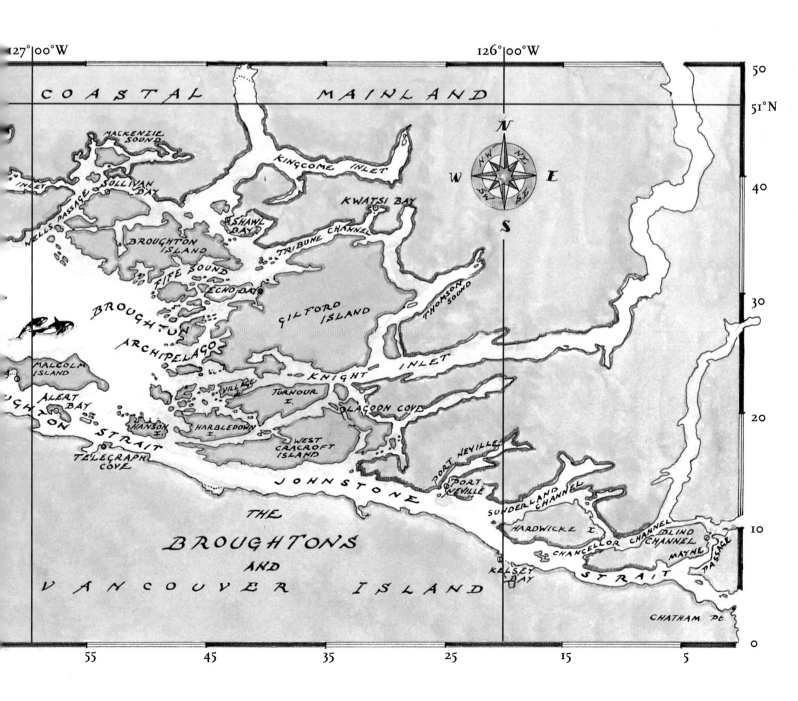

HISTORY AND WILDLIFE PROTOCOL

Canoe shaped serving dish by Sam Charlie, given to Bill —

The proliferation of white-shell midden beaches in the Broughton Archipelago give evidence to the large population of First Nations (Kwakiutl) people that lived in the area over 10,000 years ago; 4,000 years ago, more than 20,000 indigenous people lived in the region between Blunden Harbour and Broken Islands.

Local fisherman and environmentalist Bill Proctor, who has called the Broughton neighbourhood home for 60 years, knows of over 200 village sites where larger villages were populated by as many as 400 people. Daily activities for the men included fishing, hunting, building canoes, carving totem poles from cedar tree trunks and constructing homes and ceremonial houses using cedar planks and split cedar boards. Women took care of gathering food, smoking fish and game, family and home activities and producing clothing from soft cedar bark.

British explorer Capt. Cook, along with Spanish explorers Dioniso Alcala Galiano and Cayetano Valdes were the first European explorers to discover and investigate the Inside Passage of the Pacific Northwest in the late 1770s. A follow-up British expedition to claim the Pacific Northwest for the crown was led by Capt. George Vancouver; while surveying the region in HMS *Chatham* during the early 1790s, he named Broughton Strait and Broughton Archipelago for Lt. Commander William Robert Broughton, who was responsible for conducting the survey.

During the early to mid-1800s, trade (especially otter furs) with First Nation communities was significant, although after the devastating 1870s smallpox epidemic the coastal indigenous population declined by more than 60 percent. During the late 1800s and early 1900s, a large number of European settlers moved to the area and introduced farming, logging, fishing and mining; we see evidence of these occupations today in the remains of homesteads and farms, ruins of logging operations and canning factories, and abandoned mines.

PETROGLYPHS AND PICTOGRAPHS

Petroglyphs, or ancient Native Indian rock carvings, are pictures carved into rocks and cliffs, while pictographs are rock paintings using natural dyes made from roots and berries. Both include a variety of images from "mythological animals made with flowering, curving lines, to flat fish and birds and little human stick figures in a brittle dance," which give us an insight into the prehistoric world of the Indian people in the Pacific Northwest. Please respect these ancient sites, which are often found on private property and require prior permission to visit. In this volume, the accessible, recorded sites can be found in Forward Harbour, Port Neville Narrows, Robber's Knobb, Port Neville, Fort Rupert and Lizard Point, Malcolm Island. (See selected reading, Beth Hill's *Rock Carvings of the Pacific Northwest* and Judith Williams' *Two Wolves at the Dawn of Time*.)

The delightful pen and ink drawings on these pages have been kindly provided by artist Yvonne Maximchuk, and appear in Full Moon Flood Tide *by Bill Proctor and Yvonne Maximchuk.*

Yvonne is a working artist and teacher, proficient in watercolour and acrylic media as well as drawing and pottery techniques – she is also a naturalist and avid gardener and offers Art Retreats at SeaRose Studio on Gilford Island, her seaside home with an abundant coastal garden and fabulous view. Visit her web site at: www.zoombuy.net/searose.html

ANCIENT SHELL MIDDENS AND CLAM GARDENS OR TERRACES

Most Indian villages were built above large clam beaches, in good sunny spots, and shell middens were formed over thousands of years of harvesting clams and depositing their shells on the beaches. Clam gardens or terraces, however, were well-tended clam beaches protected by a ring of rocks piled along the low-tide perimeter, often with a clear space left for landing canoes. These gardens often served a dual purpose during herring season when hemlock boughs were used to trap quantities of these nutritious fish between the rocks. There are over 300 recorded sites in the Broughton Archipelago and numerous other sites from Orcas Island in Washington State to as far north as Sitka, Alaska, have also been documented. Evidence shows that these clam gardens may be totally unique in the world. (See selected reading, Bill Proctor, *Full Moon Flood Tide* and Judith Williams' *Clam Gardens: Aboriginal Mariculture on Canada's West Coast*.)

CULTURALLY MODIFIED TREES

"Culturally Modified Trees (CMTs) are large, old red cedar trees that the First Nations people flattened off on one side to split off boards usually three feet wide and about four inches thick," to use in the construction of their villages. – Bill Proctor, *Full Moon Flood Tide*.

WILDLIFE PROTOCOL: GRIZZLY AND BLACK BEARS

"Bears are most active before 10 a.m. and after 4 p.m., and they tend to bed down during the middle of the day. When walking in bear country, always be alert and look out for bear sign, and always make a bit of a noise as not to startle a bear. Bears have very poor eyesight but they have a good nose. If the wind is at your back, most bears will smell you and be gone before you ever see them. Don't ever think that you can outrun a bear, don't try to feed one and don't ever get between a mother and her cub," (Bill Proctor, *Full Moon Flood Tide*). The owners of Kwatsi Bay Marina advise visitors to take along a fog/air horn when hiking in the area, as they have found that this is one of the most effective ways to let bears know that you are around as their ears are very sensitive to the sound of a horn. For more detailed information on bear safety visit the WSPA (World Society for the Protection of Animals) at www.wspa.ca.

CMT – Burdwood Group

WILDLIFE PROTOCOL: WHALES, PORPOISES, DOLPHINS, SEALS, SEA LIONS AND BIRDS ON LAND

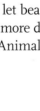

As the number of visiting boats increases, the need to minimize our impact on marine animals and birdlife is imperative, and regulations in Canada and the U.S. prohibit any harassment and disturbance, which includes the interference with an animal's ability to hunt, feed, communicate, socialize, rest, breed and care for its young. Avoid approaching closer than 100 metres to any marine mammals or birds.

When observing whales, reduce speed to less than 7 knots when within 400 metres of them. Avoid abrupt course changes, and limit your viewing time to a maximum of 30 minutes. If possible, do not approach whales from the front or behind – always approach or leave from the side, moving in a direction parallel to their direction. Stay on the off-shore side of any whales when they are travelling close to shore, and remain at least 200 metres off-shore at all times. For more detailed information, visit www.nmfs.noaa.gov/pr/education/viewing.htm.

WEATHER

At dawn a weather front passes over Forward Harbour

There are only two marine forecast areas that cover the Broughton region east to west – Johnstone Strait and Queen Charlotte Strait.

Marine forecasts and warnings are available in the Broughton region as continuous marine broadcasts on the following VHF Channel frequencies – WX1: 162.55 Weather Channel 1, Alert Bay.

Call the following continuous marine weather recordings:
Vancouver – 604-666-3655
Comox – 250-339-9861
Campbell River – 250-286-3575
Port Hardy – 250-949-7148

For further information on weather products and services visit Environment Canada at www.weatheroffice.ec.gc.ca

Environment Canada West Coast Weather Publications
Mariners Guide: West Coast Marine Weather Services.
Marine Weather Hazard Manual – West Coast: A Guide to Local Forecasts and Conditions.
The Wind Came All Ways, by Owen Lange.

Note: at the start of each chapter, the relevant forecast area and observation sites are listed.

S ummer weather from mid-June to mid-September begins with the Pacific High anchoring itself off the northern tip of Vancouver Island. This high-pressure system, which brings clear skies, sunshine and westerly winds, could arrive mid-May; however, it could also arrive in late July.

Bad weather is associated with low pressure, rain, overcast skies and easterly winds. Depending on the strength of the high, the good weather and bad weather are cyclical.

MARINE FORECAST ISSUE TIMES:

0400. 1030. 1600 & 2130. Issue times remain the same throughout the year.

MARINE WARNINGS:

Small Craft Warning	20-33 knots
Gale Warning	34-47 knots
Storm Warning	48-63 knots
Hurricane Force Wind Warning	64 knots or more

Note: The "Small-Craft Warning" means just that: winds forecast at between 20 and 30 knots can be hazardous to small craft

WIND

T he prevailing summer winds are westerly – anywhere from SW-W-NW. These westerly winds are strongest as the high-pressure ridge approaches, and can blow continuously for weeks at a time in the early summer, tapering off in July and August.

Westerly winds that begin as a sea breeze at around noon in Queen Charlotte Strait will often increase in force to 15-20 knots until early evening, dying off completely near sundown. This afternoon breeze increases as it moves into Johnstone Strait, accelerated by the typography of the strait. These winds will often reach 25-30 knots off Chatham Point by late evening. Westerly winds usually become light during the early morning hours.

Easterly winds are not as predictable when accompanied by a low-pressure front or cyclonic disturbance. This is *hunkering down* weather with overcast skies, rain and unstable winds ending in gale-force gusts.

WAVES

O cean swells, the residue of the open Pacific Ocean, may be encountered in Queen Charlotte Strait. These swells are usually from the northwest and generally are not a hazard in themselves. Hazardous wave action in this region develops as a result of the wind interacting with the tidal current. It's best to travel when the winds are in the same direction as the current. (See Current page 17.)

Summer Weather in The Broughtons can be glorious, and locals will wax lyrically on "another beautiful day in paradise" – however, it is is good to remember, that daytime conditions are generally 5° cooler than in Desolation Sound. Water temperatures are also much colder and usually not conducive to a leisurely swim!

Following is a list of average summer air temperatures recorded at Alert Bay:

May	10.4°C	(50.6°F)
June	12.5°C	(54.5°F)
July	14.1°C	(57.1°F)
August	14.4°C	(58°F)

The sunset after-glow reflects on the mirror calm waters of Tracey Harbour

FOG

Fog is a common occurrence in the summer months; the relatively warm, moist westerly wind over the cool water creates fog, which forms in Queen Charlotte Strait and is then funnelled eastward into the sounds, channels, passages and inlets. On most days, this fog will burn off/clear around noon. Fog can become a navigational hazard, especially in busy Johnstone Strait. Refrain from venturing into poor visibility if fog is forecast or you see it silently moving in – best to seek refuge before it begins to envelope your boat and threaten visibility.

RAIN

The Broughton region is known as the raincoast for good reason, and the area receives its fair share of rainfall during the fall, winter and spring months. Although summer is the driest season with glorious days of sunshine and blue skies, precipitation is still part of the weather package.

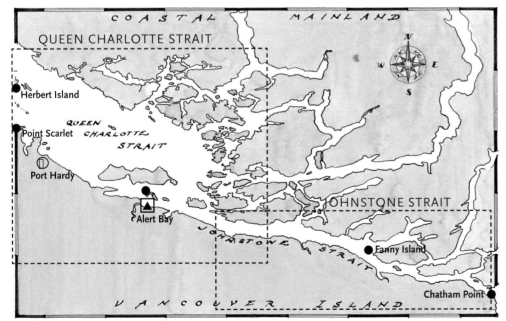

West Coast Marine Weather Forecast Areas and Observation Sites

KEY:

```
┌ ─ ─ ┐
└ ─ ─ ┘   Marine Forecast Areas
```

●   Marine Weather Reporting Station

▲   WeatherRadio 1
WX1 162.59 MHz

Ⓘ   WeatherRadio Canada
103.70 MHz

TIDES
(The Vertical Movement of Water)

Refer to *Canadian Tide and Current Tables, Volume 6*. Published annually.

Note: At the start of each chapter we list the reference and secondary ports that are within or influence the area covered. The chart below indicates the approximate position of the reference and secondary ports.

Tide tables contain essential navigational information and must be acquired prior to venturing into these waters. A working knowledge of the tides and currents, and their interplay with the wind, is fundamental to safe navigation in this region.

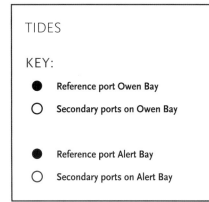

Low water exposes the rock in "Pearl Passage," Broughton Archipelago

T ides and current, although interlinked, are two quite different variables to be considered in passage planning and navigation.

Tide, the vertical movement of water, will rise (flood) or fall (ebb). Their height on Canadian charts is calculated upon chart datum. Current, the horizontal movement of water, is directionally defined and its speed calculated in knots.

The tidal range (low, low water to high, high water) in the Broughton region is signifcant. A 4.5 m (15 ft) range is common on a large or spring tide, with the highest tides occurring near full moon. These tidal ranges gradually become less on the monthly cycle, then build again. Tides are semidiurnal, having two highs and two lows each day. The ability to calculate the depth under your boat's keel accurately is important to safe passage making and when anchoring overnight.

In general the Flooding tide creates an easterly current and the Ebbing tide a westerly current; be aware however, due to the maze of channels locally, the current may flow in quite different directions.

TIDES

KEY:

● Reference port Owen Bay

○ Secondary ports on Owen Bay

● Reference port Alert Bay

○ Secondary ports on Alert Bay

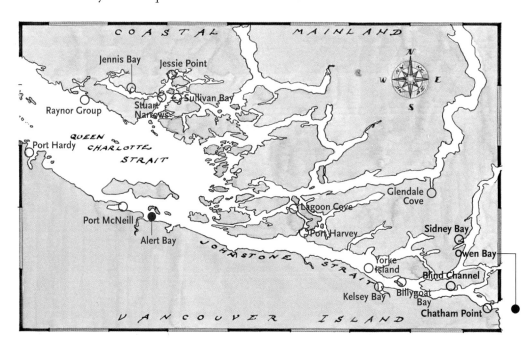

CURRENT
(The Horizontal Movement of Water)

Refer to *Canadian Tide and Current Tables, Volume 6.* Published annually.

Note: At the start of each chapter we list the reference current stations and secondary current stations that are within or influence the area covered. The chart below indicates the approximate positions of the reference and secondary current stations.

It is essential to be able to calculate the time of slack water, the direction and strength of the current and be aware of the locations where current may pose a hazard to navigation.

A whirlpool in Current Passage off Helmcken Island

Due to the large tidal range, the currents in the Broughton region are generally strong. From 2-3 knots in Queen Charlotte Strait, the current increases eastward as water is funnelled into Broughton Strait and Johnstone Strait. In the inlets, passages, sounds and channels, 4-5 knots is not uncommon. Rapid water of 5-7 knots can be found in the restricted passages and narrows and turbulent water may be present. Very swift currents of 6-10+ knots will be found in charted rapids, and turbulent water will be present in the form of upwellings, eddies and whirlpools. It is always best to time transiting rapids at slack water.

Not only does strong current and rapid turbulent water present a hazard in itself, when it is combined with moderate to strong opposing current that creates steep choppy waves, it can be extremely hazardous to small craft. Johnstone Strait is infamous when westerly winds of 20-30+ knots oppose an ebbing current – known locally as the "devils cauldron."

CAUTIONARY NOTE: *Times of slack water (turns) at the rapids may differ significantly from the times of shore-side high and low water. For the safety of boat and crew, it is of paramount importance to be able to read and interpolate the tide and current tables accurately.*

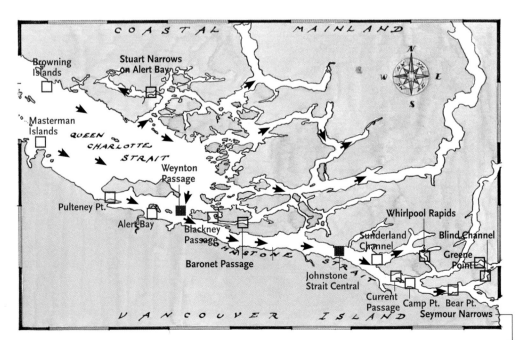

OFFICIAL PUBLICATIONS

Pulteney Point Light on the west tip of Malcolm Island

CHARTS FOR VOLUME 5, THE BROUGHTONS

3515 – Knight Inlet 80 000
        Simoom Sound 20 000

3539 – Discovery Passage 40 000
        Seymour Narrows 20 000

3543 – Cordero Channel 40 000
        Greene Point Rapids 20 000
        Dent and Yuculta Rapids 20 000

3544 – Johnstone Strait, Race and
        Current Passage 25 000

3545 – Johnstone Strait, Port Neville to
        Robson Bight 40 000

3546 – Broughton Strait 40 000
        Port McNeill 20 000
        Alert Bay 20 000

3547 – Queen Charlotte Strait,
        Eastern Portion 40 000
        Stuart Narrows 20 000
        Kenneth Passage 20 000

3548 – Queen Charlotte Strait, Central
        Portion 40 000
        Blunden Harbour 15 000
        Port Hardy 15 000

3564 – Johnstone Strait
        Port Neville 20,000
        Havannah Channel and
        Chatham Channel 20,000
        Chatham Channel 10,000

CHARTS AND NAUTICAL PUBLICATIONS

We have carefully designed this cruising guide to work in conjunction with the CHS charts and publications, and above each destination we have referenced the appropriate charts required.

For their safety, all operators of ships and boats are required to have official, up-to-date charts and publications on board that cover the area they are navigating. These charts can be referenced from Pacific Coast Catalogue, Nautical Charts and Related Publications – Canadian Hydrographic Service (CHS), which are available at any chart dealer, free of charge – visit www.charts.gc.ca.

Individual charts are the primary tools used by professional mariners and recreational boaters, and those referenced below will cover the entire area included in this volume (Volume 5):

ELECTRONIC CHARTS

Electronic charts are either raster or vector scans of CHS individual charts, produced under licence by Nautical Data International (NDI). They may be viewed independently on your computer or with the appropriate navigational software as an onboard aid to navigation — visit www.digitalocean.ca 1-800-563-0634.

We recommend the navigational software developed by Nobeltec Inc. – www.nobeltec.com 1-800-495-6279.

Note: Up-to-date paper charts and tide tables are still a legal, on-board requirement for all craft in Canadian waters.

APPROACH WAYPOINTS

Approach waypoints are latitude and longitude positions based on NAD 83 and shown in degrees, minutes and decimals of a minute. They are located in deep water from a position where the illustrated features will be readily discernable in daylight.

PUBLICATIONS

We recommend the following publications to accompany your copy of Volume 5 of *A Dreamspeaker Cruising Guide*. For further reading, consult the Selected Reading list on p. 188.

NAUTICAL PUBLICATIONS

Canadian Tide and Current Tables, Volume 6: Discovery Passage and West Coast of Vancouver Island (updated annually).
Symbols and Abbreviations, Terms – Chart 1, as used on Canadian Charts
Pacific Coast List of Lights, Buoys and Fog Signals
Sailing Directions – British Columbia Coast (South Portion)
Boating Safety Publications, Canadian Coast Guard
The Canadian Aids to Navigation System: Marine Navigation Services Directorate
Protecting British Columbia's Aquatic Environment: A Boaters Guide

EMERGENCY PROCEDURES

THE CANADIAN COAST GUARD is a multitask organization whose primary role of search and rescue is supported by the following roles: maintaining the Aids to Navigation, operating the Office of Safe Boating and, in association with Environment Canada, the Marine Weather Forecast. For a copy of the *Safe Boating Guide*, call 1-800-267-6687. For search and rescue call:

TELEPHONE: 1-800-567-5111
CELLULAR: *311
VHF CHANNEL: 16

EMERGENCY RADIO PROCEDURES
MAYDAY: For immediate danger to life or vessel.
PAN-PAN: For urgency but no immediate danger to life or vessel.
For MAYDAY or PAN-PAN transmit the following on VHF Channel 16 or 2182 kHz.

1. MAYDAY, MAYDAY, MAYDAY (or PAN-PAN, PAN-PAN, PAN-PAN), this is (vessel name and radio call sign).
2. State your position and the nature of the distress.
3. State the number of people on board, and describe the vessel (length, make/type, colour, power or sail and registration number.)

NOTE: *If the distress is not life-threatening, the coast guard will put out a general call to boaters in your area for assistance. A tow at sea by a commercial operator can be expensive. HUB International TOS Limited provides marine towing insurance as part of their Platinum Bluewater Contract – 1-877-986-5265 or www.tos.ca. C-TOW operates a marine assistance network in British Columbia waters – 1-888-354-5554 or www.c-tow.ca for further information on areas covered.*

HOW TO USE THIS BOOK

This sample layout identifies the various features of this cruising guide that will help you to reach your destination safely, and give you plenty of information.

Chapter & featured destination reference
Chapter legend
Destination locator
Approach waypoint latitude & longitude
Tips on best approach & anchorages
Cautionary note

Depth contour (approximate position). Depths reduced to lowest normal tide (zero tide)
Sepia area indicates shoreline that covers & uncovers with the tide
Solid black line indicates HW mark
Green area indicates land above HW mark
Blue area indicates shallower water
White area indicates deeper water that is safe for navigation
Red broken line indicates a safe approach course
✳Asterisk indicates approximate position of approach waypoint
Aerial approach or ambient photograph

HW: high water
LW: low water

All depths as indicated are in metres.

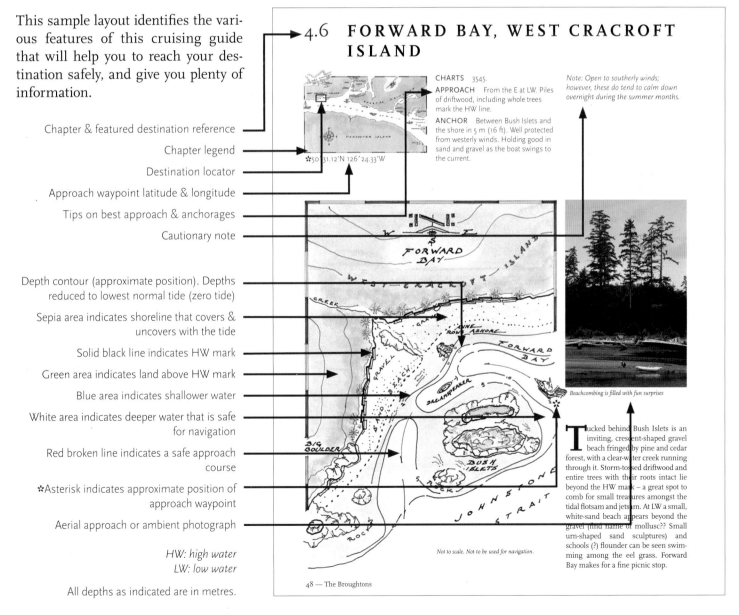

4.6 FORWARD BAY, WEST CRACROFT ISLAND

CHARTS   3545.

APPROACH   From the E at LW. Piles of driftwood, including whole trees mark the HW line.

ANCHOR   Between Bush Islets and the shore in 5 m (16 ft). Well protected from westerly winds. Holding good in sand and gravel as the boat swings to the current.

Note: Open to southerly winds; however, these do tend to calm down overnight during the summer months.

✳50 31.12'N 126 24.33'W

Beachcombing is filled with fun surprises

Not to scale. Not to be used for navigation.

Tucked behind Bush Islets is an inviting, crescent-shaped gravel beach fringed by pine and cedar forest, with a clear-water creek running through it. Storm-tossed driftwood and entire trees with their roots intact lie beyond the HW mark – a great spot to comb for small treasures amongst the tidal flotsam and jetsam. At LW a small, white-sand beach appears beyond the gravel (find name of mollusc?? Small urn-shaped sand sculptures) and schools (?) flounder can be seen swimming among the eel grass. Forward Bay makes for a fine picnic stop.

Port Hardy is the westerly limit of this guide

Chapter 2
PASSAGES NORTH OF 50°

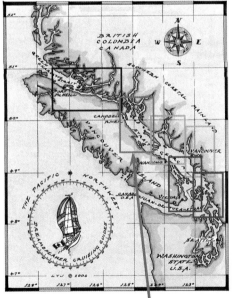

Chapter 2
ROUTES NORTHWEST THROUGH THE RAPIDS

The following *Dreamspeaker* titles will guide you north:

Volume 4   *The San Juan Islands*
Volume 1   *The Gulf Islands & Vancouver Island –*
                  Victoria & Sooke to Nanaimo
Volume 3   *Vancouver, Howe Sound & the Sunshine Coast —*
                  Princess Louisa Inlet and Jedediah Island
Volume 2   *Desolation Sound & the Discovery Islands*

The Pacific Northwest greets all nations

Volume 2–Desolation Sound & the Discovery Islands

The following text and chart opposite are intended as a synopsis for passage planning. Passage planning is a serious component of safe navigation. Take time to consider the conditions you will be encountering, and take precautions accordingly.

The region north of 50°, as depicted in the chart, is comprehensively covered in *A Dreamspeaker Cruising Guide Volume 2 – Desolation Sound and the Discovery Islands*.

For the recreational boater travelling from home ports in southern British Columbia and Washington State to The Broughtons, the journey is a challenge and commitment in itself. With a distance of some 90 nautical miles from Vancouver, B.C., and twice that from Seattle, WA, this trip takes a good deal of planning. South of 50°, fuel, moorage, provisioning and marine services are relatively numerous and comprehensively covered by *A Dreamspeaker Cruising Guide Volumes 1, 3 and 4*.

North of 50°, *A Dreamspeaker Cruising Guide Volume 2 – Desolation Sound and the Discovery Islands* will serve for planning the passages through the initial channels and rapids. Fuel, moorage, provisions and marine services are not as numerous, and Campbell River is the last real urban centre with well-developed marine services and a regional airport with feeder floatplane services to the outlying communities and resorts.

There are two passages north – the western and eastern routes, with a central diversion through the Okisollo Channel. All have tidal gates in the form of rapids and swift currents in the channels, a limited choice of fuel, moorage and provisioning options and an excellent selection of anchorages.

Dreamspeaker's route was north to Lund from Vancouver, then northwest to Campbell River before embarking on a passage via Seymour Narrows and Discovery Passage to begin the cruise to The Broughtons. This is a good shakedown for any vessel, usually the first big one of the season, and Campbell River is the perfect location to obtain boat parts and fix any mechanical problems prior to your cruise further north.

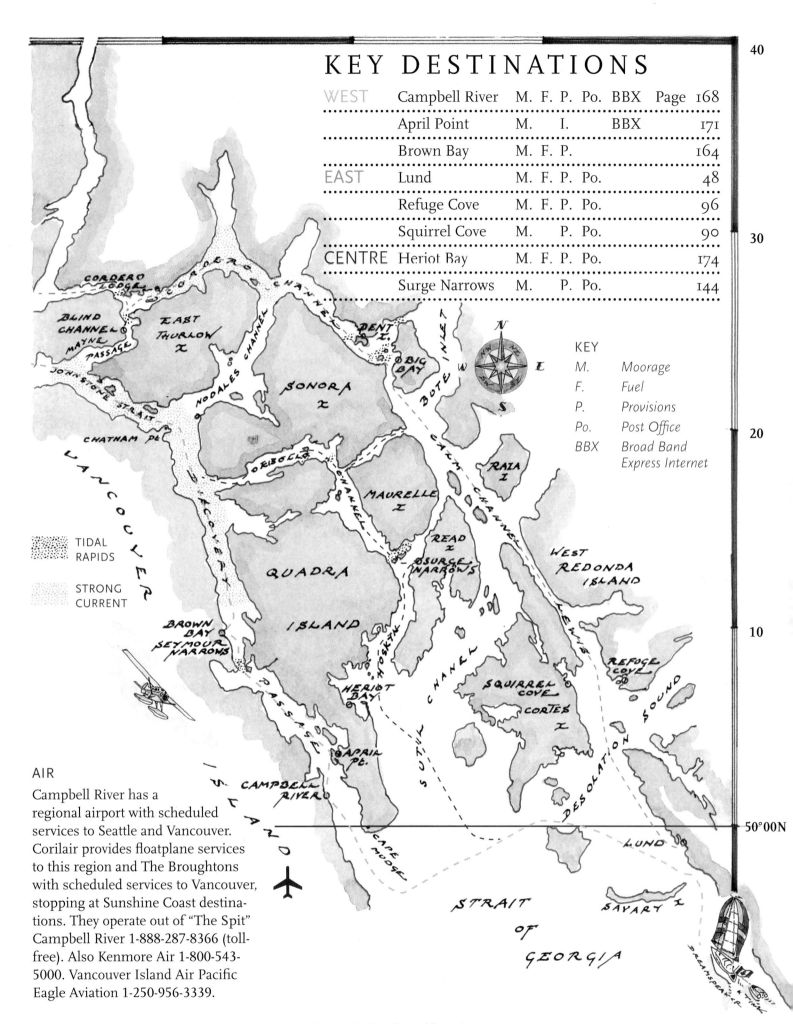

KEY DESTINATIONS

KEY

M.	Moorage
F.	Fuel
P.	Provisions
Po.	Post Office
BBX	Broad Band Express Internet

TIDAL RAPIDS

STRONG CURRENT

AIR

Campbell River has a regional airport with scheduled services to Seattle and Vancouver. Corilair provides floatplane services to this region and The Broughtons with scheduled services to Vancouver, stopping at Sunshine Coast destinations. They operate out of "The Spit" Campbell River 1-888-287-8366 (toll-free). Also Kenmore Air 1-800-543-5000. Vancouver Island Air Pacific Eagle Aviation 1-250-956-3339.

Not to scale. Not to be used for navigation.

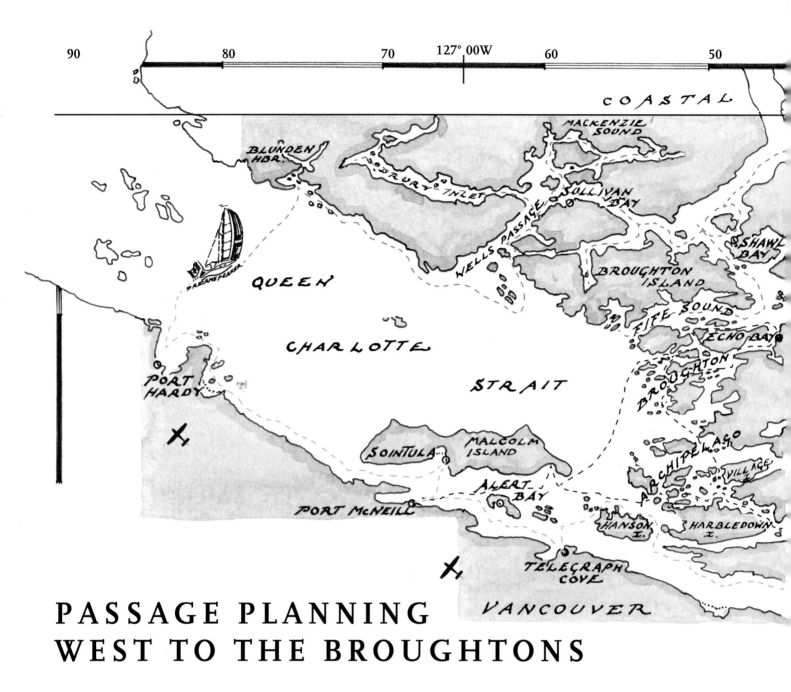

PASSAGE PLANNING
WEST TO THE BROUGHTONS

Note: There are regional airports at Port McNeill and Port Hardy with fix wheel, floatplane, and helicopter charter services to all the destinations in the Broughton region.

The Volume 5 chapters follow the route taken by *Dreamspeaker* and her crew while researching this guide.

Taking up where *A Dreamspeaker Cruising Guide Volume 2 – Desolation Sound and the Discovery Islands* left off, Volume 5 begins in the waters of Mayne Passage and travels west from Blind Channel via Johnstone and Broughton Straits and the friendly communities of Vancouver Island.

After an immersion of First Nations culture in Alert Bay, Cormorant Island, Volume 5 travels north into the "Village of Islands" in the Broughton Archipelago – two chapters of remote anchorages, First Nation villages and fun family-run resorts.

Returning south to refuel and provision in Port McNeill, the adventure continues after a visit to the community of Sointula on Malcolm Island. *Dreamspeaker* travels west to Port Hardy and across Queen Charlotte Strait to Blunden Harbour, then east to explore the labyrinth waters of the coastal mainland, visiting the floating community and marina at Sullivan Bay and venturing into the fjord-like splendour of Kingcome and Knight Inlets. Finally, there's a lovely layover at Lagoon Cove Marina and a shelter from a westerly gale in Port Harvey.

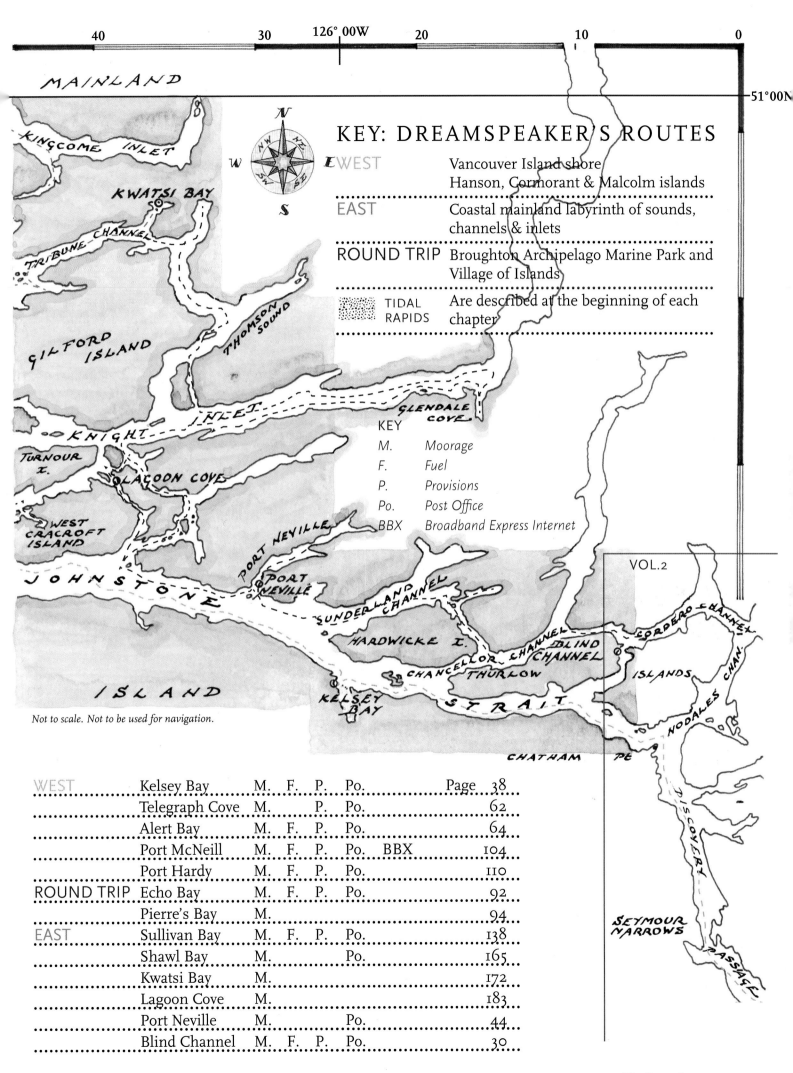

KEY: DREAMSPEAKER'S ROUTES

WEST — Vancouver Island shore
Hanson, Cormorant & Malcolm islands

EAST — Coastal mainland labyrinth of sounds, channels & inlets

ROUND TRIP — Broughton Archipelago Marine Park and Village of Islands

TIDAL RAPIDS — Are described at the beginning of each chapter

KEY

M.	Moorage
F.	Fuel
P.	Provisions
Po.	Post Office
BBX	Broadband Express Internet

Not to scale. Not to be used for navigation.

Chancellor Channel from Billygoat Bay, Helmcken Island

Chapter 3

JOHNSTONE STRAIT EAST

Chapter 3
JOHNSTONE STRAIT EAST

The unique burger stand in Kelsey Bay

TIDES – *Volume 6,*
Canadian Tide and Current Tables
Reference Port – Owen Bay
Secondary Ports – Blind Channel,
Cordero Island
Reference Port – Alert Bay
Secondary Ports – Billygoat Bay, Kelsey
Bay

CURRENTS

Reference Station – Seymour Narrows
Secondary Stations – Blind Channel,
Greene Point Rapids, Whirlpool Rapids
Reference Station – Johnstone Strait
Central
Secondary Station – Current Passage

WEATHER

Weather Station – WX1 162.55 MHZ
Area – Johnstone Strait
Reporting Stations – Fanny Island,
Chatham Point

CAUTIONARY NOTES: *Johnstone Strait*
is notorious for strong, summer westerly
winds. The swift currents in East
Johnstone Strait will create potentially
dangerous seas when wind-against-
current conditions prevail. On a large
tide, East Johnstone Strait averages 5
knots of current on both the ebb and
flood. Consult your chart for the Traffic
Separation Scheme (TSS) and stay clear
of the shipping lanes, as the strait is a
busy commercial artery.

Currents can range from 5-7 knots on
the northern route via Blind Channel
and Greene Point Rapids through
Chancellor and Wellbore Channels. The
prudent navigator will run with the
current and endeavour to transit rapids
at slack water. Due to turbulence caused
by the strong current, a dinghy or yacht
tender should always be stowed on deck.

This is a chapter on transiting, which needs to be well planned as it presents a potential challenge to the cruising boater. Johnstone Strait is famous for its strong westerly winds, while the rapids, channels and passages are noted for their strong currents and turbulent waters. The scenery, however, is dominated by snow-capped mountain ranges and stunning vistas.

Routes west are via Mayne Passage and Johnstone Strait, with potential shelter at Helmcken Island and Kelsey Bay. The alternative route is north via Blind Channel and Greene Point Rapids and west via Chancellor and Wellbore Channels through Whirlpool Rapids to the shelter of Douglas Bay in Forward Harbour.

BLIND CHANNEL RESORT AND MARINA is a major staging post for boaters planning their cruise to The Broughtons. We made an early morning start from Blind Channel to take advantage of light winds and the ebb current to Helmcken Island where we investigated the two small anchorages, which provided protected overnight anchorage and a cozy spot to hide while waiting out the adverse tide in Current Passage.

Travelling with the current to Kelsey Bay the following morning, we found a safe haven for local fish boats and transient boaters; its entrance might not look that inviting in a blow, but once inside there is good protection and a friendly community that welcomes visitors. Sayward Village is a pleasant 15-minute walk from the dock, and the lovely Salmon River Estuary Trails are teeming with birdlife.

Note: On our return journey from The Broughtons, we enjoyed a thrilling downwind sail as the westerly wind and flood tide carried us through Sunderland Channel to a rendezvous with friends in Forward Harbour.

FEATURED DESTINATIONS

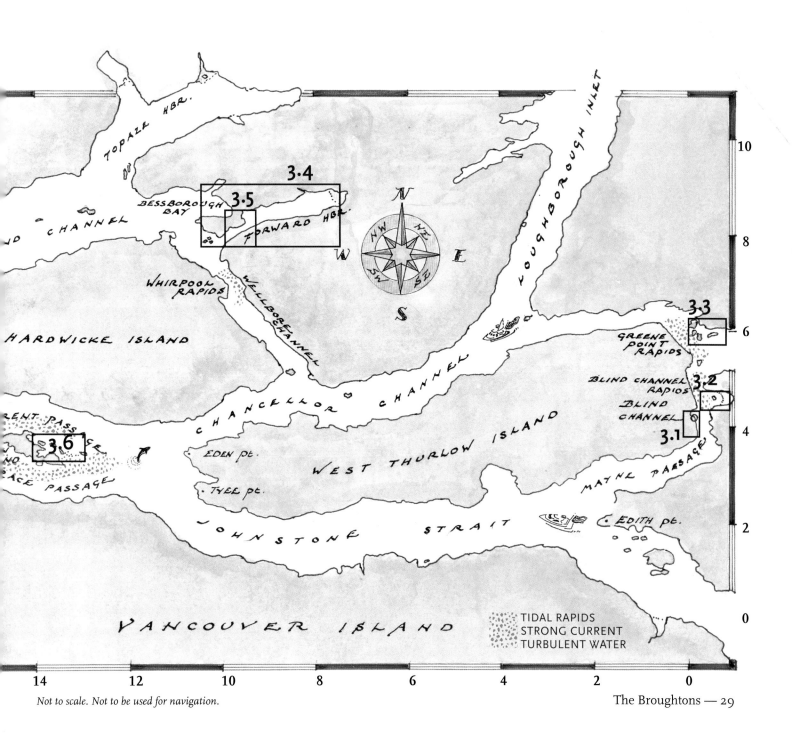

Not to scale. Not to be used for navigation.

3.1 BLIND CHANNEL RESORT AND MARINA

✣50°24.90'N 125°29.90'W

CHARTS   3543. 3312, p. 24.

APPROACH   With caution, because a back eddy, running counter to the current in Mayne Passage, creates a strong current setting into the marina facility.

MARINA   The Blind Channel Resort and Marina, toll-free 1-888-329-0475 or VHF Channel 66A, has extensive visitor moorage with WiFi internet access.

FUEL   Open all year round, the fuel dock is operated by the resort. Propane and kerosene are also available.

Lovely Blind Channel Resort and Marina

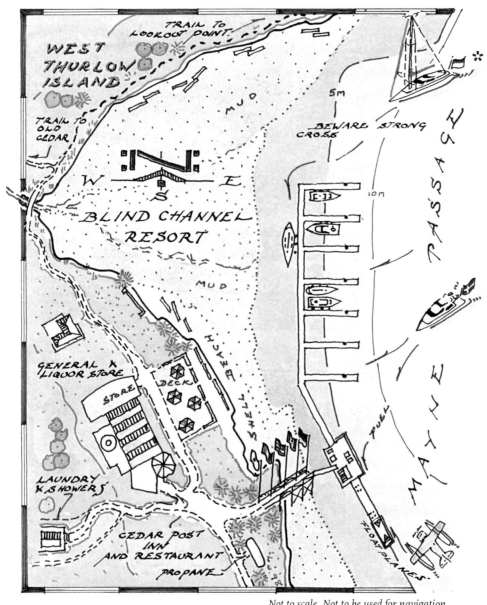

Not to scale. Not to be used for navigation.

Pristine docks, colourful artwork and terra cotta pots spilling over with flowers welcome you to BLIND CHANNEL RESORT AND MARINA, owned and operated by three generations of the Richter family. In business since 1970, this resort has a restaurant and patio, store, post office, B.C. LIQUOR STORE and waterside cottages with full facilities. Moorage comes with 24-hour power and piped spring water. The marina offers free moorage of two hours to boaters while they shop or dine at the resort. Shower and laundry facilities are also available.

The well-stocked store offers delicious baked goods, picnic fare and fresh bread daily in high season. It also carries a variety of basic provisions, frozen meats and an adequate selection of fresh produce. "Spring water ice" is produced on site, and fishing licences, charts, guides, books and unique gifts are also sold. Pick up a hiking trail map and visit the 800-year-old cedar in the forest behind the resort.

Edgar and Annemarie Richter's artistic talents can also be seen in the CEDAR POST INN, where gourmet and home-cooked Bavarian-style meals are served, along with a selection of wines. In summer, reservations are essential.

BLIND CHANNEL RESORT is a major staging point
for boaters beginning their cruise W to The Broughtons
or for those at the end of their Desolation Sound cruise.
For Dreamspeaker it was the last stop at the end of a
Broughtons cruise before heading S.

3.2 CHARLES BAY, BLIND CHANNEL RAPIDS, EAST THURLOW ISLAND

✤ (A) 50°25.02'N 125°29.70'W
✤ (B) 50°25.44'N 125°30.03'W

CHARTS 3543.

APPROACH (A) Charles Bay, from Mayne Passage at LW slack. (B) From the N, off Shell Point. Transit Blind Channel Rapids, on or near slack water.

ANCHOR Due N of Eclipse Islet. Swing in the back eddies in depths of 2-4 m (6-13 ft). Holding good in mud.

At anchor off the shingle beach, Charles Bay

Good crabbing and well-protected anchorage can be found across the way from BLIND CHANNEL RESORT in secluded Charles Bay. Sheltered from southeasterly and northwesterly winds and the effects of the Green Point and Blind Channel Rapids, this small haven offers peace. Beautiful Eclipse Islet, encircled by clear water, provides an idyllic picnic spot. You can pick fresh sea asparagus, poke around the rocks or just laze on the colourful pebble beach watching boat traffic in Mayne Passage challenge the Blind Channel Rapids. The bay, although open to Mayne Passage, lies in the wind shadow of W Thurlow Island and is, therefore, well protected from the prevailing summer westerly winds.

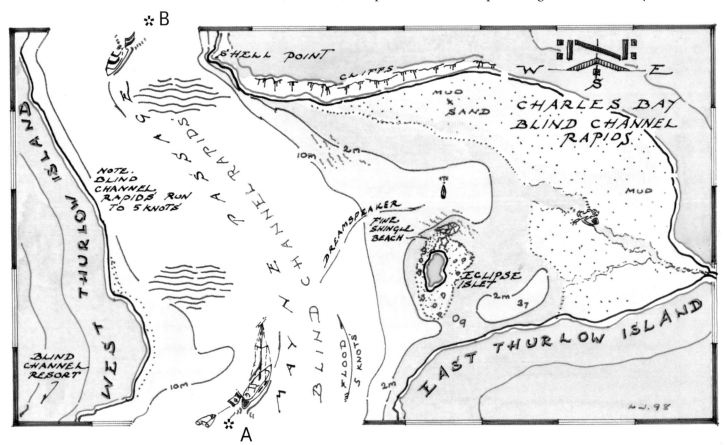

✣50°26.40'N 125°20.60'W

CHARTS   3543. 3312, p. 24.

APPROACH   From the S, the channel between the S islands is fringed by kelp. A rock lies off the W tip of the easternmost island.

ANCHOR   Good sheltered anchorage, away form the turbulence and eddies in Cordero Channel, can be found in the cove. Depths of 6-12 m (19-39 ft), holding over a mud, sand and weed bottom.

Sunset over West Thurlow Island

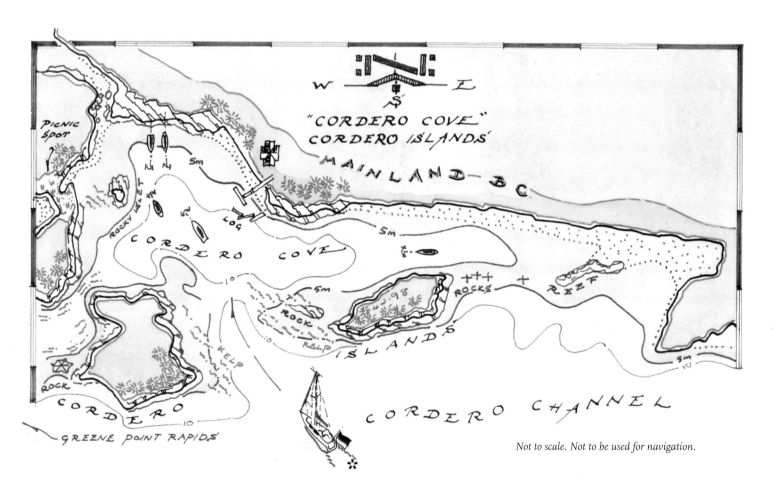

Not to scale. Not to be used for navigation.

This surprise anchorage is protected from northwesterly winds and the swift current in Cordero Channel by three charming islands. The SE basin also affords some protection in southeast winds.

With a pleasant view out to bustling Cordero Channel, "Cordero Cove" (named by us) is an ideal spot for exploring, picnicking, shell collecting and just lazing in the cockpit. Many tranquil hours can be spent basking on the smooth-rock islet in the cove's NW corner.

You'll be lulled by water music as water gushes through the narrow gap and tumbles over rocks at HW. The best spot to spread your picnic blanket is on the downy moss and grass patch on the westernmost island, with a great view over to the Greene Point Rapids.

FORWARD HARBOUR

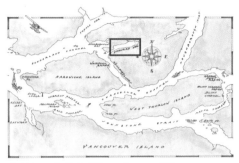

✢ (A) 50°28.65'N 125°47.05'W
✢ (B) 50°28.11'N 125°46.37'W

CHARTS 3544.

APPROACH The approaches to Forward Harbour lie (A) NW and (B) SE of Midgham Islets. The entrance channel between Louisa Point and Robson Point is wide and clear.

ANCHOR In Bessborough Bay only as an alternative in easterly winds. Open to the full westerly fetch of Cumberland Channel. Forward Harbour entrance channel has a small bight on the northern shore, which can accommodate 2 boats. Good all-round protection – a stern line ashore is recommended. For Douglas Bay see p. 35. In the head of the harbour, deep anchorage is available for larger boats and vessels, with plenty of swinging room.

MARINA FORWARD HARBOUR FISHING LODGE has moorage for transient boaters by reservation. Their docks have 20 m (65 ft.) of water below at LW and can accommodate boats up to 24 m (80 ft). Water and wireless internet are available (power coming in 2007). Call ahead 250-287-6778 or email info@forwardharbour.com; they monitor VHF Channel 6.

The entrance channel to Forward Harbour

An ancient rock petroglyph site, good anchorage and transient moorage facilities at the friendly fishing lodge can be found at the head of commodious Forward Harbour.

The lodge offers a limited dinner menu in its restaurant by reservation (upgraded to a full menu in 2007) and has shower, laundry and telephone facilities. Trips to view the local grizzlies and petroglyphs are offered to overnight moorage guests, and their fully guided ATV Adventure Wilderness Tours visit Heydon Lake and Topaze Harbour; search for cedar balls, see bears on the beach, canoe, take a refreshing swim before lunch and enjoy the selection of wildlife and birds that call this lovely area home.

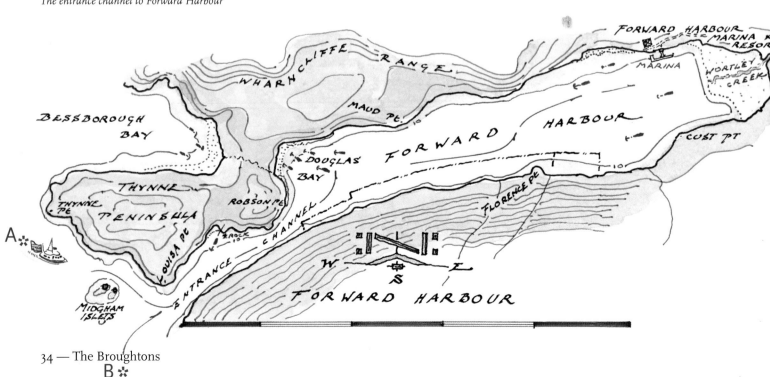

B ✢

CHARTS 3543.

APPROACH The approach to Forward Harbour lies NE or SE of Midgham Islets; Douglas Bay is free of obstructions.

ANCHOR Off the sand and gravel beach in Douglas Bay, in 4-10 m (13-32 ft) with enough room for 8-10 boats to swing comfortably. The bay is protected from all but outflow winds, with holding good in sand and gravel.

CAUTIONARY NOTE: *Boats will tend to swing towards the northern shore when gale force westerly winds combine with the current.*

✱50°28.75'N 125°45.09'W

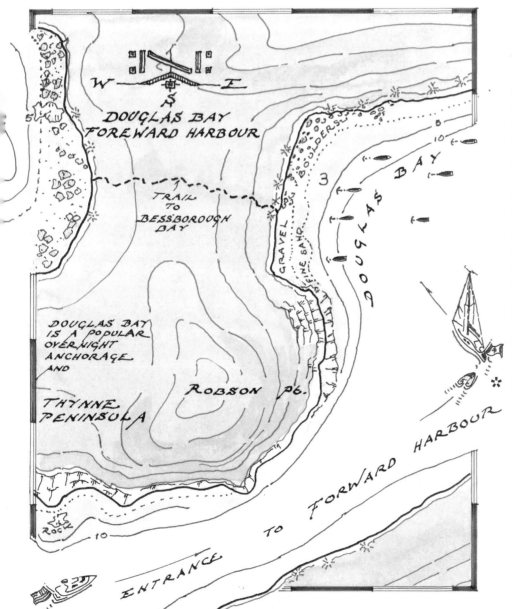

A popular overnight anchorage for boaters at the start or end of their Broughton cruise, Douglas Bay offers a fine sand and gravel beach backed by pine and maple trees. From here, an interesting flotsam and jetsam trail zigzags through the forest to Bessborough Bay and its sandy swimming beach.

We visited in the aftermath of a westerly gale, and the white sand was covered with blobs of bracken-coloured jellyfish and mounds of kelp and seaweed, which the slim-legged sandpipers picked through delicately. The head of the bay was a beachcomber's paradise, with everything from huge reels of plastic piping to wayward fenders and lengths of blue rope. Only then did we realize how the ritual of displaying *beach finds* along the trail had become a summer tradition.

3.6 HELMCKEN ISLAND

❀ (A) 50°24.14'N 125°51.19'W
❀ (B) 50°24.24'N 125°51.94'W

CHARTS   3544.

APPROACH   (A) Billygoat Bay from the W between the 2 islets. The range mark is to starboard. Beware of the reef and a rock to the E. (B) "Deer Cove" is a clear run in from the NE.

ANCHOR   (1) At the head of the bay in depths of 5-6 m (16-19 ft). Good protection from westerly winds with holding good in mud. (2) Beyond the old log dump, off the gravel beach (outside the eel grass) in depths of 7-8 m (22-26 ft). Holding is moderate in gravel and mud. Although this bay is more open than (A), it is well protected from westerly winds.

Note: A good spot to hide while waiting out foul weather in Johnstone Strait.

Deer are a common shoreline sight

These two cozy anchorages certainly came in handy after an unsuccessful attempt to navigate east beyond Current Passage on a flooding tide.

We tucked into the head of Billygoat Bay and shared the tranquil anchorage with jumping fish, kingfishers and plump seals sunning themselves on the rocks. The view NE to Chancellor Channel is lovely and the fresh seaweed picked from the shoreline rocky outcrops was delicious.

"Deer Cove" (named by us for the resident deer) is the more scenic of the two spots with views NE and SE down Johnstone Strait with mighty Mount Waddington in the distance. Stretch your legs and your pooch's with a hike on the old logging roads.

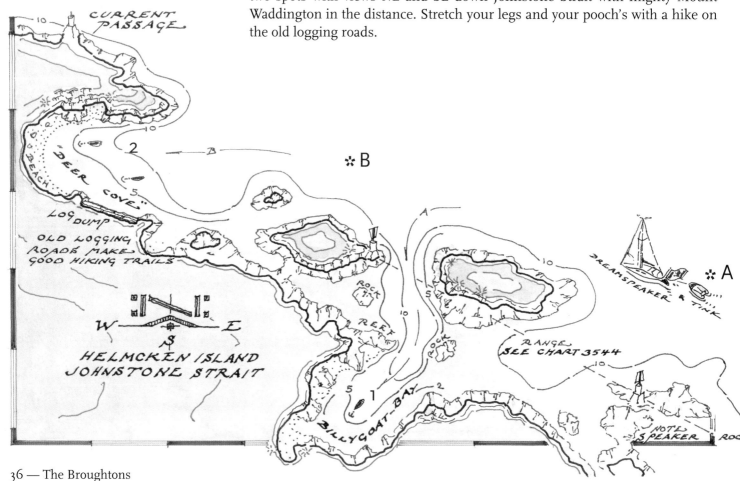

Snug in Kelsey Bay while gale force winds blow in Johnstone Strait

✳ 50°23.86'N 125°57.55'W

CHARTS 3544.

APPROACH With extreme caution. A floating breakwater extends out from a stone breakwater. Enter between the starboard mark (red) and the rusting ship hulls that lie to the S.

PUBLIC WHARF 3 fingers extend SE behind the breakwater; during the summer months, rafting up is the norm. In a westerly blow, all boats rock and roll although the outer portion of "C" dock is the most exposed. Call Sayward Futures Society 250-282-0018; they stand by on VHF Channel 6.

BOAT LAUNCH Ramp is private.

Starboard mark on the tip of the floating breakwater

CAUTIONARY NOTE: *On the ebb tide a strong back eddy runs across the entrance. This back eddy is less strong on a flood tide.*

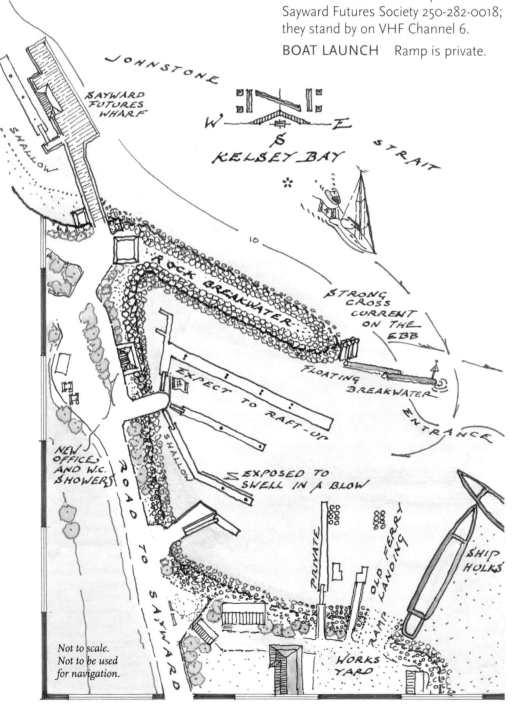

Not to scale.
Not to be used
for navigation.

A safe haven for local fish boats, Kelsey Bay and its entrance might not be that inviting in a blow, but once inside, there is protection from the winds in Johnstone Strait and a friendly community who welcomes visiting boaters. Washrooms and shower and laundry facilities are available at the head of the PUBLIC WHARF. Although it is a pleasant walk into the nearby Village of Sayward, a ride from one of the local fishermen is often the norm, and the local supermarket van will transport you and your groceries back to the dock.

The Sayward Futures Society is working hard to make the Port of Kelsey Bay attractive to cruising boaters, and welcomes visitors to its office and TOURIST INFORMATION CENTRE located on the old GOVERNMENT WHARF north of the rock breakwater. The Society's building is also home to a gift store offering local products and a whale watching and wildlife tour operation; internet access is also available. The view across Johnstone Strait is spectacular, and the day we visited, a large pod of Orcas at play in the strait thrilled a crowd of viewers on the dock.

SAYWARD VILLAGE AND SALMON RIVER ESTUARY TRAILS

For chart approach and moorage information, see Kelsey Bay (opposite).

✣50°23.76'N 125°56.33'W

3.7 FOR DETAIL

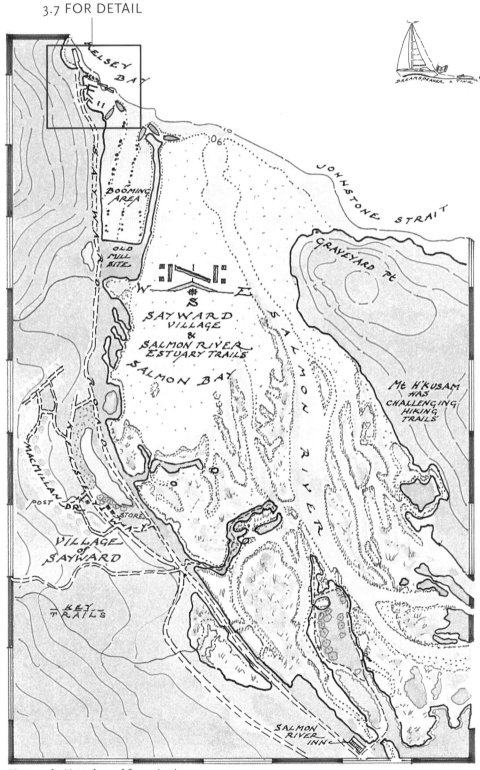

Not to scale. Not to be used for navigation.

Neat and tidy homes, manicured lawns and flower-filled hanging baskets welcome visitors to the friendly Village of Sayward, a pleasant 15-minute walk from Kelsey Bay. Here you will find the post office and a well-stocked supermarket, which also includes a B.C. LIQUOR STORE outlet. Picnic in the shaded, grassy park fronted by a lagoon filled with wildlife, or take a leisurely stroll along the lovely Salmon River Estuary Trails, teeming with birdlife. A solid, wooden lookout provides views over the Salmon River and its maze of tributaries out to Johnstone Strait.

A windswept marsh fronts Sayward Village

Chapter 4

JOHNSTONE STRAIT WEST

Eastbound – surfing in Johnstone Strait

Chapter 4
JOHNSTONE STRAIT WEST

Fisheries searching for that illusive salmon

TIDES – *Volume 6,*
Canadian Tide and Current Tables
Reference Port – Alert Bay
Secondary Ports – Port Neville, Port
Harvey

CURRENTS

Reference Station – Johnstone Strait
Central
Secondary Station – Forward Bay
Note – Strong currents of up to 4 knots
occur at the entrance to Port Neville.
On a large tide, currents of up to 2
knots occur in Havannah Channel.

WEATHER

Weather Station – WX1 162.55 MHZ
Area – Johnstone Strait
Reporting Station – Fanny Island

CAUTIONARY NOTES: *Strong westerly*
winds forecast for Johnstone Strait equate
to equally strong winds in Sunderland
and Havannah Channels. Although the
current runs a maximum of 1.5 knots in
West Johnstone Strait, in a wind-against-
current situation this section of the strait
is reputed for uncomfortable, short
choppy seas. These can be potentially
hazardous for small craft.

All craft travelling east or west between Hardwicke and the Broken Islands have to transit the western portion of Johnstone Strait. It would be prudent to plan your journey on an ebb tide and before the westerly winds get up, as there is little shelter in Johnstone Strait or Sunderland Channel. If shelter is required, visit lovely Port Neville with its resident deer and historic post office and store, which is also a museum and art gallery. Stay overnight and enjoy a potluck supper or investigate the peaceful, upper reaches of Port Neville.

Many boaters wishing to shorten their Johnstone Strait transit will head north via Havannah and Chatham Channel to Lagoon Cove Marina (Chapter 14) or continue west to explore the anchorages and shell-midden beaches in Cleo Channel and the wild-life-filled wetlands in Potts Lagoon.

We opted for the morning ebb to Forward Bay, West Cracroft Island, before heading west into Broughton Strait (see Chapter 6). Tucked behind Bush Islets, the bay offers a charming picnic stop and an inviting, crescent-shaped gravel beach fringed by storm-tossed driftwood.

It was not until our homeward-bound journey that we discovered Port Harvey, a quiet inlet between East and West Cracroft Islands. Seeking shelter from a 45-knot westerly gale, we found protected and comfortable anchorage at the head of the inlet, with good holding in sticky mud and a peaceful night's sleep.

FEATURED DESTINATIONS

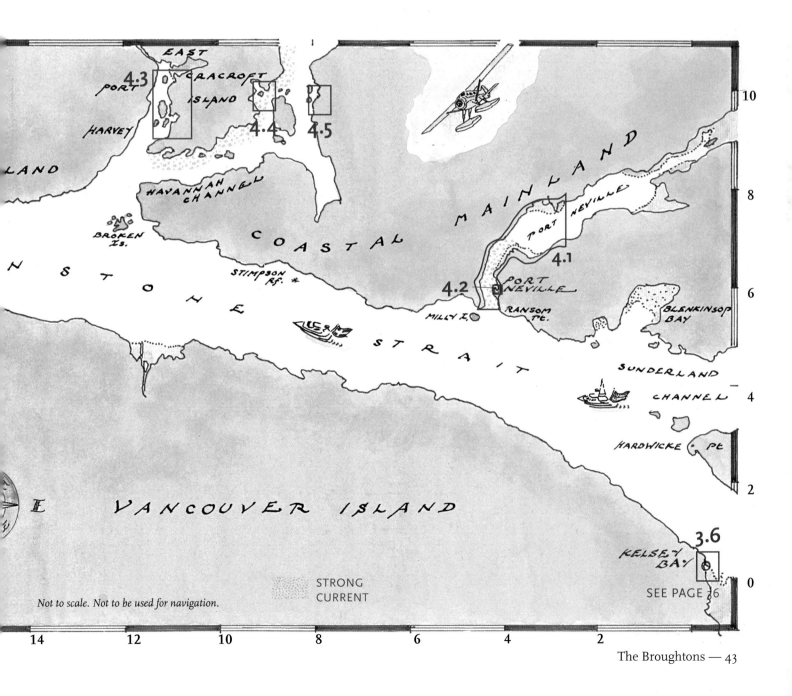

Not to scale. Not to be used for navigation.

STRONG CURRENT

4.1 PORT NEVILLE

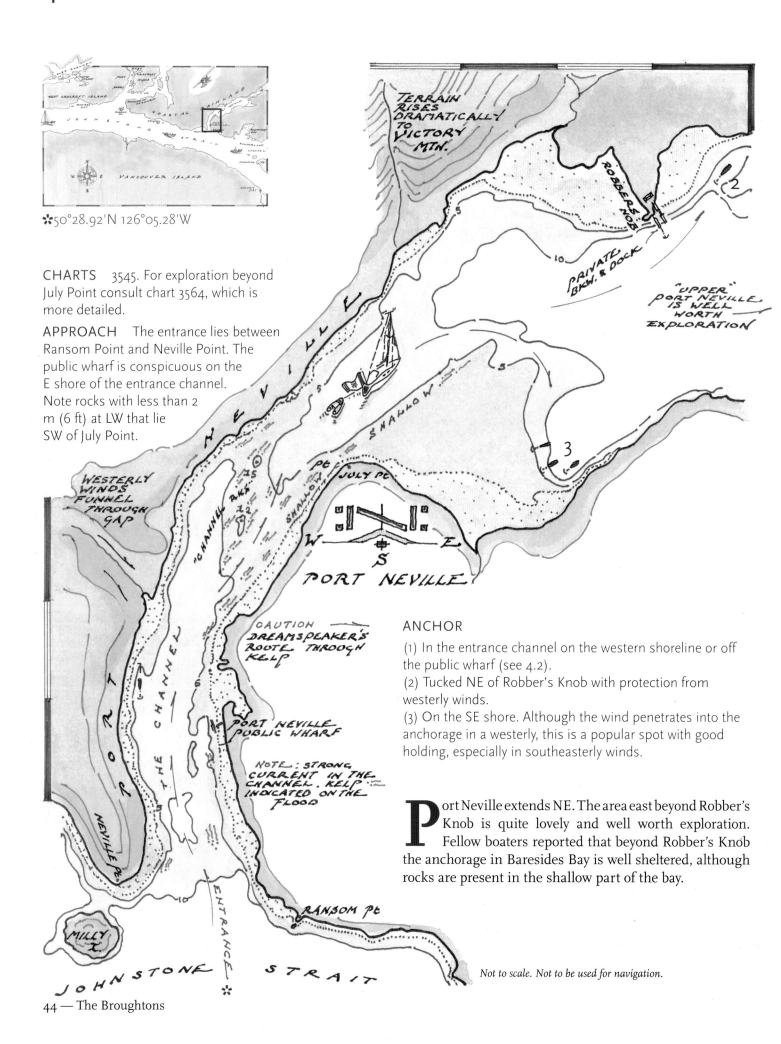

✳ 50°28.92'N 126°05.28'W

CHARTS 3545. For exploration beyond July Point consult chart 3564, which is more detailed.

APPROACH The entrance lies between Ransom Point and Neville Point. The public wharf is conspicuous on the E shore of the entrance channel. Note rocks with less than 2 m (6 ft) at LW that lie SW of July Point.

Map labels:
TERRAIN RISES DRAMATICALLY TO VICTORY MTN.

ROBBERS KNOB

PRIVATE BKW. & DOCK

"UPPER" PORT NEVILLE IS WELL WORTH EXPLORATION

NEVILLE

SHALLOW

SHALLOW PE

JULY PE

WESTERLY WINDS FUNNEL THROUGH GAP

"CHANNEL RKS"

PORT NEVILLE

THE CHANNEL

NEVILLE PE

CAUTION — DREAMSPEAKER'S ROUTE THROUGH KELP

PORT NEVILLE PUBLIC WHARF

NOTE: STRONG CURRENT IN THE CHANNEL. KELP INDICATED ON THE FLOOD

MILLY I.

RANSOM PE

ENTRANCE ✳

JOHNSTONE STRAIT

ANCHOR

(1) In the entrance channel on the western shoreline or off the public wharf (see 4.2).

(2) Tucked NE of Robber's Knob with protection from westerly winds.

(3) On the SE shore. Although the wind penetrates into the anchorage in a westerly, this is a popular spot with good holding, especially in southeasterly winds.

Port Neville extends NE. The area east beyond Robber's Knob is quite lovely and well worth exploration. Fellow boaters reported that beyond Robber's Knob the anchorage in Baresides Bay is well sheltered, although rocks are present in the shallow part of the bay.

Not to scale. Not to be used for navigation.

APPROACH   From the SW.
The public wharf and store are
conspicuous.

ANCHOR   Off the public wharf.

PUBLIC WHARF   A well-maintained
dock with inside depths of a 2 m (6
ft) minimum; fishing boats have been
known to raft three deep here. You can
reach Lorna Hansen by calling Ransom
Point on VHF Channel 6 or call her cell
phone, 250-949-1535.

*Note: The flood and ebb current is strong
in the channel; approach the wharf with
the boat's bow to the current.*

The public wharf and store sign are conspicuous on the SW shore

Named by Captain George Vancouver in 1792, Port Neville had one of the first post offices on the coast, thanks to Hans Hansen and his family, who settled at the entrance channel in 1891. Enjoyed by five generations of Hansens, the gardens, manicured lawns, and original orchards are fringed by a fine sand-and-pebble beach with glorious sunsets.

Today, the museum and art gallery (formerly the post office and store) is run by Lorna Hansen and her daughter, Erica (when she is not away at school). They invite boaters who tie up at the public wharf that dates from the Union Steamship days, to visit their property. Please respect their property – leash and clean up after your dog, and no smoking in the grounds or in the museum. Impromptu dinner and dessert potlucks are the norm in the busy summer months – no alcohol please. All are welcome, including those at anchor.

Note: Lorna will hold mail for cruising boaters, but make sure that your name and information are clear. Mail is picked up and delivered each Wednesday. Send c/o Lorna, Port Neville Post Office, B.C. VOP 1MO Canada.

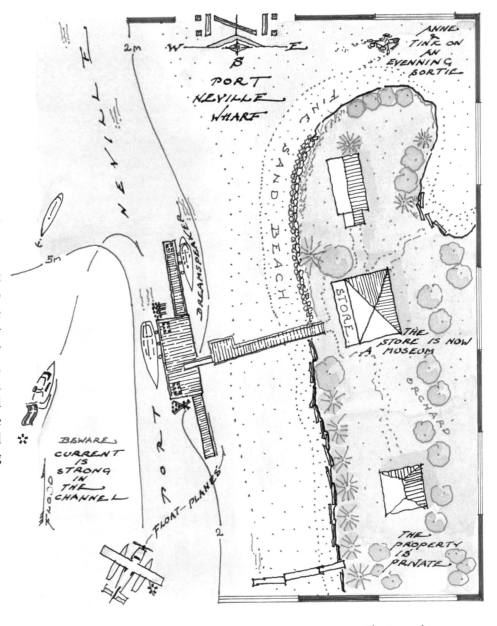

4.3 PORT HARVEY, EAST AND WEST CRACROFT ISLAND

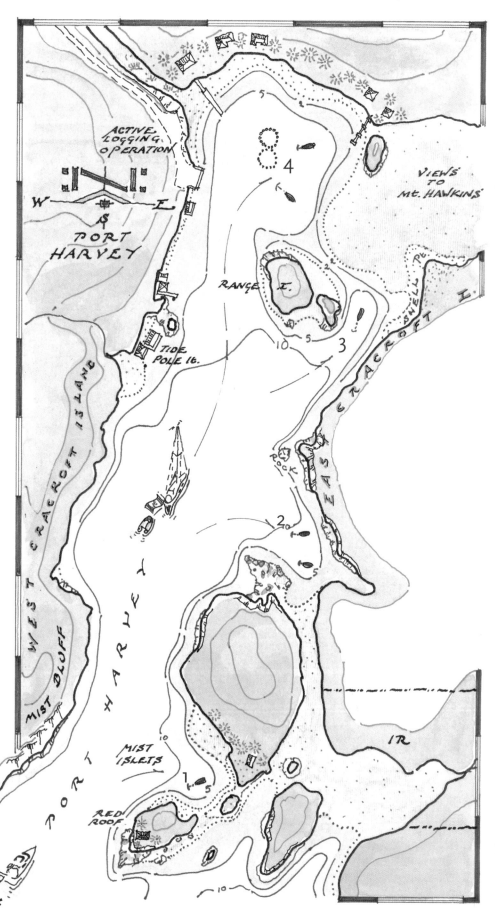

✳ 50°32.86'N 126°16.88'W

CHARTS 3545.

APPROACH Off Harvey Point. The run in along the W shore is clear; note the logging operations and log dumps that line the shore.

ANCHOR

(1) East of Mist Bluff, a local one-boat anchorage.

(2) Looks protected, but westerly winds do gust in, which puts your boat on a lee shore.

(3) One boat can tuck in behind Range Island – take care how you place the hook and gauge the boat's swinging room.

(4) The safest place to anchor is at the head of Port Harvey, to the E of the aquaculture rings in depths of 6-8 m (19-26 ft). With room to swing, the view out to Mount Hawkins is lovely, and the holding is excellent in sticky mud. *Dreamspeaker* and her crew survived a night of gale force westerly winds in relative comfort.

View out to Mount Hawkins

Not to scale. Not to be used for navigation.

BURIAL COVE, 4.4
EAST CRACROFT ISLAND

CHARTS 3545.

APPROACH (A) From the SW, between Round Island and East Cracroft Island.

ANCHOR In 5-10 m (16-32 ft) at the head of the cove, with holding good in mud. Well protected from westerly winds.

✣(A) 50°33.54'N 126°12.88'W
✣(B) 50°33.50'N 126°11.65'W

In settled weather both anchorages are fun picnic spots. For protection from westerly wind, use Burial Cove, and for easterly wind, use Matilpi Indian Islands.

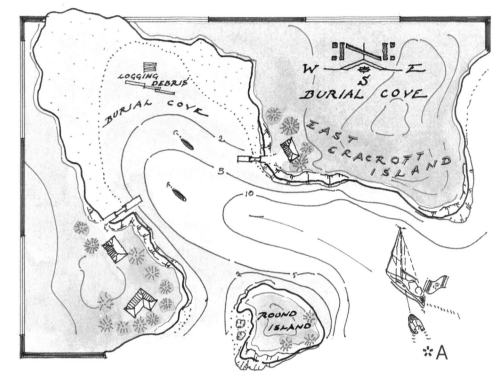

✣A

MATILPI INDIAN ISLANDS 4.5

CHARTS 3545.

APPROACH (B) From the W. It is a clear run in 10 m (32 ft) between the northern island and the charted rocks.

ANCHOR Off the white-shell beach in 5-10 m (16-32 ft). Holding good in mud. With a stern line ashore this anchorage is well protected from easterly winds and open to westerly winds.

The land and islands surrounding the anchorage are First Nations Reserves. The shell beach is an excellent example of a midden.

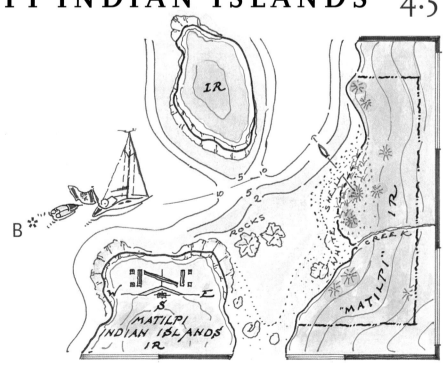

B ✣

4.6 FORWARD BAY, WEST CRACROFT ISLAND

CHARTS   3545.

APPROACH   From the E at LW. Piles of driftwood, including whole trees mark the HW line.

ANCHOR   Moderate protection from westerly winds can be had between Bush Islets and the shore in 5 m (16 ft). Holding good in sand and gravel.

❋50°31.12'N 126°24.33'W

Not to scale. Not to be used for navigation.

Beachcombing is filled with fun surprises

Tucked behind Bush Islets is an inviting, crescent-shaped gravel beach fringed by a pine and cedar forest, with a clear-water creek running through it. Storm-tossed driftwood and entire trees with their roots intact lie beyond the high water mark – a great spot to comb for small treasures amongst the tidal flotsam and jetsam. At low water, a small white-sand beach appears beyond the gravel. Forward Bay makes for a fine picnic stop.

Morning mist hangs in the bight off Klaoitsis Island

KLAOITSIS ISLAND, CLEO CHANNEL

✻50°34.17'N 126°28.27'W

CHARTS 3545.

APPROACH From Cleo Channel, the waypoint marks the initial channel prior to turning to starboard into "Laurence Passage" (named by us) or straight ahead to Potts Lagoon.

ANCHOR These anchorages are best explored at LW. Locations (1) and (2) are 2 bights protected from westerly winds, while (3) gives protection from southeasterly winds.

Dreamspeaker's crew spent an enjoyable day exploring the nooks and crannies between the islets off Klaoitsis Island, with breakfast in the northern anchorage between Wilson Pass and "Laurence Passage" and a picnic lunch on the semi-circular shell beach. We chose the less-crowded northern basin of Potts Lagoon for an overnight anchorage, peacefully swinging to the current. From here, you can visit Potts Lagoon by dinghy or kayak, but keep an eye on the tides if you plan to explore the upper reaches with its inviting marshlands and meadows. We were cautioned to keep a lookout for visiting black bears that come to enjoy the fruits of the lagoon and its wetlands. Float homes and the ruins of an old jetty line the S shoreline.

Not to scale.
Not to be used
for navigation.

POTTS LAGOON, 4.8
WEST CRACROFT ISLAND

CHARTS 3545.

APPROACH The waypoint given is E of Klaoitsis Island. Both entrances to the N and S basins of the lagoon are quite apparent.

ANCHOR (4) The N basin is less crowded and more open to the W, although protected from the SE. The holding is good in sand and mud, in depths of 3-6 m (9-19 ft). (See 4.7)

(5) The popular S basin has good all-around protection with good holding in mud, in depths of 3-6 m (9-19 ft).

Old jetty and floats in Potts Lagoon

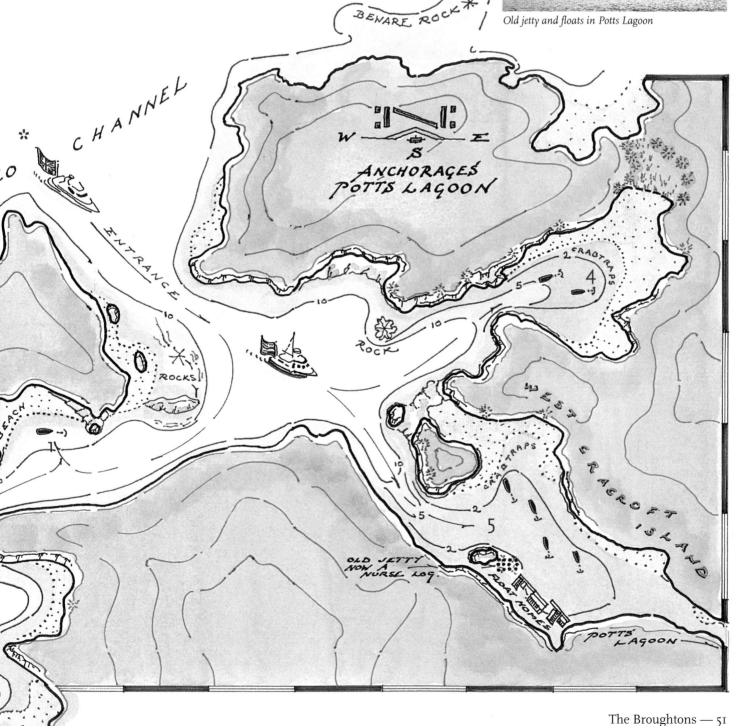

Cruise liners in Broughton Strait, off Cracroft Point, prior to entering Johnstone Strait

Chapter 5

BROUGHTON STRAIT

Whale Museum, Telegraph Cove

Chapter 5
BROUGHTON STRAIT

TIDES – *Volume 6,*
Canadian Tide and Current Tables
Reference Port – Alert Bay

CURRENTS

Reference Station – Seymour Narrows
Secondary Station – Baronet Passage

Reference Station – Johnstone Strait
Central
Secondary Station – Blackney Passage,
Alert Bay

Reference Station – Weynton Passage

WEATHER

Weather Station – WX1 162.55 MHZ
Area – Queen Charlotte Strait
Reporting Station – Alert Bay

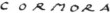

CAUTIONARY NOTES: *Be aware of the large number of commercial vessels and cruise liners that ply the waters in Broughton Strait, especially in the summer months.*

A current of up to 5 knots in Blackney Passage causes circular tide rips and turbulent water in both the passage and off Cracroft Point. Weynton Passage has a maximum 6-knot current and boaters should exercise caution when exploring the waters between Plumper and Pearse Islands, which lie on either side of the pass. Pearse Passage, between Cormorant and Pearse Islands, experiences a maximum 4-5 knot current. While docking in Alert Bay, keep in mind the 3-4 knot current in the bay.

This area is known for strong tidal currents and fog. Gale-force winds and accompanying seas can build at any time. Pre-planning and following marine weather predictions are essential.

Although this area is dominated by strong currents, Broughton Strait is protected from the worst of the westerly winds and seas in Queen Charlotte Strait by Malcolm Island to the north and the string of islands that lie south of Cormorant Channel.

A good spot for whale watching is outside the boundary of Robson Bight Ecological Reserve, a favourite "rubbing beach" for orcas. Boat Bay and Growler Cove, on West Cracroft Island, provide convenient picnic and overnight anchorage.

Cormorant Channel Marine Park, located between Broughton Strait in the south and Cormorant Channel and Blackfish Sound in the north, encompasses Stephenson Islet in Weynton Passage and a number of islands and islets from both Pearse and Plumper Islands. This delightful park supports a rich variety of wildlife and is the primary habitat of the northern resident orca population. It is also well used by parties of kayakers on the Johnstone Strait sea-kayaking circuit.

The charming boardwalk village of Telegraph Cove is not always easy to visit by boat, as transient moorage is limited. The Whale Interpretive Centre's *Bones Project* is an educational work, fascinating for all ages.

Friendly Alert Bay offers excellent provisioning and the sweetest water on the coast. With the impressive U'mista Cultural Centre, the ceremonial *Big House*, and the captivating display of totem poles in the 'Namgis burial ground, this is a destination not to be missed.

Mitchell Bay, Malcolm Island, is well protected from westerly winds and seas in Cormorant Channel. *Dreamspeaker* anchored here prior to entering the Broughton Archipelago.

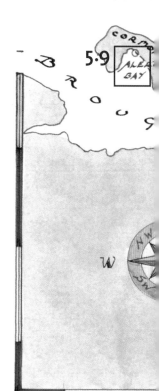

18

FEATURED DESTINATIONS

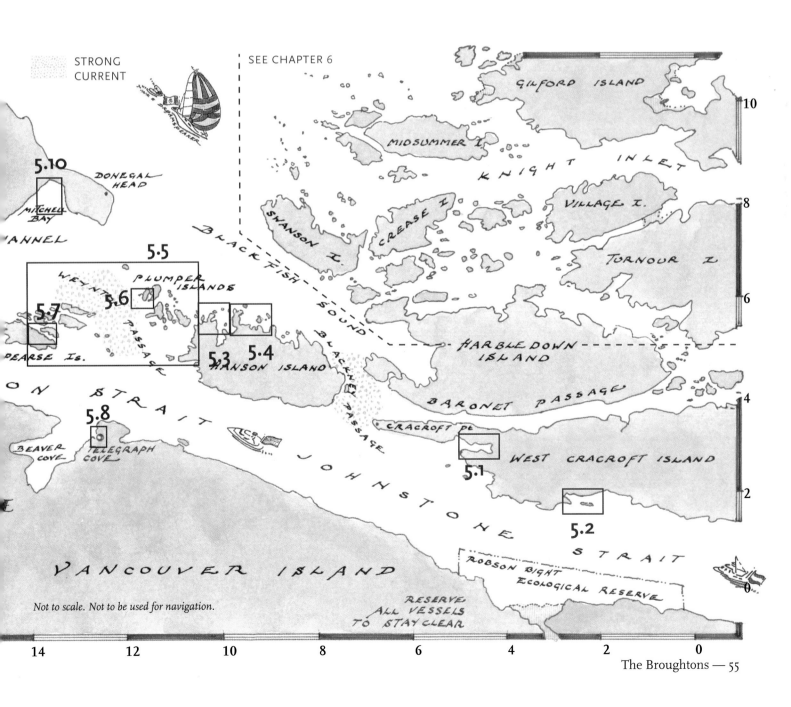

STRONG CURRENT

SEE CHAPTER 6

Not to scale. Not to be used for navigation.

5.1 GROWLER COVE, WEST CRACROFT ISLAND

✳ 50°32.36'N 126°38.16'W

CHARTS 3546.

APPROACH The waypoint lies to the N of Sophia Islands. The run lies in centre channel.

ANCHOR In 5-10 m (16-32 ft), below a distinctive rock cliff or further into the head of the cove. Holding good in mud.

Note: Growler Cove affords moderate protection from westerly winds.

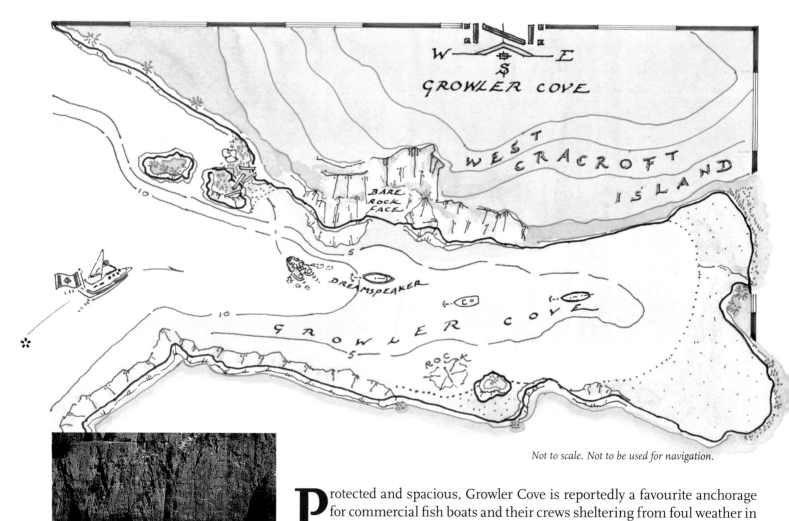

Not to scale. Not to be used for navigation.

Kayakers silhouetted against the bare rock cliff

Protected and spacious, Growler Cove is reportedly a favourite anchorage for commercial fish boats and their crews sheltering from foul weather in Johnstone Strait. The gently curved gravel beach is backed by driftwood logs, and a grassy picnic patch beside the stream is fronted by a small garden of sea asparagus. We were amused to find a concealed *forest toilet*, complete with an authentic seat and lid and a recycled fishnet fashioned into a hammock and slung between two trees.

BOAT BAY, 5.2
WEST CRACROFT ISLAND

CHARTS 3545.

APPROACH From the E at LW rounding "Tink's Island" (named by us) into Boat Bay. Rocks covered by kelp extend out from Camp Point, trapping driftwood logs and other debris.

ANCHOR There is fair protection from westerly winds, although open to the SE. Anchor in 5 m (16 ft) where holding is good in mud and sand.

Note: The small float and camp are reserved for the wardens of the Robson Bight (Michael Bigg) Ecological Reserve (across from Boat Bay) who advise boaters of the reserve's boundaries and regulations. The two wardens that visited Dreamspeaker were knowledgeable, friendly and enthusiastically committed to educating visitors on the lifestyle of killer whales.

✱50°31.31'N 126°33.07'W

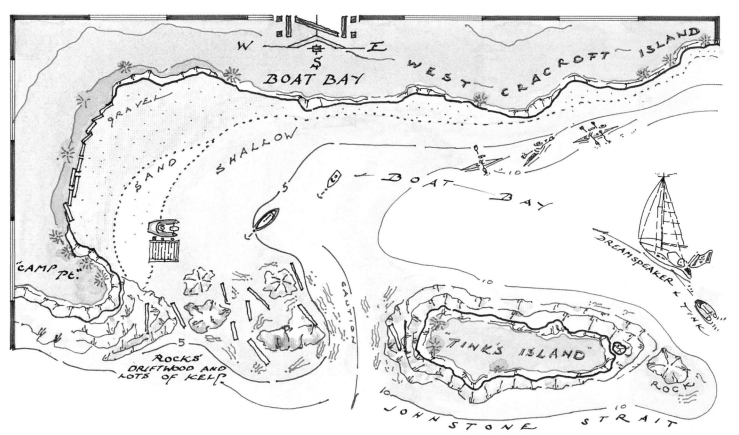

The ecological reserve located on the Vancouver Island shores opposite Boat Bay was established in 1982 as a sanctuary and to preserve important killer-whale habitat that also includes an upland buffer zone. Resident killer whales have long used Robson Bight as one of their rubbing beaches, and boats must keep at least half a nautical mile from the posted sign. Approach whales only from the side, never from the front or rear, and keep your engine in neutral or idle.

The friendly Robson Bight wardens in Boat Bay

5.3 DOUBLE BAY, HANSON ISLAND

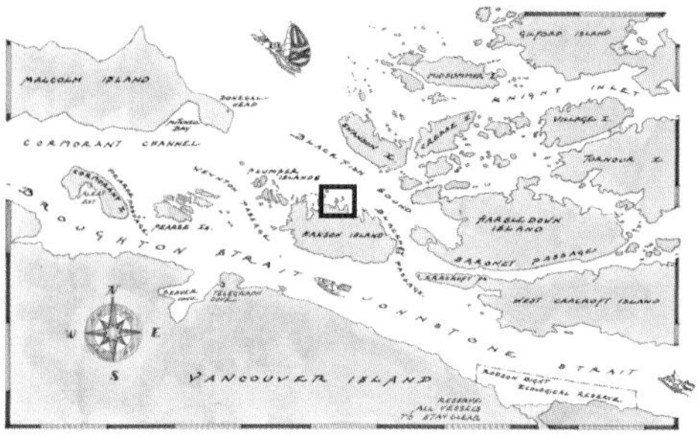

✲50°35.50'N 126°45.98'W

CHARTS 3546.

APPROACH From the N. The sign DOUBLE BAY RESORT atop a rock marks the starboard side of the entrance channel.

ANCHOR In the shelter of the group of islets and rocks in 5-10 m (16-32 ft), although somewhat open to a swell from Blackfish Sound. Holding good in mud and shell.

Note: The dock and moorage at DOUBLE BAY RESORT is private and reserved exclusively for resort guests.

Anchorage at the head of Double Bay, below the private resort, is deep and not recommended because of the noisy generator that resides there! For good depths and lovely views out to Blackfish Sound, drop the hook inside the cluster of rocks and islets to the north. The bay to the southeast is fun to investigate by dinghy at high water; at low water it dries to reveal a sizable shell and sand beach.

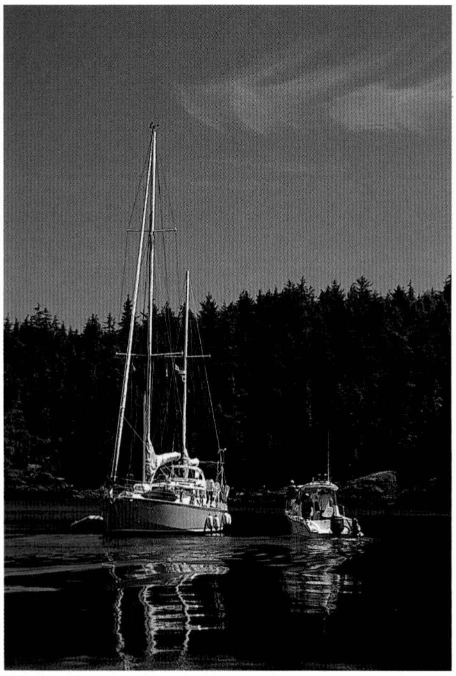

Mother ship and tender in Double Bay

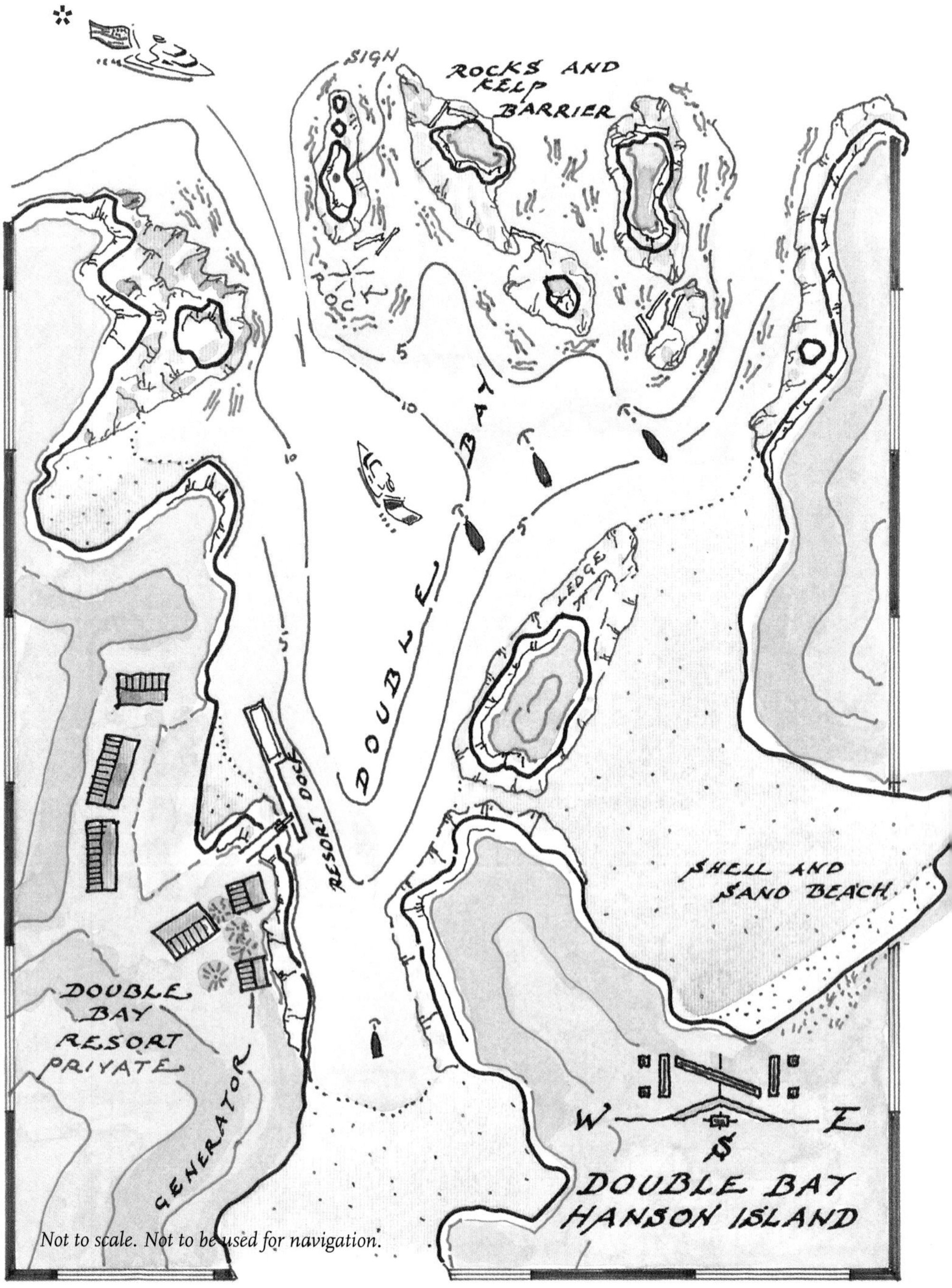

Not to scale. Not to be used for navigation.

SPOUT ISLETS, HANSON ISLAND 5.4

CHART 3546.

APPROACH (A) From the NE at LW. The run in is clear. (B) From the NE at LW, beware of the rock ledge to the SE and isolated rock to the W.

ANCHOR (1) Tuck into the W shore of "Spout Bay" (named by us). (2) Anchor as indicated in "Spout Cove" (named by us).

Note: Both locations afford only moderate protection from swell and westerly winds.

✵(A) 50°35.36'N 126°44.66'W
✵(B) 50°35.16'N 126°43.94'W

Spacious "Spout Bay" is a popular anchorage with ample room for a dozen boats. Tuck into the western shoreline and swing to the current, put out a stern anchor or take a stern line ashore. "Spout Cove" is a snug alternative with a beautiful islet to explore. Anchor at the head of the cove or south of the rock and kelp barrier. Surrounded by a rocky shoreline, this peaceful spot was quite comfortable for an overnight anchorage – just the occasional blowing of a passing orca pod and a lulling swell to rock one to sleep.

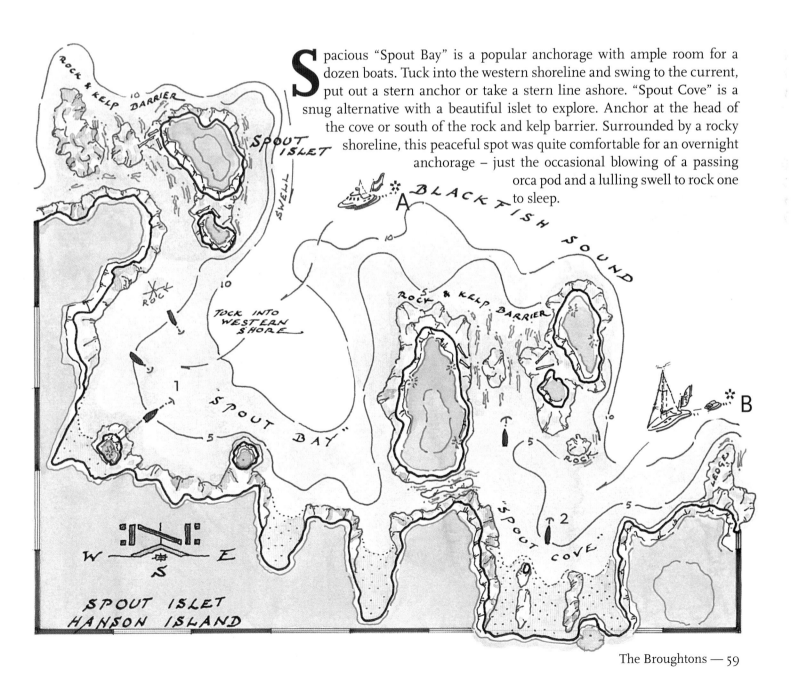

5.5 CORMORANT CHANNEL MARINE PARK

See 5.6 and 5.7 for detail opposite.

CAUTIONARY NOTE: *Weynton Passage is a current station. This area is known for strong tidal currents and fog. Gale-force winds and accompanying seas can build at any time. Pre-planning and following marine weather predictions are essential.*

❈(A) Plumper Group:
    50°35.24'N 126°48.87'W
❈(B) Pearse Islands:
    50°34.51'N 126°51.14'W

Located between Broughton Strait in the south and Cormorant Channel and Blackfish Sound in the north, CORMORANT CHANNEL MARINE PARK encompasses a number of islands and islets from both Pearse and Plumper Islands. It also includes Stephenson Islet in Weynton Passage.

Well-used by parties of kayakers on the Johnstone Strait sea-kayaking circuit, the park supports a rich variety of wildlife and is the primary habitat of the northern resident orca population.

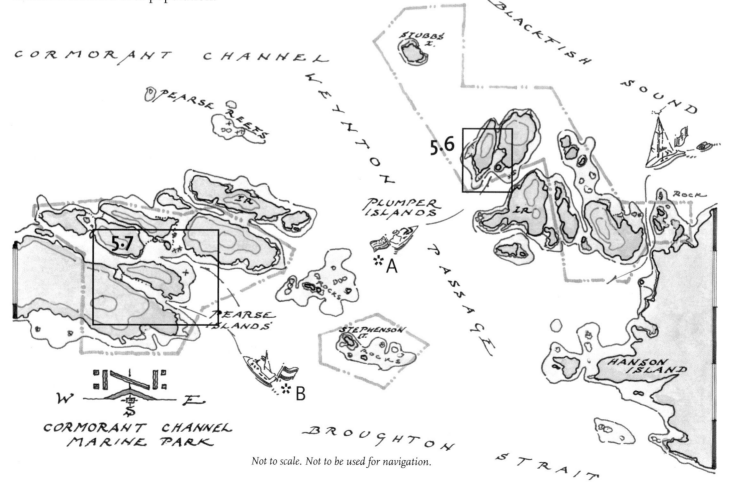

Not to scale. Not to be used for navigation.

PLUMPER GROUP, CORMORANT 5.6
CHANNEL MARINE PARK

A peaceful pool surrounded by kelp

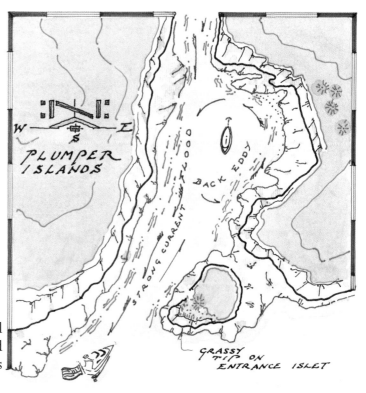

PLUMPER ISLANDS

STRONG CURRENT IN FLOOD

BACK EDDY

GRASSY TIP ON ENTRANCE ISLET

CHARTS   3546.

APPROACH   From the S at LW. The two islands lie to the NW of Ksuiladas Island.

ANCHOR   As indicated, in 5 m (16 ft); strong current is present.

Dreamspeaker swung to the current in the small pool created by the back eddy. Some boaters might find this anchorage a little unnerving; however, there is good protection from westerly and easterly winds.

PEARSE ISLANDS, CORMORANT 5.7
CHANNEL MARINE PARK

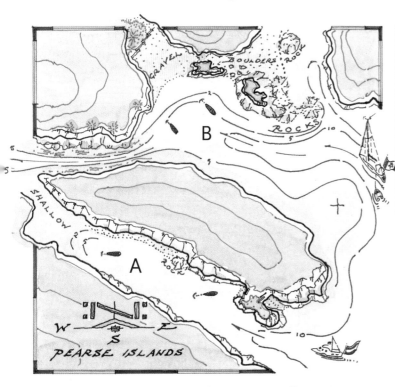

GRAVEL BAR

BOULDERS ROCK

ROCKS

SHALLOW

ROCK

B

A

PEARSE ISLANDS

Note: A good rendezvous spot for a number of boats.

A small gravel beach to stretch your legs

CHARTS   3546.

APPROACH   From the SE. Both approaches are deep and without obstruction. The channel between the two islands is navigable in the centre channel, although the current flows pretty swiftly.

ANCHOR   (A) This long, narrow and deep anchorage shallows at its head. (B) Keep an eye out for rocks off the NE shore. Swing in the centre, off the gravel beach, and enjoy the open view out to Broughton Channel and the mountains beyond. Good protection from westerly winds. Depths and holding vary.

5.8 TELEGRAPH COVE, VANCOUVER ISLAND

✣50°32.89'N 126°50.08'W

Approach to Telegraph Cove with gas dock to starboard

Moorage backed by the Killer Whale Café

Little room to manoeuvre in the centre channel

The charming boardwalk village of historic Telegraph Cove is not always easy to visit by boat; visitors often take a day-trip from Port McNeill, using public transportation, as it's well worth a visit. Taking a chance, we contacted TELEGRAPH COVE MARINA before reaching the entrance channel. It was our lucky day, and we were able to secure a slip big enough to accommodate *Dreamspeaker*'s 36-foot length for the night.

Although the architecture on this side of the cove is in total contrast to the historic village opposite, we appreciated the resort's clean shower and laundry facilities. THE SEAHORSE CAFÉ AND GALLERY at the head of Dockside 29 has a lovely view of the cove and serves great coffee and delicious breakfast and lunch dishes, from a bowl of granola, fruit and yoghurt to an egg-on-a-muffin or an artichoke panini.

The cove was named in 1911 when a telegraph station was built there; it also operated as a logging camp, saltery and a sawmill, which eventually supplied lumber for the boats, docks, bridges and railways on northern Vancouver Island. At that time, the community of Telegraph Cove had over 60 residents who were served by the Union Steamships. Pick up the lovely black-and-white sketch book by Teresa Petite and relive history with an informative boardwalk tour of the original timber buildings and homes.

Provisioning is possible at the well-stocked GENERAL STORE, which also has a B.C. LIQUOR STORE outlet. Buy a picnic lunch and spread a blanket on the lawn, enjoy the atmosphere and some fine pub grub at the OLD SALTERY PUB or pop into the KILLER WHALE CAFÉ, which serves very tasty lunch and evening dishes.

Jim and Mary Barrowman's WHALE INTERPRETIVE CENTRE is located in the old Freight Shed near the cove's entrance. Dubbed the "Bones Project," this educational work-in-progress is fascinating for all ages, as skeletons are cleaned and displayed on site. Volunteers encourage visitors to ask questions and will happily take you on a *bones tour*. We left the centre far more knowledgeable about marine mammals and the fascinating internal make up of a diverse number of whale species.

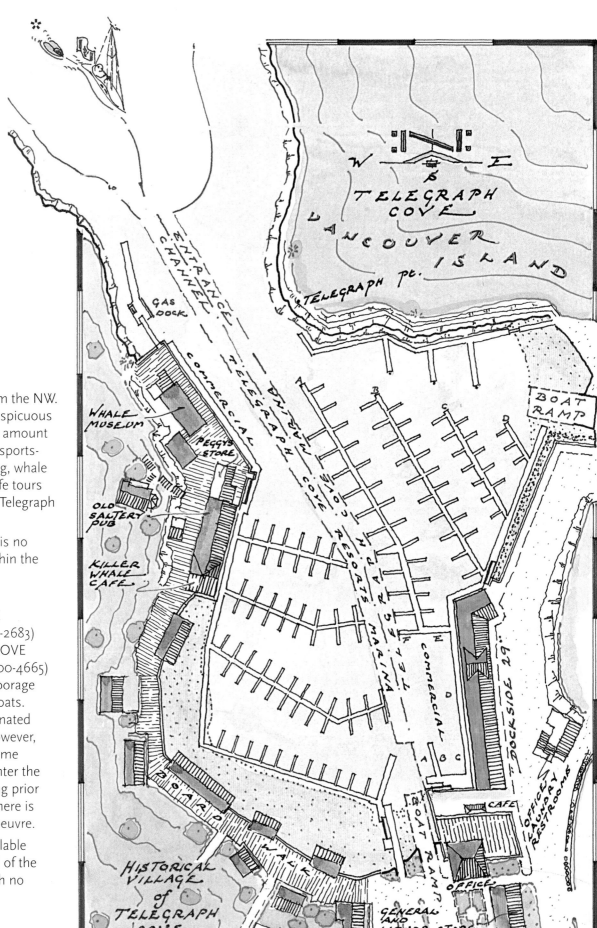

CHARTS 3546.

APPROACH From the NW. The entrance is conspicuous (in summer) by the amount of commercial and sports-boat traffic. Kayaking, whale watching and wildlife tours also operate out of Telegraph Cove.

ANCHOR There is no room to anchor within the cove.

MARINA Both TELEGRAPH COVE MARINA (1-877-835-2683) and TELEGRAPH COVE RESORTS (1-800-200-4665) are private, with moorage for sports fishing boats. They have no designated visitor moorage; however, some slips do become available. Do not enter the cove without making prior arrangements, as there is little room to manoeuvre.

FUEL Gas is available at the northern end of the boardwalk, although no diesel.

5.9 ALERT BAY, CORMORANT ISLAND

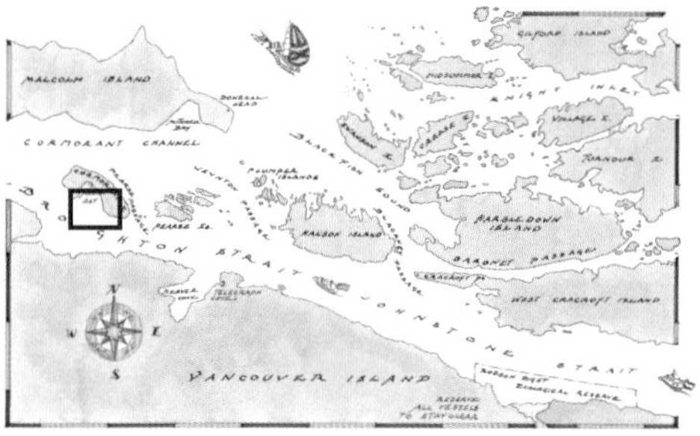

✣50°34.89'N 126°55.91'W

Even in Waddington Bay Dreamspeaker *finds a quiet nook.*

The colourful seawall

The historic Nimpkish Hotel and Pub

Historic Alert Bay and its friendly community are well worth a visit. With so much to see and do, stay overnight in the protected anchorage at the head of the bay or at the public wharf inside the breakwater north of the ferry terminal. A fun alternative is to take the scheduled ferry from Port McNeill on Vancouver Island; we enjoyed both.

South of the ferry terminal, the colourful Village of Alert Bay welcomes visitors to tie up at the convenient public wharf. From here, it's a short walk to Front Street and the island's ALERT BAY PUBLIC LIBRARY AND MUSEUM housing an excellent archival collection of historic and modern photographs. The well-appointed ALERT BAY VISITOR INFO CENTRE and art gallery offers internet access and a selection of free booklets and information leaflets. Call 250-974-5024 or contact them at info@village.alertbay.bc.ca or visit their website at www.alertbay.ca.

From the centre, take a self-guided tour of Alert Bay's historic buildings that date back to the mid-1800s, or walk along the Ecological Park trails and boardwalk built over a natural swamp at the top of the island, which hosts birds of many species. The variety of memorial poles displayed in the nearby 'Na̲mgis First Nation burial ground is captivating and ranges from vibrant, recently erected figures to those in the final stages of decomposition; poles are not repainted nor repaired, as the First Nation belief is that "all things must return to nature."

Excellent provisioning is available at the well-stocked supermarket and deli where you will find a choice of fresh produce, dry goods and hardware sections and even nautical charts. A liquor store and post office are nearby, and the sidewalk gift stores and art galleries carry local artists' works.

Front Street also offers a variety of fine, locally-run cafés and restaurants, including BILL'S CAFÉ across from the wharf, the historic OLD CUSTOMS HOUSE RESTAURANT and PASS'N TIME RESTAURANT, with a covered view-patio. The NIMPKISH HOTEL AND PUB, re-located by barge in 1925, has the perfect beach setting for sunset drinks, appetizers and dinners.

Located north of the ferry terminal, at the western end of Front Street, the U'MISTA CULTURAL CENTRE is a must see. Built in 1980, it houses one of

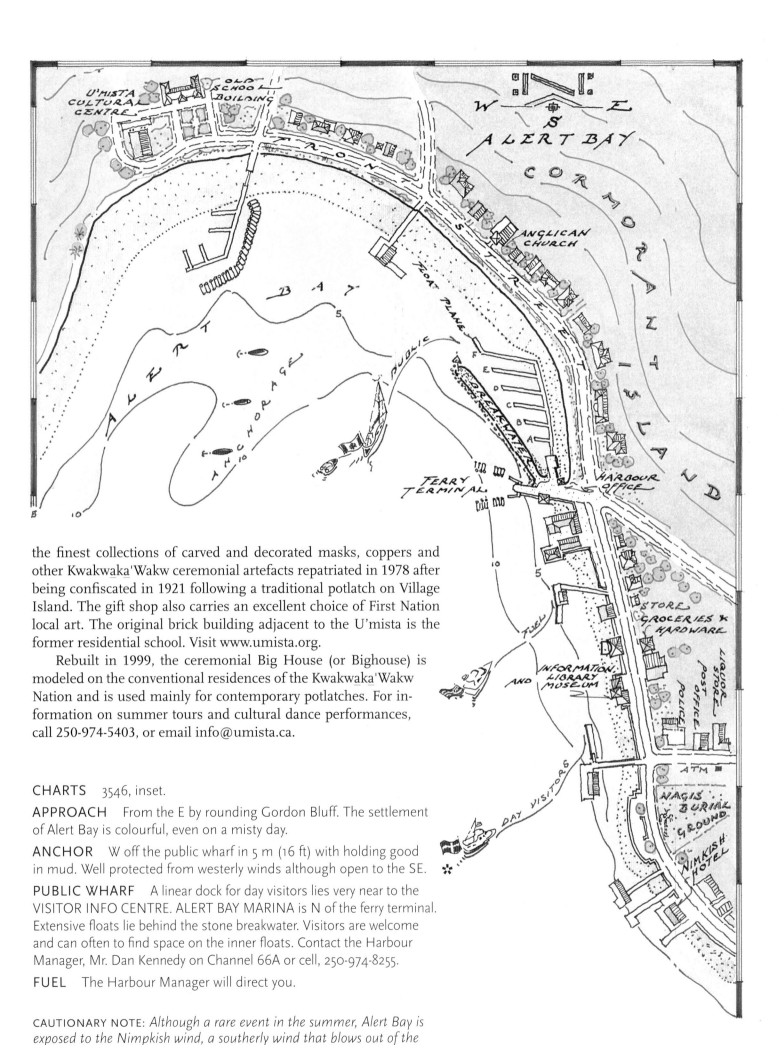

the finest collections of carved and decorated masks, coppers and other Kwakwaka'Wakw ceremonial artefacts repatriated in 1978 after being confiscated in 1921 following a traditional potlatch on Village Island. The gift shop also carries an excellent choice of First Nation local art. The original brick building adjacent to the U'mista is the former residential school. Visit www.umista.org.

Rebuilt in 1999, the ceremonial Big House (or Bighouse) is modeled on the conventional residences of the Kwakwaka'Wakw Nation and is used mainly for contemporary potlatches. For information on summer tours and cultural dance performances, call 250-974-5403, or email info@umista.ca.

CHARTS   3546, inset.

APPROACH   From the E by rounding Gordon Bluff. The settlement of Alert Bay is colourful, even on a misty day.

ANCHOR   W off the public wharf in 5 m (16 ft) with holding good in mud. Well protected from westerly winds although open to the SE.

PUBLIC WHARF   A linear dock for day visitors lies very near to the VISITOR INFO CENTRE. ALERT BAY MARINA is N of the ferry terminal. Extensive floats lie behind the stone breakwater. Visitors are welcome and can often to find space on the inner floats. Contact the Harbour Manager, Mr. Dan Kennedy on Channel 66A or cell, 250-974-8255.

FUEL   The Harbour Manager will direct you.

CAUTIONARY NOTE: *Although a rare event in the summer, Alert Bay is exposed to the Nimpkish wind, a southerly wind that blows out of the Nimpkish Valley.*

Memorial totem poles displayed in the 'Namgis burial ground, Alert Bay

MITCHELL BAY, MALCOLM ISLAND 5.10

At anchor off the public wharf

CHARTS   3546.

APPROACH   From the S, best at LW if intending to anchor. The public wharf and settlement are conspicuous with a logging operation, local buoys, driftwood and the coast road.

ANCHOR   Off the gravel beach between the boulders and seaward of the local buoys in 5-10 m (16-32 ft). Holding good in gravel and kelp.

PUBLIC WHARF   Local fish boats and runabouts occupy the wharf. It would be best to anchor off and take the dinghy ashore.

✳50°37.78'N 126°51.26'W

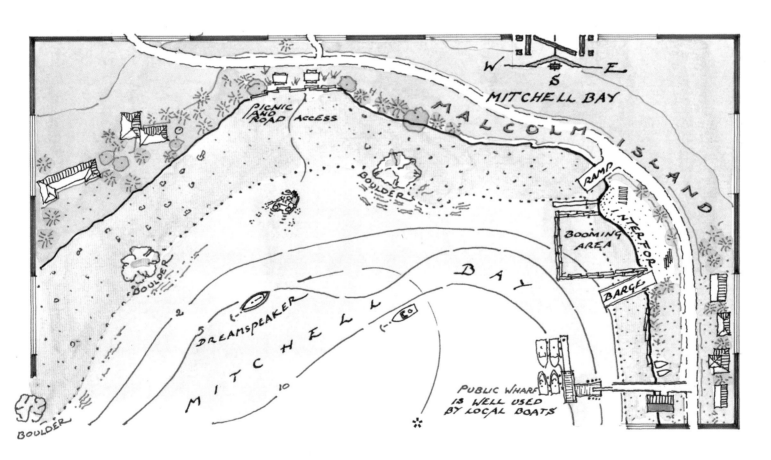

Note: Gusty winds sweep the bay when there are strong westerly winds in Queen Charlotte Strait.

Nestled between the trees on the southeast point of Malcolm Island lies the small, neat community of Mitchell Bay. The anchorage is backed by driftwood and a curved gravel beach with a picnic area and public access to the island road that begins at Pulteney Point in the west and ends at Donegal Head in the east. With *Dreamspeaker* securely anchored for the night, we sat in the cockpit at sunset to witness an exhilarating and loud display of herons, bald eagles and seagulls fighting to intercept the huge schools of fish caught in the kelp and whirling cross current. Early the next morning, we observed several locals out fishing in the traditional way – with rowboats and canoes.

5.11 BROUGHTON ARCHIPELAGO MARINE PARK

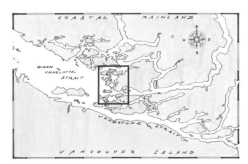

See chapters 6 & 7

The Marine Park is extremely popular with kayaking enthusiasts worldwide

Broughton Archipelago – The perfect place to meditate on the universe

Established in 1992 as a B.C. Protected Area, BROUGHTON ARCHIPELAGO MARINE PARK is British Columbia's largest marine park (116.79 km²/ 72.5 m²), and is located 30 km (18.6 m) east of Port McNeill, northern Vancouver Island; it is situated on the west side of Queen Charlotte Strait, near the mouth of Knight Inlet.

Broughton Archipelago Marine Park offers fabulous boating, kayaking and wildlife viewing opportunities and is extremely popular with kayaking enthusiasts worldwide. Although the many passages in the park are affected by the swift ebbing currents that force the waters of Queen Charlotte Strait through its countless islets and small islands, visitors can still find sheltered waters and a selection of protected anchorages backed by the magnificent, snow-topped coastal mountains to the east.

The area has a rich 12,000-year history, as its sheltered waters, abundant sea life and natural vegetation were the mainstay of the Kwakiutl First Nation who established numerous village communities in the Broughton Archipelago. The many shell-midden beaches and clam gardens among the park's captivating maze of islands and islets give evidence to cruisers and kayakers of the bountiful lifestyle before the area was discovered by European explorers in the late 1700s and settled by pioneers in the late 1800s and early 1900s. The remains of these sites, plus culturally modified trees (large old red cedar trees known as CMTs), and an ancient pictograph painted on a rock wall in Village Channel can also be found in the park. The pictograph is on the north side of Berry Island, near a small rock pool known as the "Chief's Bathtub." *Note that all heritage sites are protected by law – please treat these areas with respect.*

Note: See Chapter 6 Broughton Archipelago South p. 71, and Chapter 7 Broughton Archipelago North p. 85 for details of marine park destinations.

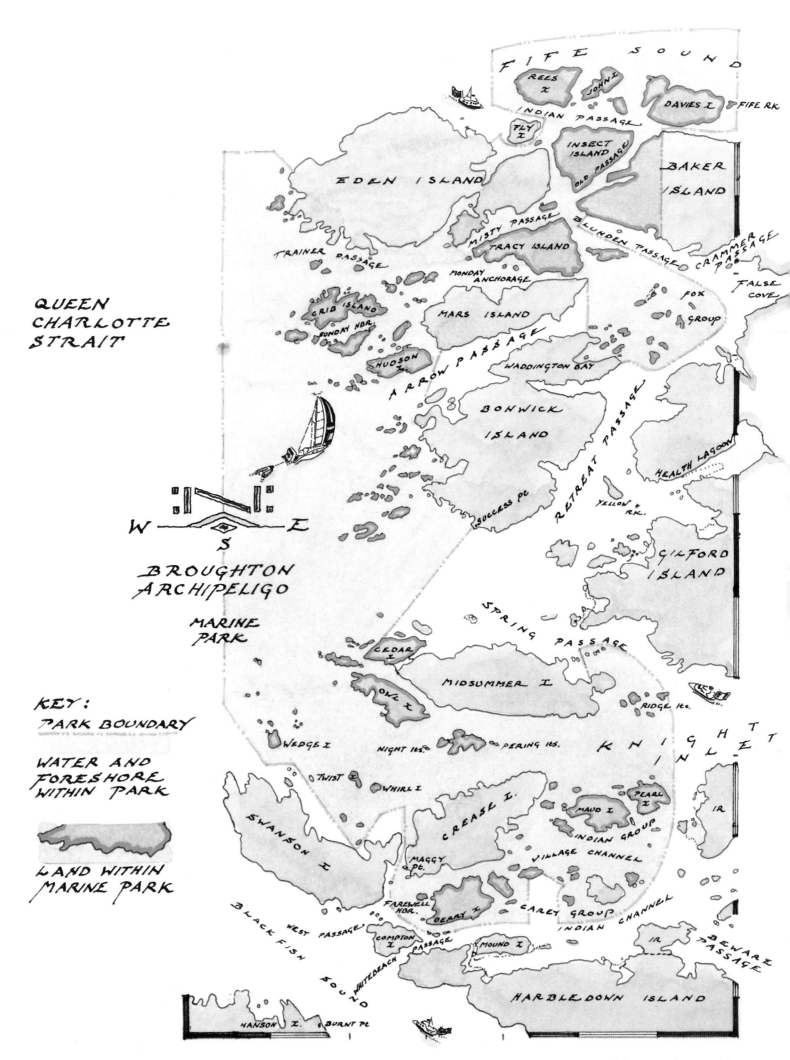

QUEEN
CHARLOTTE
STRAIT

BROUGHTON
ARCHIPELIGO

MARINE
PARK

KEY:
PARK BOUNDARY

WATER AND
FORESHORE
WITHIN PARK

LAND WITHIN
MARINE PARK

FIFE SOUND

REES I

JOHN I

DAVIES I

FIFE RK

INDIAN PASSAGE

TLY I

INSECT ISLAND

OLD PASSAGE

BAKER ISLAND

EDEN ISLAND

MISTY PASSAGE

TRACY ISLAND

BLUNDEN PASSAGE

CRAMMER PASSAGE

FALSE COVE

TRAINER PASSAGE

MONDAY ANCHORAGE

CRIB ISLAND

SUNDAY HBR.

MARS ISLAND

FOX GROUP

HUDSON I.

ARROW PASSAGE

WADDINGTON BAY

BONWICK ISLAND

RETREAT PASSAGE

HEALTH LAGOON

SUCCESS PT.

YELLOW RK.

GILFORD ISLAND

SPRING PASSAGE

CEDAR I

MIDSUMMER I.

OWL I

RIDGE ICS.

WEDGE I

NIGHT ICS.

PERING ICS.

KNIGHT INLET

TWIST

WHIRL I

PEARL I

MAUD I

CREASE I.

INDIAN GROUP

SWANSON I

MAGGY PT.

VILLAGE CHANNEL

FAREWELL HBR.

DEARY I

CAREY GROUP

INDIAN CHANNEL

BLACKFISH SOUND

WEST PASSAGE

COMPTON I

WHITEBEACH PASSAGE

MOUND I

BEWARE PASSAGE

HARBLEDOWN ISLAND

HANSON I.

BURNT PT.

W   E
   S

The Broughtons — 69

A serene evening anchorage aglow in Broughton Archipelago

Chapter 6

BROUGHTON ARCHIPELAGO SOUTH

Chapter 6
BROUGHTON ARCHIPELAGO SOUTH

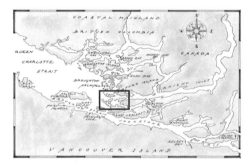

The Village of 'Mi'mkwamlis (Mamaliliculla) slowly retreating back to nature

TIDES – *Volume 6,*
Canadian Tide and Current Tables
Reference Port – Alert Bay
Secondary Port – Cedar Island

CURRENTS
No specific reference or secondary stations cover this chapter; however, currents run swiftly through the channels and passages, creating a certain amount of current in most anchorages.

WEATHER
Weather Station – WX1 162.55 MHZ
Area – Queen Charlotte Strait
Reporting Station – Alert Bay

CAUTIONARY NOTES: *Countless marked and unmarked rocks and reefs are well scattered throughout this southern portion of the Broughton Archipelago; explore the area at low water when the dangers are visible – fog will also obscure the proliferation of rocks.*

The locations of rocks and reefs are often well marked by the presence of kelp, which also indicates the direction of currents; a path between kelp will often denote a deep-water passage.

There are two routes into the southern portion of Broughton Archipelago from Blackfish Sound – the popular southern choice through Whitebeach Passage is clear and unobstructed, while the less straightforward northern route via West Passage experiences current swirls from unexpected directions and should be navigated only at low water, when the rocks are visible.

Once inside this magnificent village of islands, the uninterrupted vista of the island groups is quite breathtaking, and further exploration reveals splendid views around every headland. Cruising through the Broughton Archipelago helps to bring the area's ancient Native history to life, and at low water the clam gardens and middens with sun-bleached, white-shell beaches pinpoint the sites of the numerous Native villages and food gathering areas. Kayaking parties paddling between the islands have now replaced the hundreds of dugout canoes that plied these waters, ferrying locals and commodities between the now-deserted villages. Please treat these sites and any artefacts with respect at all times.

Strewn with an abundance of marked and unmarked islets and rocks, aptly named Beware Passage, located between Village and Turnour Islands, also has strong currents and should be navigated with caution, preferably at low water. When transiting south to Cleo Channel, Beware Cove is the only suitable fine-weather anchorage in the passage.

Prior to leaving this captivating maze of islands, drop anchor off protected Crease Island and explore charming Goat Islet. Adorned with a mass of wild flowers in the springtime, this small islet provides the perfect picnic spot with a view, shaded by a single tree.

STRONG CURRENT

WEDGE I

TWIST

SWANSON I.

BLACK FISH

WEST PASSAGE

SOU

HANSON I.

BURN

6.

9

8

FEATURED DESTINATIONS

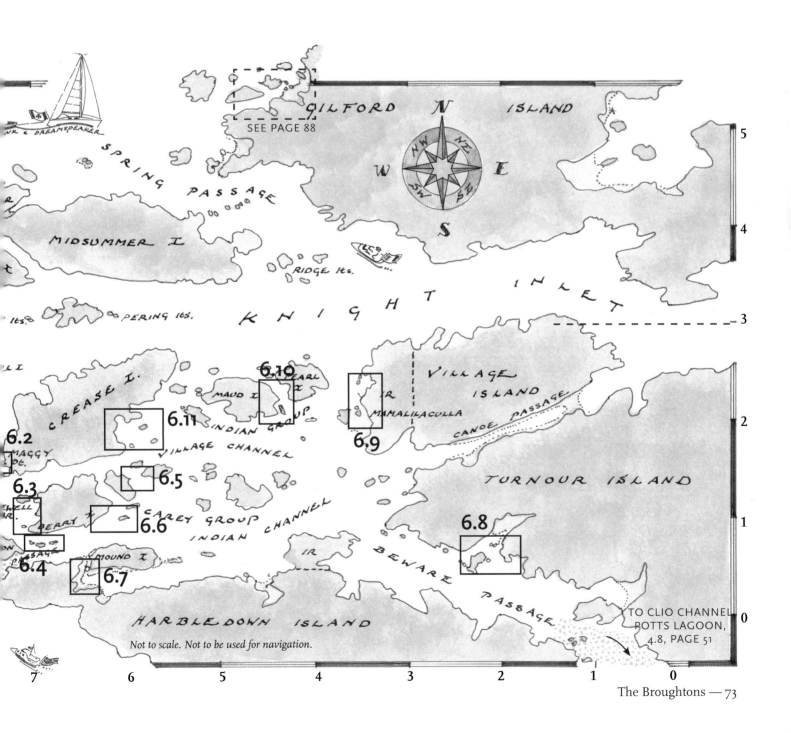

6.1 WEST PASSAGE BETWEEN SWANSON AND COMPTON ISLANDS

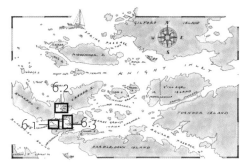

❃(A) 50°35.82'N 126°41.74'W
❃(B) 50°36.46'N 126°40.90'W
❃(C) 50°35.99'N 126°40.52'W

CHARTS 3546.

APPROACH (A) From Blackfish Sound. After rounding Slate Point with an eye out for Punt Rock to the W, leave Star Islets either to the S or to the N with caution, as this passage is navigable, but fringed with kelp.

MARINA Compton Island Marina is a seasonal facility for kayaks and small craft.

Kayaks at Maggy Point

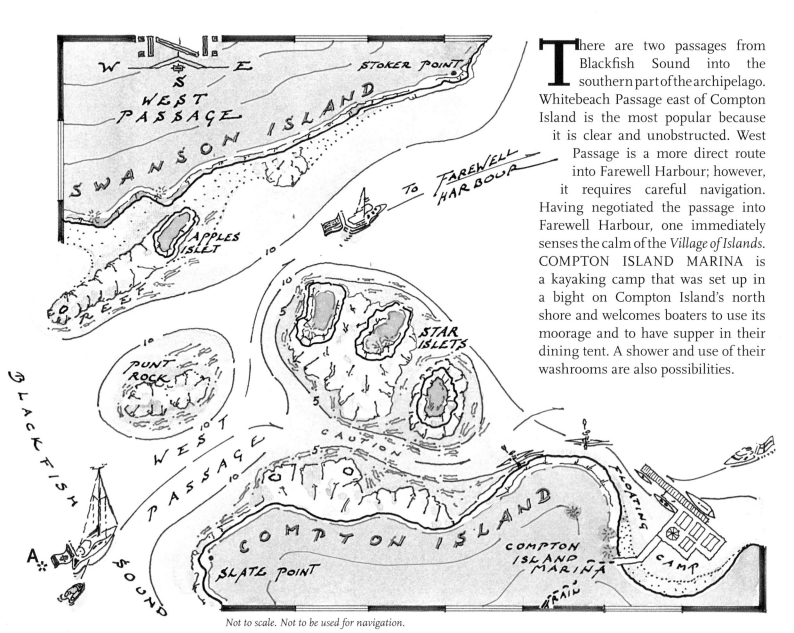

There are two passages from Blackfish Sound into the southern part of the archipelago. Whitebeach Passage east of Compton Island is the most popular because it is clear and unobstructed. West Passage is a more direct route into Farewell Harbour; however, it requires careful navigation. Having negotiated the passage into Farewell Harbour, one immediately senses the calm of the *Village of Islands*. COMPTON ISLAND MARINA is a kayaking camp that was set up in a bight on Compton Island's north shore and welcomes boaters to use its moorage and to have supper in their dining tent. A shower and use of their washrooms are also possibilities.

Not to scale. Not to be used for navigation.

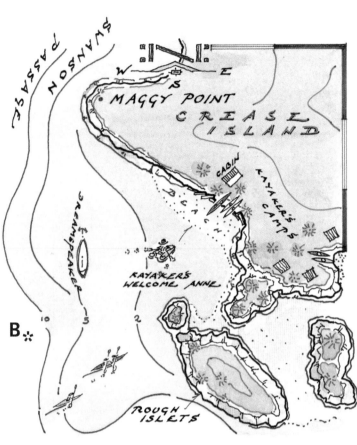

CHARTS 3546.

APPROACH (B) From within Farewell Harbour leaving Rough Islets to the E or from Swanson Passage in the N. Both are clear and without obstruction.

ANCHOR In depths of 3-6 m (9-19 ft) with protection from the west. Holding is good in sticky mud and kelp.

Within the Broughton Archipelago Marine Park boundaries, this delightful spot is useful as a picnic or overnight stop and is also home to an established summer kayak camp complete with a covered cookhouse just off the beach, rustic shower and toilet facilities and tent platforms in the trees. While on a row of discovery in *Tink*, we were invited by the camp's friendly group of paddlers to share their happy hour fruit cocktails and appetizers – luxury camping at its best.

For overnight anchorage in Farewell Harbour, the spots indicated S of Kumax Island give good protection.

FAREWELL HARBOUR, 6.3
BERRY ISLAND

CHARTS 3546.

APPROACH (C) From the W. The private fishing lodge on a rocky point, central to the bay, is conspicuous.

ANCHOR To the N of the lodge, S of Kumax Island in 4-10 m (13-32 ft). Excellent holding in sticky mud. Well protected from the E with moderate protection from the W.

Note: The lodge float is private.

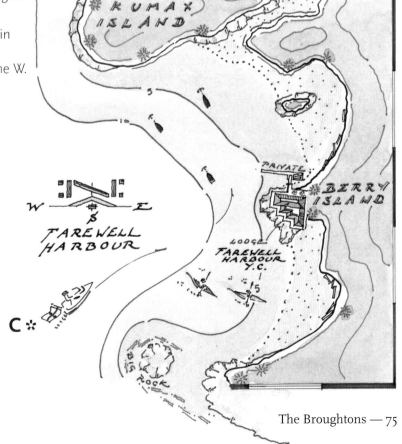

Farewell Harbour Lodge and private dock

6.4 SARAH ISLETS

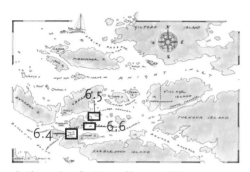

❋ (A) 50°35.84'N 126°40.43'W
❋ (B) 50°36.55'N 126°38.77'W
❋ (C) 50°35.94'N 126°39.02'W

CHARTS 3546.

APPROACH   (A) From Farewell Harbour. The passage N of Sarah Islets is lined with kelp and the most conspicuous landmark is the white-shell mound on the eastern islet.

ANCHOR   To the N of Sarah Islets, in a kelp-free spot. This is a comfortable anchorage in settled weather, where a boat will swing to the current in depths of 6-8 m (19-26 ft). Protected from the S with some protection from the E and W, with fair holding in sand and shell.

Tranquility personified in Sarah Islets

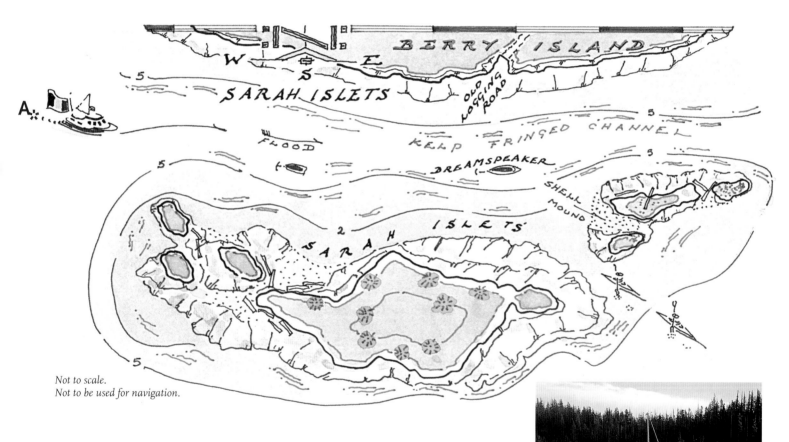

Not to scale.
Not to be used for navigation.

We found three spots in the approach to Indian Channel, Sarah Islets and the anchorages south of Madrona Island and Leone Islets. The channel between Sarah Islets and Berry Island is an ideal spot to anchor for the night in settled weather, if you're looking for a secluded alternative to Farewell Harbour. Kayakers use the narrow pass between the midden and the islets. With views east down Indian Channel, the islet and the white-shell mound are fun to explore. Take a break from the boat and beachcomb, picnic or harvest the fresh sea asparagus.

A sunset beam illuminates Dreamspeaker

CHARTS   3546.

APPROACH   (B) From Village Channel or alternatively from Indian Channel.

ANCHOR   Between Madrona Island and the small islet to the S, in a still pool of 4 m (13 ft) with little current and fair protection all round. Holding is fair in sand/gravel/kelp. In the evening, a glowing sunset illuminates the steep rock bluff on Madrona Island.

Note: Due to continuous generator noise from the nearby fish farm, we recommend this anchorage only when a westerly wind is blowing!

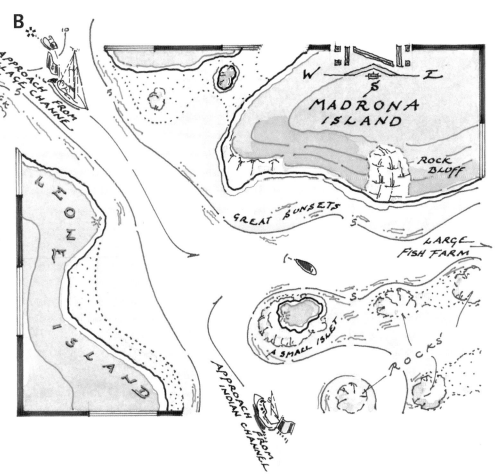

"LEONE ISLETS," LEONE ISLAND 6.6

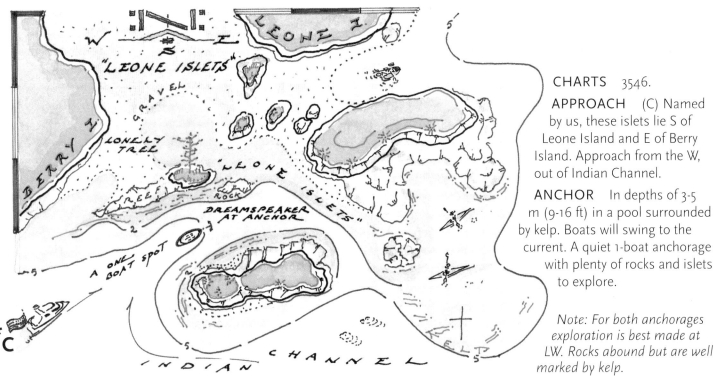

CHARTS   3546.

APPROACH   (C) Named by us, these islets lie S of Leone Island and E of Berry Island. Approach from the W, out of Indian Channel.

ANCHOR   In depths of 3-5 m (9-16 ft) in a pool surrounded by kelp. Boats will swing to the current. A quiet 1-boat anchorage with plenty of rocks and islets to explore.

Note: For both anchorages exploration is best made at LW. Rocks abound but are well marked by kelp.

6.7 "MOUND BAY," MOUND ISLAND

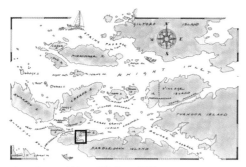

✷50°35.31'N 126°38.92'W

CHARTS 3546.

APPROACH From Indian Channel. The entrance lies between two unnamed islets to the E of Mound Island.

ANCHOR As indicated in depths of 4-10 m (13-32 ft), this commodious bay is well protected from westerly winds with good holding in mud.

Note: Some shelter can be found in the bay in moderate SE winds.

Good holding in mud with a stow-aboard sea star!

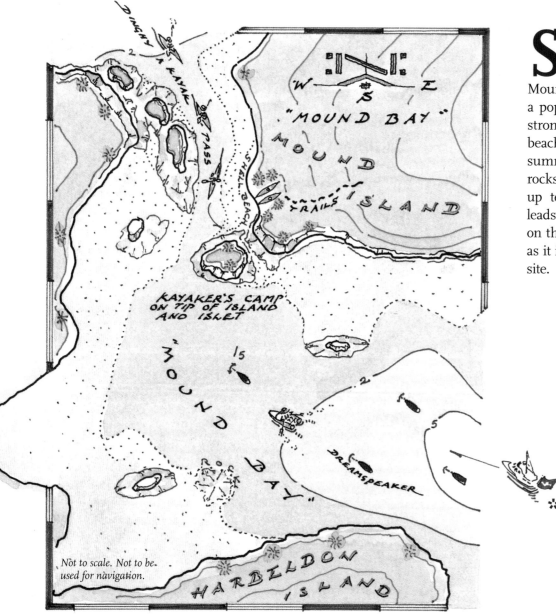

Not to scale. Not to be used for navigation.

Spacious and protected, the anchorage in "Mound Bay" (named by us) is tucked between Mound and Harbeldon Islands and is a popular hide-out for boaters during strong westerly winds. The small shell beach off Mound Island is backed by a summer kayak camp, with soft mossy rocks and islets for picnicking or setting up tents. The forest trail reportedly leads to a sanctuary of old-growth trees on the island. Please respect this area, as it is an ancient First Nations' burial site.

BEWARE COVE, TURNOUR ISLAND 6.8

CHARTS   3545.

APPROACH   From the W. The entrance channel N of Cook Island is clear. The alternative entrance from the S has a narrow and kelp-lined channel.

ANCHOR   To the NE of Cook Island in depths of 4-6 m (13-19 ft) with good holding in mud and shell. The cove is open to all winds, although it provides moderate protection from the NW.

Note: Beware Cove is a temporary anchorage with good views out. The cove is outside the marine park boundaries.

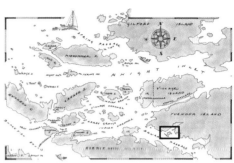

✴50°35.57'N 126°33.32'W

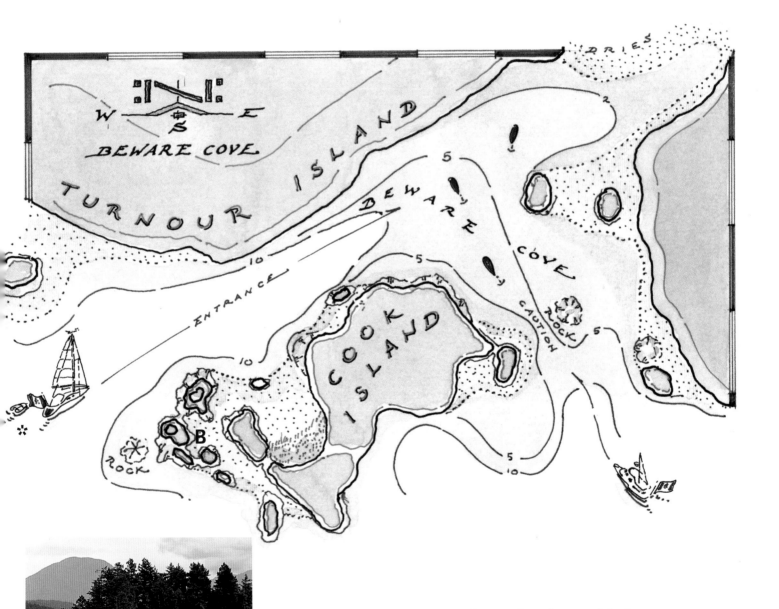

Local knowledge helps to know where to anchor in a SE blow

Beware Passage is aptly named for its strong currents and abundance of marked and unmarked islets and rocks, and therefore should be navigated with caution, preferably at low water. Beware Cove was the only suitable anchorage found in the passage on a transit south to Cleo Channel on a cold and overcast day. Cook Island looked inviting to explore on a sunny day.

Dreamspeaker *anchored in the bay north of the village*

A good example of a large, clam-shell midden beach

CHARTS   3546.

APPROACH   From Elliot Passage. Pass between the makeshift breakwater and the Barrier Islets to the N.

ANCHOR   In approximately 5 m (16 ft) with good holding in mud and shell. Protected from all but strong NW winds. There is a mooring buoy in the bay marked "Welcome," although there is no guarantee that is has been serviced.

Note: 'Mi'mkw<u>a</u>mlis is also accessible by dinghy from many of the anchorages featured in this chapter. No village tours were available when we visited.

⚓50°37.33'N 126°35.07'W

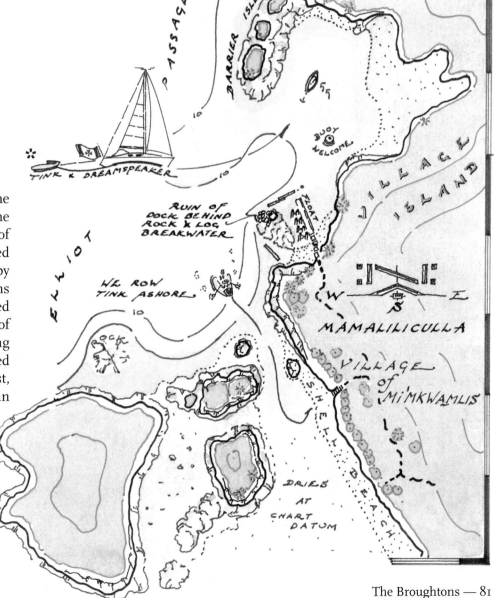

Anchoring *Dreamspeaker* in the bay, we rowed *Tink* past the breakwater and the remains of a float that leads to the now-abandoned village trail. In the fine rain, a wispy mist enveloping the overgrown ruins and fallen totem poles only added to the hushed, ghostlike mood of 'Mi'mkw<u>a</u>mlis. Fronted by a long shell beach and somewhat protected by the island and islets to the west, this once-thriving village, built on an ancient midden, housed a large First Nations community that in the early 1900s even included a schoolhouse. The book, *Totem Poles and Tea,* gives Hughina Harold's honest insight into village life in the 1930s, as does an account by M. Wylie Blanchet in the classic, *The Curve of Time.*

6.10 "PEARL PASS"

✽50°37.11'N 126°35.95'W

CHARTS 3546.

APPROACH From the S. Favour the Maud Island shore as rocks extend into the pass entrance.

ANCHOR In 2-5 m (6-16 ft) between the kelp patches, as indicated. Good protection in moderate westerly winds. In strong winds, swells surge in from the north.

Note: The kelp barrier at the head of the anchorage prevents further navigation.

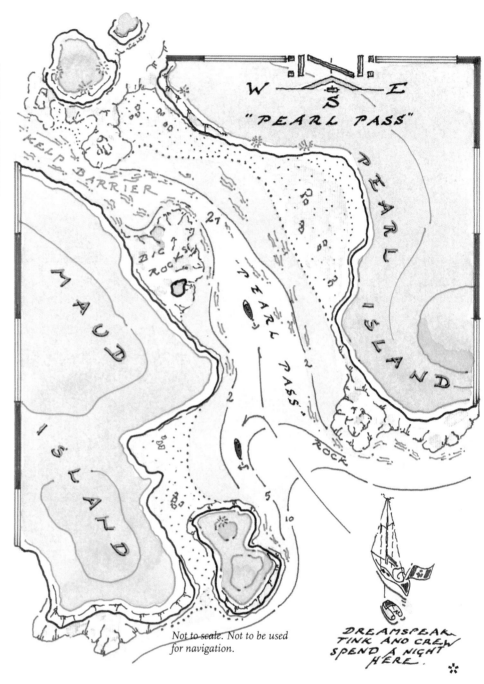

Not to scale. Not to be used for navigation.

A primeval morning at low water

Rocks and trees surround the kelp-lined but cozy two-boat anchorage that we named "Pearl Pass," tucked inside the entrance channel between Maud and Pearl Islands. With a fine view out to Village Channel, and our neighbours sharing their surprise halibut catch with us, a pleasant night was had by all.

GOAT ISLET, CREASE ISLAND 6.11

✽50°36.78'N 126°38.17'W

Not a goat in sight, however, a lone tree stands proud!

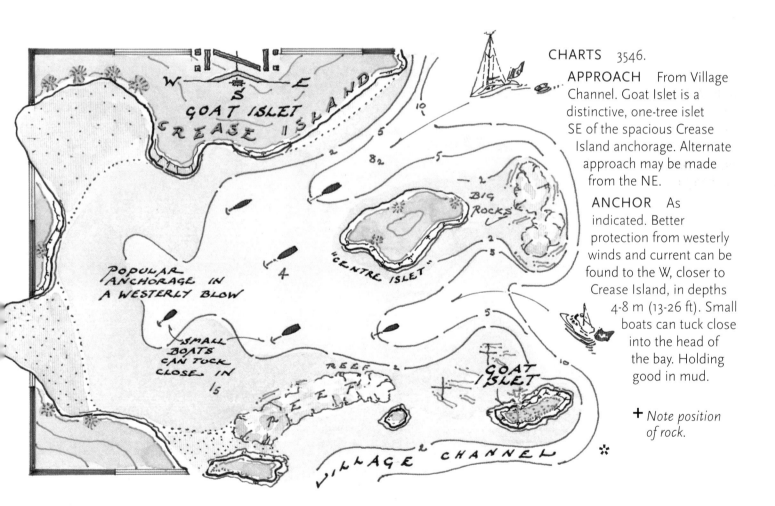

CHARTS 3546.

APPROACH From Village Channel. Goat Islet is a distinctive, one-tree islet SE of the spacious Crease Island anchorage. Alternate approach may be made from the NE.

ANCHOR As indicated. Better protection from westerly winds and current can be found to the W, closer to Crease Island, in depths 4-8 m (13-26 ft). Small boats can tuck close into the head of the bay. Holding good in mud.

✚ *Note position of rock.*

Adorned with a mass of wild flowers in the springtime, charming Goat Islet provides boaters with the perfect spot to picnic in the summer months. Explore the small island and enjoy the view out to Village Channel before spreading a blanket on the soft grass, shaded by a single tree. An experienced and friendly fisherman named Jim Davis, who anchors his boat there in the summer months, recommended this sheltered anchorage.

Ocean Dawn, *Anne and Goldy, Billy and Dreamspeaker* in
"Freshwater Bay" backed by Bill Proctor's homestead and museum

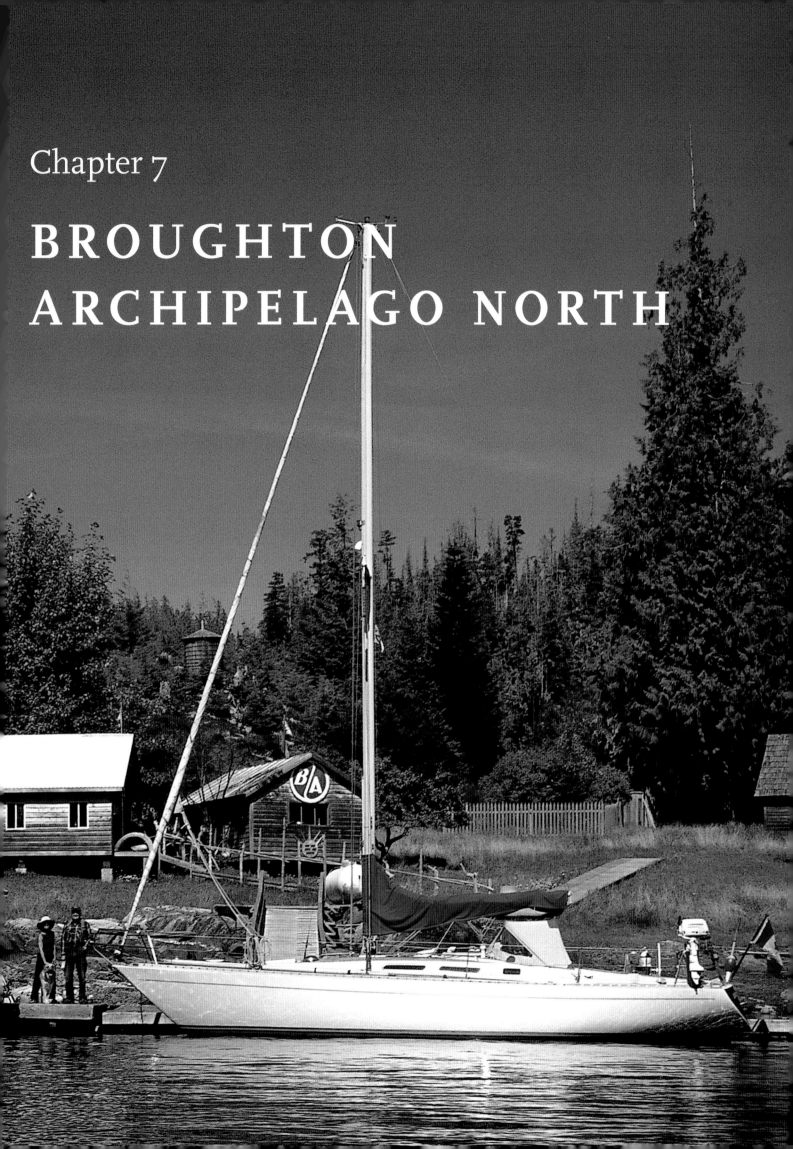

Chapter 7

BROUGHTON ARCHIPELAGO NORTH

Chapter 7
BROUGHTON ARCHIPELAGO NORTH

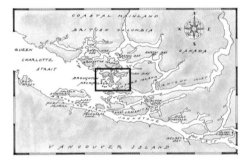

TIDES – *Volume 6,*
Canadian Tide and Current Tables
Reference Port – Alert Bay
Secondary Port – Sunday Harbour

CURRENTS

No specific reference or secondary stations cover this chapter; however, currents run swiftly through the channels and passages, creating a certain amount of current in most anchorages.

WEATHER

Weather Stations – WX1 162.55 MHZ
Weather Radio Canada 103.70 MHZ
Area – Queen Charlotte Strait
Reporting Stations – Alert Bay,
Port Harvey

Venturing into fog

CAUTIONARY NOTES: *The outer islands of the Broughton Archipelago that fringe Queen Charlotte Strait offer little protection from summer westerly winds; shelter should be found before wind and seas build. Although this northern section of the Broughton Archipelago is well charted, there are many unmarked rocks and it is best navigated at low water when the majority of dangers are visible. Morning fog is a prevailing condition in this area.*

Squeezed between Queen Charlotte Strait and Gilford Island, the northern isles of the Broughton Archipelago offer picturesque anchorages with snug coves east of Seabreese Island, Health Bay and Lagoon, and the inviting islets hugging Bonwick Island's western shore. Dusky Cove is a delight to explore in settled weather.

Waddington Bay, wedged into the northern tip of Bonwick Island, is well protected but a little crowded in the summer. Nearby, is a small anchorage we named "Kelp Bight," where we overnighted with great views.

Home to the now legendary fisherman, storyteller, author and environmental advocate Bill Proctor, Gilford Island is the largest in the enchanting Broughton region. Echo Bay provides a sheltered harbour, small marine park, and transient moorage, along with showers, laundry, provisioning and fuel. WINDSONG SEA VILLAGE RESORT (opposite) is a collection of float homes with an array of interesting characters. Beneath a breathtaking, 200-foot sheer cliff on the eastern shoreline of the bay, the view out to Cramer Passage is sensational.

A cruise in The Broughtons would not be complete without a night at PIERRE'S BAY LODGE AND MARINA, renowned for its Saturday night pig roasts. THE LIGHTHOUSE BAKERY AND THE COURTYARD offers home baking, light lunches and a gift store. West via Indian Passage takes you to Eden Island and "Lady Boot Cove," Monday Harbour and Joe Cove, a quiet, sheltered anchorage.

9

8

FEATURED DESTINATIONS

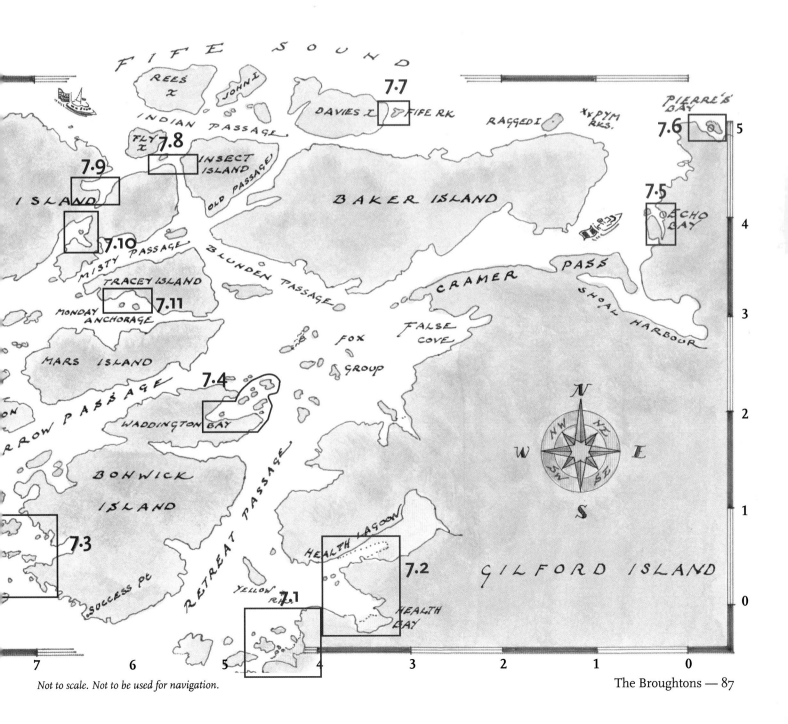

Not to scale. Not to be used for navigation.

7.1 COVES EAST OF SEABREESE ISLAND

✳50°40.79'N 126°36.79'W

CHARTS   3546.

APPROACH   Best approached at LW. The waypoint lies just S of Gilford Rock. When heading S, thread your way slowly between Islet 1 and 2. For the northern anchorages, head E between Islet 2 and 3.

ANCHOR   In any of the four small coves indicated. Holding is excellent in mud with depths of 4-8 m (13-26 ft). Suitable for 1-2 boats; all anchorages offer good protection from the SE and moderate protection from the W.

Not even a sea breeze ripples the water

It was a pleasant sail from Success Point to the snug coves east of Seabreese Island. Black bears, previously sighted by our boat neighbours, were being elusive, although watchful bald eagles and osprey looked on while Bonaparte gulls indulged in a one-legged nap, and sleepy seals lazed on the warm rocks. Illuminated by the sun's radiant afterglow, this cluster of islets provided the perfect setting for an overnight stay.

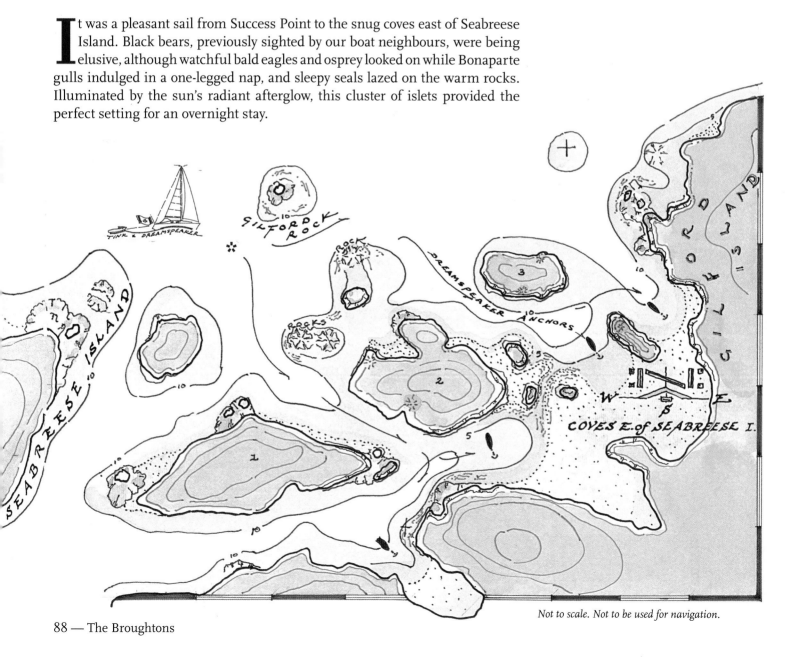

Not to scale. Not to be used for navigation.

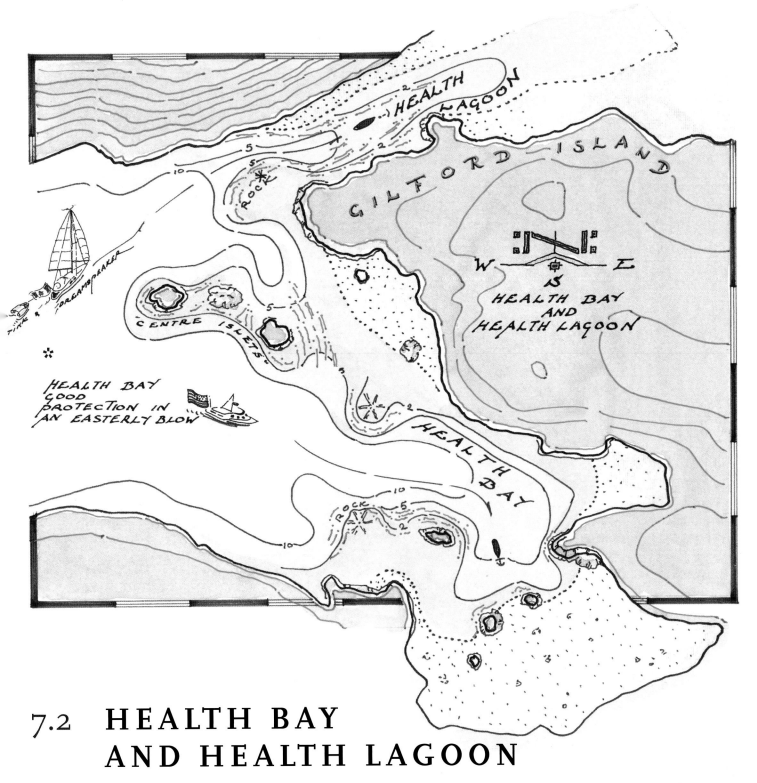

Map labels: HEALTH LAGOON · GILFORD ISLAND · "CENTRE ISLETS" · ROCK · HEALTH BAY · ROCK · DREAMSPEAKER

HEALTH BAY
GOOD
PROTECTION IN
AN EASTERLY BLOW

N
W — E
S
HEALTH BAY
AND
HEALTH LAGOON

7.2 HEALTH BAY AND HEALTH LAGOON

CHARTS 3546.

APPROACH Health Bay and Lagoon from the W. Health Bay lies to the SE of "Centre Islets" (named by us). The run in is clear. Health Lagoon lies to the NE of "Centre Islets." Enter N of the rock in the entrance for a picnic stop, or anchor overnight in settled weather.

The head of the lagoon shallows rapidly, revealing a muddy foreshore at LW.

ANCHOR As indicated, in depths of 3-6 m (9-19 ft) where holding is excellent in sticky mud. Health Bay offers good protection from the SE and with moderate protection from the W.

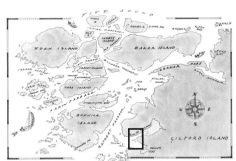

✻50°41.14'N 126°35.35'W

Drop anchor in the good, sticky mud of Health Bay and explore the lagoon by dinghy or kayak. Alternatively, laze in the cockpit surrounded by the bay's tree-lined and rocky shore, well patronized by the local community of basking seals and their doe-eyed pups.

7.3 DUSKY COVE, BONWICK ISLAND

✤50°40.88'N 126°40.19'W

CHARTS 3546.

APPROACH At LW, between the Leading Islets. Be aware that the islets' ledges, like icebergs, extend farther out below water.

ANCHOR (1, 2, & 3) Alternate temporary anchorages. (4) In Dusky Cove, depths of 3-6 m (9-19 ft) where holding is good in sand. The anchorage is surprisingly commodious and well protected from the SE. The ring of islets breaks the swell and light winds from the W. This is not a good spot in a moderate-to-strong westerly blow.

A lot of rocks and Christmas trees!

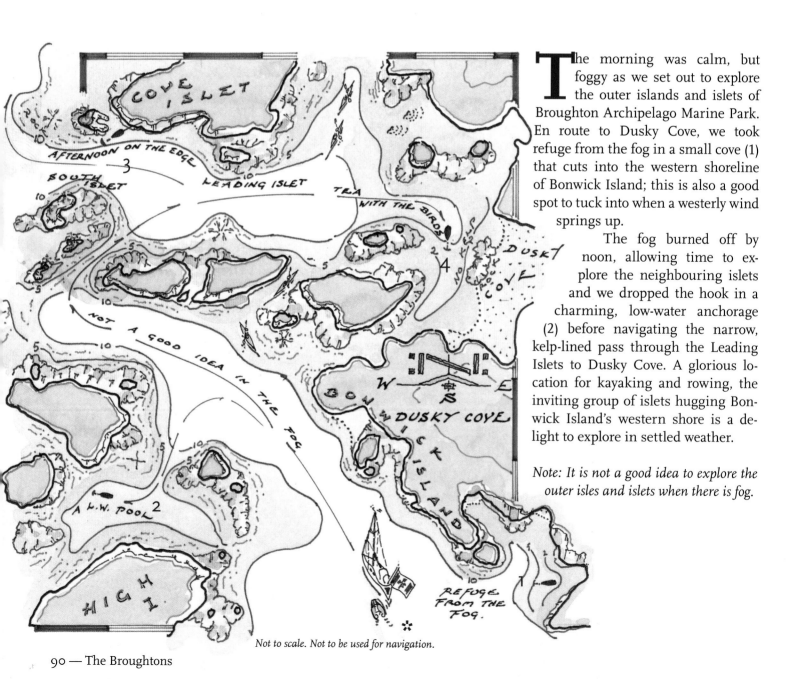

The morning was calm, but foggy as we set out to explore the outer islands and islets of Broughton Archipelago Marine Park. En route to Dusky Cove, we took refuge from the fog in a small cove (1) that cuts into the western shoreline of Bonwick Island; this is also a good spot to tuck into when a westerly wind springs up.

The fog burned off by noon, allowing time to explore the neighbouring islets and we dropped the hook in a charming, low-water anchorage (2) before navigating the narrow, kelp-lined pass through the Leading Islets to Dusky Cove. A glorious location for kayaking and rowing, the inviting group of islets hugging Bonwick Island's western shore is a delight to explore in settled weather.

Note: It is not a good idea to explore the outer isles and islets when there is fog.

Not to scale. Not to be used for navigation.

There again, trees are often useful when catching up on notes.

CHARTS   3546.

APPROACH   (A) From Arrow Passage. Leave "Fox Island" to starboard. (B) From Retreat Passage, leave the rocks and reef that extend well off "Fox Islet" (named by us) to port. The entrance channel is clear.

ANCHOR   Good holding in mud in depths of 4-8 m (13-26 ft). The alternative anchorages outside Waddington Bay should be approached cautiously and at LW.

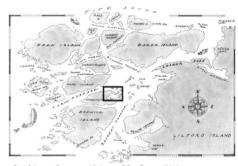

✿(A) 50°43.37'N 126°36.00'W
✿(B) 50°42.92'N 126°36.07'W

An orderly semi-circle of neatly positioned power and sailboats and a sleek motor yacht, anchored stern-to on the islet, glistened in the sunlight as we entered popular Waddington Bay. A small alternative anchorage south of "Fox Island" provided a quiet overnight stop with fine views out. We spent a blissful morning exploring the islets in *Tink*, lounging on our grassy picnic rocks with their fragrance of wild onion and mint and shaded by a lone tree. At low water, a mini shell beach is revealed between the two rocks.

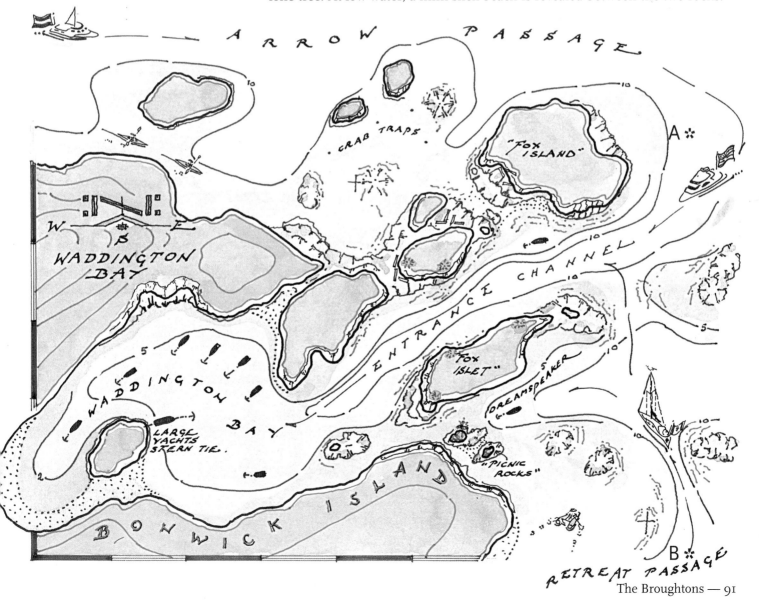

7.5 ECHO BAY, GILFORD ISLAND

✣50°45.34'N 126°29.95'W

The entrance to Echo Bay is highly conspicuous

Visitor moorage at Echo Bay Resort and Marina

The vibrant float home at Windsong Sea Village and Resort

Accessible by boat or float plane, Gilford Island is the largest of the islands that make up the enchanting Broughton Archipelago. Echo Bay, originally called Echo Cove, provides a sheltered harbour and lovely vistas.

The bay was occupied by First Nations communities for over 10,000 years until the devastating smallpox epidemic. Those who survived moved away 150 years ago leaving rust-coloured pictographs on the steep cliff face and an extensive midden that forms a lovely white-shell beach at the head of the bay, which is part of ECHO BAY MARINE PARK.

Since 1910, the bay has been home to pioneers and their families who ran the store and fuel dock. It also housed a fish-buying camp, a shingle mill and a beer parlour. The school, located in the park, is still operational.

ECHO BAY RESORT AND MARINA is located on the west side of the bay and has ample moorage, shower and laundry facilities, a fuel dock, grocery store and post office (Wednesday pick up and drop off). The well-stocked store carries all the basics including fresh produce and dairy products, bread, baked goods (homemade cinnamon buns daily) and ice cream. Ice, charts, books, fishing accessories and some household goods are also available. Garbage is charged by weight.

Wednesday evenings are set aside for BBQ ribs and potluck side dishes, which often include the catch of the day from a friendly boater. If you and the crew are in the mood for socializing, gather your crockery, cutlery and beverages and meet on the covered party dock.

On the bay's eastern shoreline, nestled beneath a breathtaking, 61 m (200 ft) sheer cliff, WINDSONG SEA VILLAGE RESORT is a vibrant collection of west coast float homes and 213 m (700 ft) of dock space for visiting boats; filtered local spring water is available. You'll be sure to encounter an array of interesting characters at happy hour when visitors and locals gather around the dock picnic table. The sunset view out to Cramer Passage is sensational. An antique bathtub and large rainforest showerhead provide a unique bathing experience. The art gallery and gift store sell local art, crafts, books and jewellery, including excellent beadwork; just ask for Carol, "The Bead Lady."

For a must-have experience, visit fisherman, story-teller, author and envi-

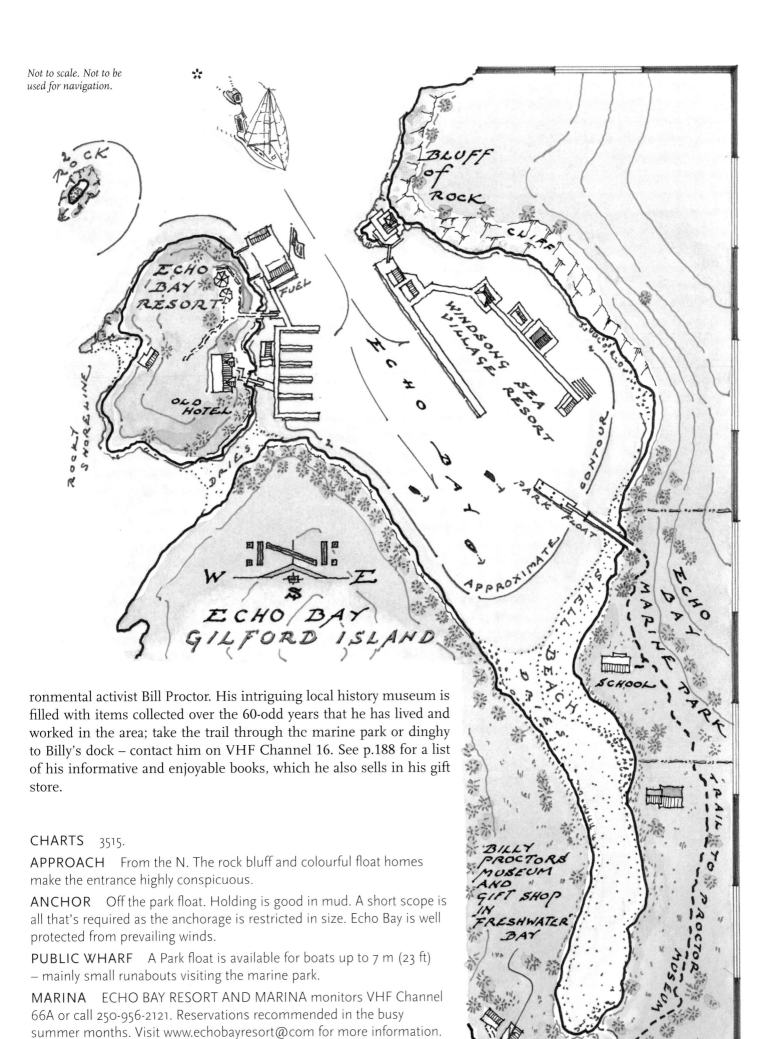

Not to scale. Not to be used for navigation.

ROCK

ECHO BAY RESORT

FUEL

OLD HOTEL

ROCKY SHORELINE

DRIES

W E

S

ECHO BAY GILFORD ISLAND

BLUFF of ROCK

CLIFF

WINDSONG SEA VILLAGE RESORT

ECHO BAY

APPROXIMATE

PARK FLOAT

CONTOUR

WILLOW

SHELL BEACH

DRIES

ECHO BAY MARINE PARK

SCHOOL

TRAIL TO PROCTOR MUSEUM

BILLY PROCTORS MUSEUM AND GIFT SHOP IN FRESHWATER BAY

ronmental activist Bill Proctor. His intriguing local history museum is filled with items collected over the 60-odd years that he has lived and worked in the area; take the trail through the marine park or dinghy to Billy's dock – contact him on VHF Channel 16. See p.188 for a list of his informative and enjoyable books, which he also sells in his gift store.

CHARTS 3515.

APPROACH From the N. The rock bluff and colourful float homes make the entrance highly conspicuous.

ANCHOR Off the park float. Holding is good in mud. A short scope is all that's required as the anchorage is restricted in size. Echo Bay is well protected from prevailing winds.

PUBLIC WHARF A Park float is available for boats up to 7 m (23 ft) – mainly small runabouts visiting the marine park.

MARINA ECHO BAY RESORT AND MARINA monitors VHF Channel 66A or call 250-956-2121. Reservations recommended in the busy summer months. Visit www.echobayresort@com for more information.

WINDSONG SEA VILLAGE RESORT offers transient visitor moorage and monitors VHF Channel 16.

7.6 PIERRE'S BAY LODGE AND MARINA,

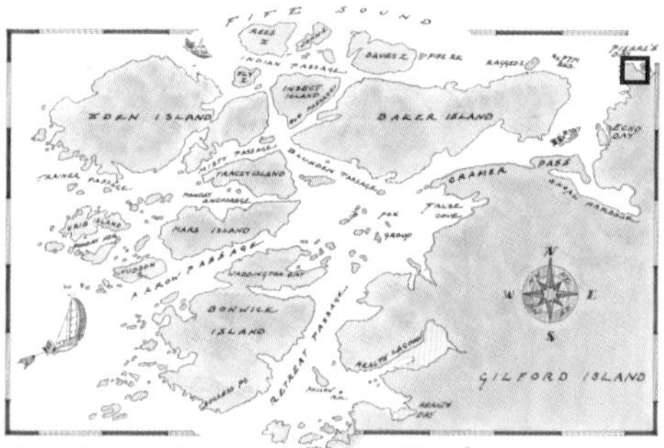

✲50°46.26'N 126°29.09'W

Pierre's Bay Lodge on approach – a boat is exiting to the right

Saturday night pig roast – Three would-be Mexicans, one named Pierre!

A cruise in the Broughton Islands would not be complete without a night or two at welcoming PIERRE'S BAY LODGE AND MARINA. Owners Pierre and Tove Landry delight in special events and theme evenings. Their renowned Saturday night Pig Roasts take place in the barbeque tent from July to the first Saturday in September; pre-booking your moorage and meal is highly recommended. Pierre cooks the roast to perfection while Tove keeps everything and everyone *shipshape*. Guests provide potluck side dishes to share, along with personal beverages, crockery and cutlery.

Happy hour is at 5 p.m. every day for those who wish to join in. Other special evenings include a Chili Cook-off, Italian nights, and Christmas in July – complete with a traditional turkey dinner and decorations. Marina and lodge guests are also invited to indulge in hearty homestyle meals served in the waterfront dining room Monday to Friday, and live music often is included in the evening's festivities.

"Lady Di's" vibrant LIGHTHOUSE BAKERY at the head of the dock provides a leading mark for boaters and tasty, home baking daily. Choose from a feast of fruit pies, cinnamon buns and butter tarts; special requests can be made to order. Alfresco deli-style lunches are served daily in the "Lighthouse Courtyard" where you can also browse in the small, imaginatively stocked gift store filled with local art, wood-turned sculptures, clothing and jewellery.

Note: Check their website for current events and alternative activities at www.pierresbay.com.

"PIERRE'S BAY"

CHARTS   3515.

APPROACH   From the W, leaving the rock off Powell Point to the S. The colourful lighthouse structure and lodge are conspicuous. There are no obstructions on the run into the marina.

ANCHOR   A temporary anchorage in Scott Cove has moderate protection from the W and SE. Good holding in mud in depths of 3-5 m (9-16 ft).

MARINA   PIERRE'S BAY LODGE AND MARINA offers extensive moorage with wide, wooden docks. Power and water are available, and shower and laundry facilities behind the lodge are provided for marina guests. Reservations are necessary in the busy summer months, using VHF Channel 66A or email info@pierresbay.com.

Views out at sunset

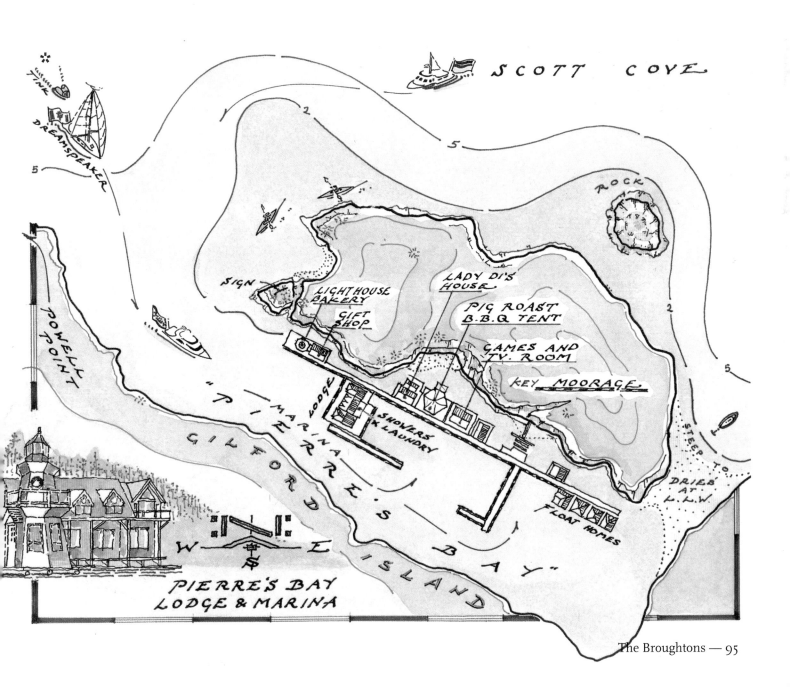

SCOTT COVE

TINK
DREAMSPEAKER
5
5

ROCK

SIGN

LIGHTHOUSE BAKERY
GIFT SHOP

LADY DI'S HOUSE

PIG ROAST B.B.Q TENT

GAMES AND T.V. ROOM

KEY MOORAGE

POWELL POINT

LODGE

SHOWERS & LAUNDRY

"MARINA

"PIERRE'S

GILFORD

BAY"

ISLAND

FLOAT HOMES

STEEP TO

DRIES AT L.L.W.

W — E
N
S

PIERRE'S BAY
LODGE & MARINA

7.7 FIFE ROCK, DAVIES ISLAND

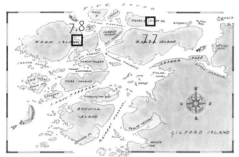

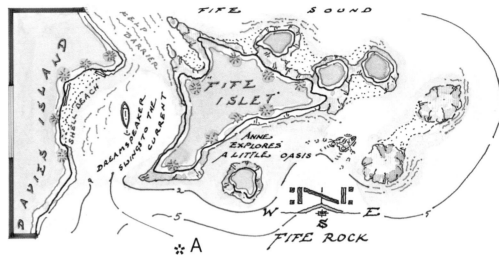

❋ A

❋(A) 50°46.04'N 126°34.29'W
❋(B) 50°45.45'N 126°39.03'W

CHARTS 3515.

APPROACH (A) From the S. The gap between Davies Island and Fife Rock has no obstructions. The presence of kelp suggests that a passage N, beyond the shell beach, may not be possible.

ANCHOR A 1-boat day stop best explored at LW. Great for a picnic or shelter from westerly winds; if the winds are strong, however, swells from Fife Sound would curl around Davies Island into the anchorage. Holding good in shell/mud/kelp in depths of 3-7(4) m (9-23 ft).

Note: Fife Rock is the size of an islet with trees and grass, rocky outcrops and isolated rocks.

A little oasis adjacent to Davies Island, Fife Rock offers calm waters for rowing or kayaking, a shell beach to stretch your legs and many delightful pocket-beaches to explore at low water.

"LADY BOOT COVE," EDEN ISLAND 7.8

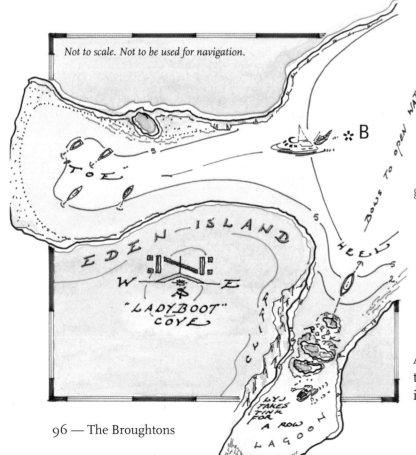

Not to scale. Not to be used for navigation.

❋ B

CHARTS 3547.

APPROACH (B) From the NE. After rounding Fly Island, 2 coves form the chart profile of a lady's stiletto-heeled boot. Both approaches are free of obstruction.

ANCHOR *Heel* – A great day stop; drop the hook at LW and stern-tie to the rock.

Toe – A commodious overnight basin. Both are well protected from westerly winds although open to the NE. Holding is good in mud/shell/kelp, in depths of 4-8 m (13-26 ft).

"Lady Boot Cove," aptly named by the Douglasses in *Exploring the South Coast of British Columbia* (see p. 188), provides sheltered, overnight anchorage at the head of the *toe*. Although there is little room to swing at the entrance to the *heel,* this cozy picnic stop offers lovely views out and is fun to explore by dinghy.

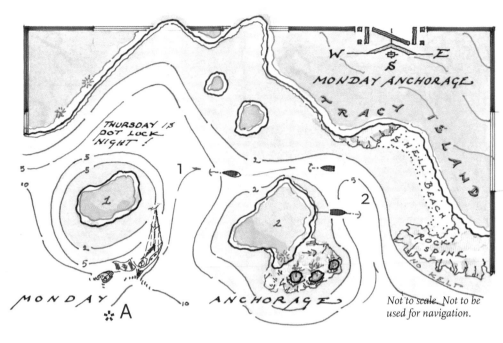

Not to scale. Not to be used for navigation.

❊ (A) 50°43.99'N 126°38.92'W
❊ (B) 50°45.91'N 126°37.83'W

CHARTS 3546.

APPROACH (A) From the W at LW. The islets have a clear passage between them.

ANCHOR (1) with protection from Islet 1.
(2) With protection from Islet 2. Shelter from a westerly blow would be marginal unless anchored with a stern line as shown; this indicates the best spot to drop the hook. Holding in mud 4-6 m (13-19 ft).

In her book *The Curve of Time*, Muriel Wylie Blanchet describes how their small boat was blown into Monday Anchorage after dragging anchor in Sunday Harbour. There, she took shelter in a small anchorage she called "Tuesday Cove."

On a sunny day, the white-shell beach on the eastern shoreline of Monday Anchorage is perfect for picnicking and beachcombing. We like to think that it is the same cove that Muriel and her family enjoyed.

7.10 "EDEN'S POOL," EDEN ISLAND

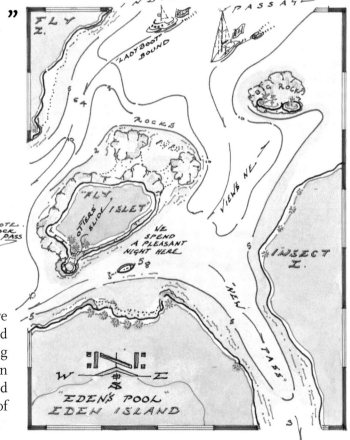

CHARTS 3547.

APPROACH From Indian Pass. Head for the passage between Insect and Eden Islands. Rocks lie to the NE of "Fly Islet" (named by us).

ANCHOR In a pool of calm water between "Fly Islet" and Eden Island. Swing to the current in depths of 6-8 m (19-26 ft). Good protection from westerly winds.

With views out to the northeast and southwest, we dropped anchor in a small anchorage that we named "Eden's Pool" and spent a peaceful night swinging to the current. Boats en route to "Lady Boot Cove" from Indian Passage take the pass between Fly Island and "Fly Islet" (named by us) while boats heading to Monday Anchorage make use of "New Pass" (named by us) between Insect and Eden Islands.

The wood float in the east finger of the cove provides convenient tie-up

JOE COVE, EDEN ISLAND 7.11

FUEL At ECHO BAY RESORT AND MARINA below the store. They also supply propane.

CHARTS 3547.

APPROACH From the SE; the entrance and run into the anchorage at the head of the cove is clear without obstructions until you reach the 2 rocks at the entrance to the anchorage (sometimes marked with a can or buoy).

ANCHOR In the N finger in depths of 3-5 m (9-16 ft). Holding in mud. The old wooden float in the east finger provides a spot for boats up to 10.5 m (35 ft) to tie up on either side.

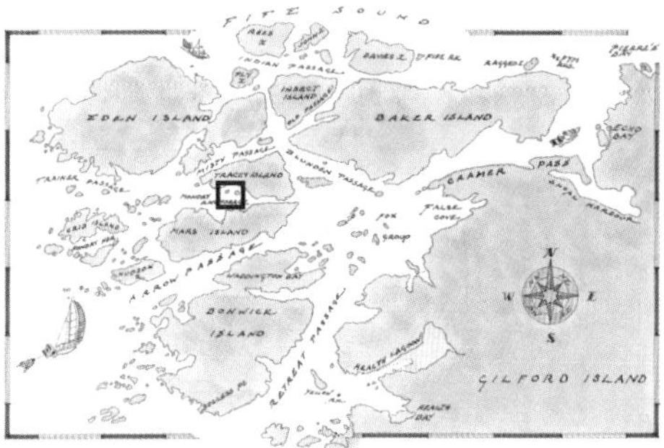

✲50°44.92'N 126°39.70'W

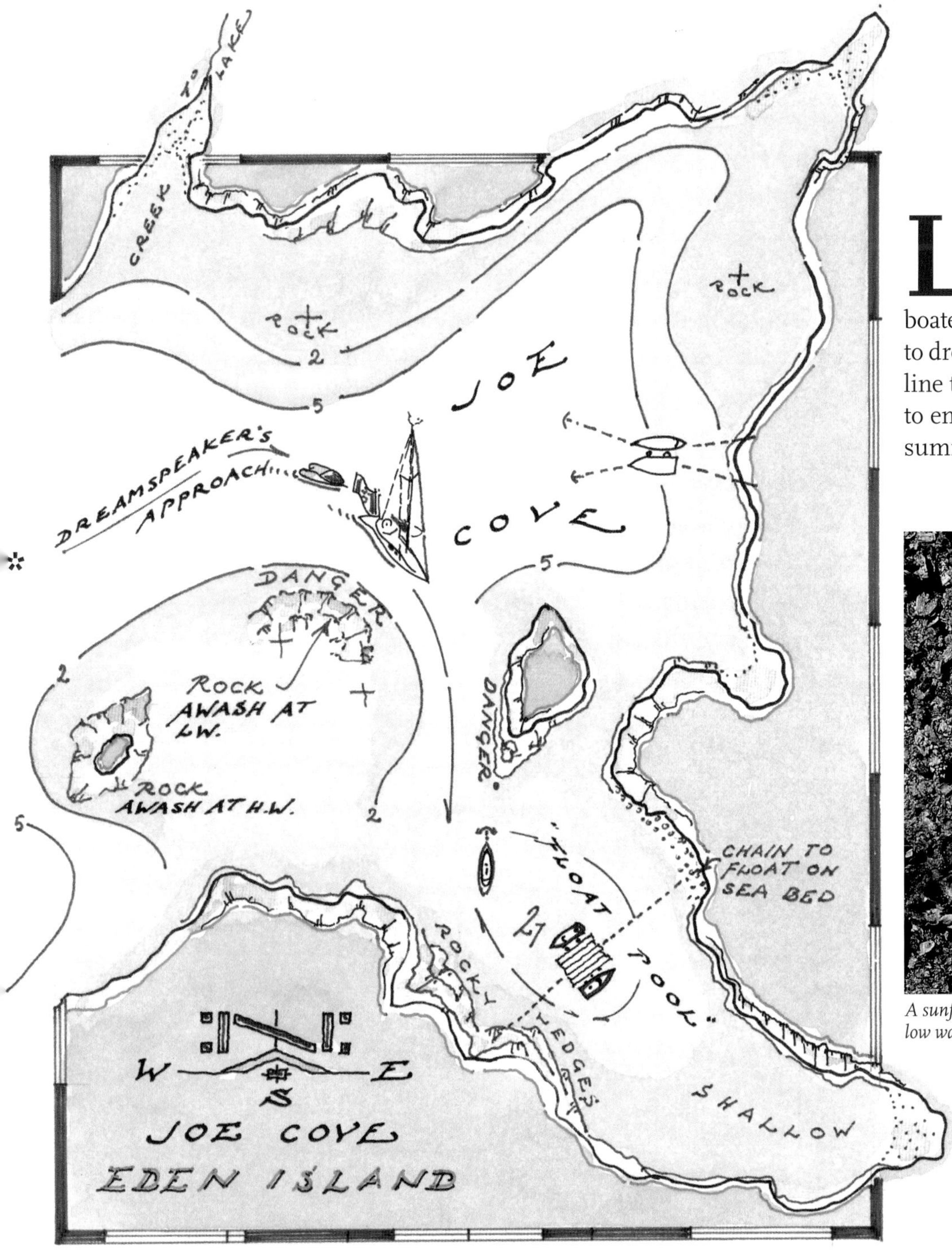

Not to scale. Not to be used for navigation.

Long and slim, Joe Cove has a protected anchorage at its head that is popular with recreational boaters seeking a quiet, sheltered spot to drop the hook or even tie up. A stern line to the shore will allow more boats to enjoy this peaceful spot in the busy summer months.

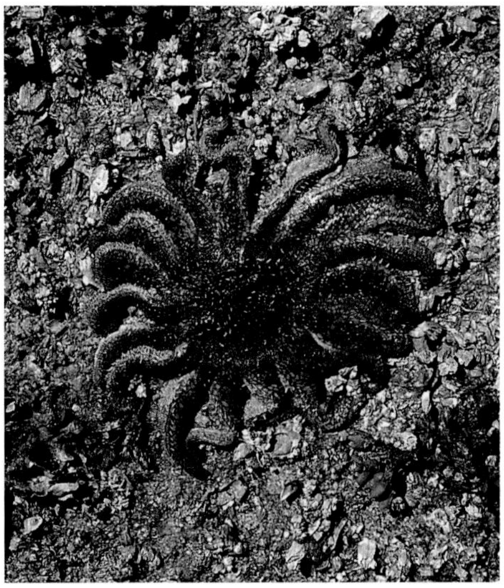

A sunflower star (twenty-rayed sea star) exposed at low water

A stormy evening in Broughton Strait, looking out from the anchorage in Port McNeill

Chapter 8

QUEEN CHARLOTTE STRAIT SOUTH

Cottage craft, Malcolm Island

Chapter 8
QUEEN CHARLOTTE STRAIT SOUTH

TIDES – *Volume 6,*
Canadian Tide and Current Tables
Reference Port – Alert Bay
Secondary Ports – Port Hardy, Port McNeill

CURRENTS
Reference Station – Johnstone Strait Central
Secondary Station – Pulteney Point, Masterman islands.

WEATHER
Weather Station – WX1 162.55 MHZ
Area – Queen Charlotte Strait
Reporting Station – Alert Bay

CAUTIONARY NOTES: *Swift currents appear to be ever present in Broughton Strait; these currents can run up to 3 knots in the channel off Pulteney Point.*

Take the ebb tide North, to Beaver Harbour and Port Hardy, remembering that wind against current always makes for an uncomfortable trip. Travelling on an ebb tide with an easterly wind in Queen Charlotte Strait would be ideal.

This chapter primarily covers the northern Vancouver Island shore and includes the urban amenities of Port McNeill and Port Hardy and a visit to Sointula on Malcolm Island.

Port McNeill proclaims to be the *Gateway to the Broughtons* and is conveniently situated with protected moorage and all amenities and services within two blocks of downtown. Port McNeill Boat Harbour and the municipal marina are well patronized by transient boaters. Downtown includes a hospital, pharmacy, post office, banks, an ATM, art galleries, gift stores, restaurants and cafés, well-stocked marine stores and a supermarket. This is a major provisioning stop, and the scheduled ferry service connects with nearby Alert Bay and Sointula on Malcolm Island. Boaters will find deluxe laundry facilities with complimentary internet service.

The thriving community of Sointula was established in 1901; enjoy the *harmony* (the Finnish word for which the island was named) when visiting. Visitors are welcome at the nearby public wharf. Take advantage of the fine Malcolm Island trails, and rent a bike or hike to Bere Point and the whale-rubbing rocks.

Once a Hudson's Bay Company trading post, fort and coal mining site, and now a thriving Indian Reserve, the Village of Fort Rupert welcomes visitors to its art galleries where you can experience traditional crafters at work. Lovely Beaver Harbour fronting the village has a choice of small, cozy anchorages; our favourite was tucked between the beautiful white-shell beaches of Cattle and Shell Islands and is a terrific spot for beach-hopping and wildlife.

A comprehensive service centre for boaters and fishermen, Port Hardy has an airport nearby, and Bear Cove is the southern terminal for the Vancouver Island-Prince

18

FEATURED DESTINATIONS

Rupert ferry. The town is a popular rendezvous stop for visitors and crew.

The town centre around Market, Rupert and Granville Streets has every type of shop or service a boater might need – supermarkets, hardware and marine stores, a post office, hospital and pharmacy. Gift stores and art galleries are in abundance and the museum is excellent. Restaurants in the area are highly recommended for their choice of fresh fish and seafood, and the chef will often turn your catch into a gourmet meal. The more protected "Inner Basin" offers boaters moorage at the public wharf and THE QUARTERDECK INN AND MARINA RESORT comes complete with clean shower and laundry facilities, a well-stocked marine store and a kid-friendly pub and restaurant. Fuel is also available.

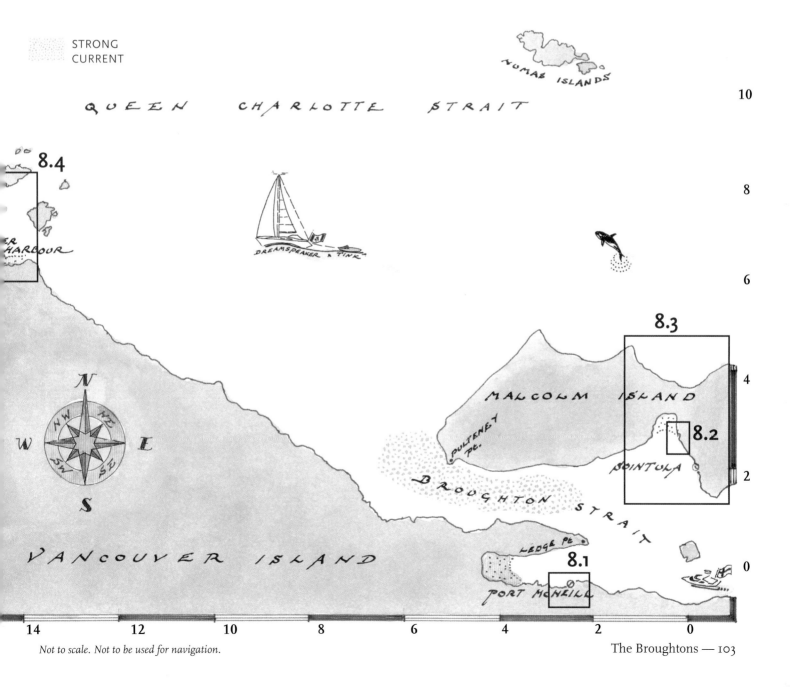

STRONG
CURRENT

NUMAS ISLANDS

QUEEN CHARLOTTE STRAIT

8.4

ER HARBOUR

DREAMSPEAKER & TINK

8.3

MALCOLM ISLAND

PULTENEY PT.

8.2

BROUGHTON STRAIT

SOINTULA

N
NW NE
W E
SW SE
S

LEDGE PT.

8.1

VANCOUVER ISLAND

PORT MCNEILL

10

8

6

4

2

0

14   12   10   8   6   4   2   0

Not to scale. Not to be used for navigation.

8.1 PORT MCNEILL, VANCOUVER ISLAND

✳ 50°35.64'N 127°05.09'W

Looking south from the anchorage to Port McNeill Boat Harbour

'Gateway to The Broughtons'

PORT MCNEILL BOAT HARBOUR is conveniently situated downtown with protected moorage, amenities, and services within two blocks. Slips fill early in the busy summer months. Rafting up is often the norm, and the dock attendants do a sterling job matching boat types and sizes to make everyone feel comfortable. Facilities include Broadband Express internet service, a tidal grid, a pump-out station, showers and washrooms and a book-swap at the harbour office. Laundry facilities with complimentary internet are on the corner of Beach and Broughton, run by AUTO PARTS PLUS opposite, which also carries marine supplies. While your wash dries, visit the INFO CENTRE (connected to the museum with a communal door on the inside and two separated entrances on the outside) and excellent forestry and logging museum.

Port McNeill has a hospital, pharmacy, post office, banks and an ATM. The scheduled ferry service connects with nearby Alert Bay and Sointula; both are well worth the trip (see pp. 64 and 106). Provisioning is a breeze in the downtown core; just choose your shopping cart, shop until it's full, transport your goods to the boat, then neatly park your trolley at the top of the dock for pickup. The well-stocked IGA MARKETPLACE is locally owned and operated, the SHOP RITE DEPARTMENT STORE carries a diverse selection of products, and the GOVERNMENT LIQUOR STORE has a good selection of wines. Bustling MCNEILL'S RESTAURANT on Beach became our favourite haunt; it has an outdoor patio that catches the afternoon sun and is the perfect spot for sundowners overlooking the harbour. Their daily specials are a good value and the breakfast is hearty, while the garlic mashed potatoes and balsamic house dressing both won our gold stars. BO-BANEES RESTAURANT in the mall was a fun alternative, despite no view.

THE GALLERY on Broughton is hard to resist and carries fine quality gifts, First Nations jewellery, specialty cards and books, gourmet food and charming home accessories; and the buyers are always on the lookout for new, fun items. Quality First Nations art, sculptures, masks and jewellery by established artists can be found at JUST ART, a tranquil gallery for taking time out and just browsing.

Dreamspeaker *rafted at the commercial public wharf*

CHARTS   3546, inset.

APPROACH   From the E, north of the Ferry terminal. Seaplanes operate frequently in this area and take off and land parallel to the breakwater.

ANCHOR   Good anchorage can be found in the bay N of the shoreside facilities. Favour the western shoreline. Holding good in mud, in depths of 5-8 m (16-26 ft). *(See cautionary note.)*

PUBLIC WHARF   The boat harbour lies behind the stone breakwater and is used mainly by commercial vessels and overflow moorage in the summer months. Port McNeill Boat Harbour is efficiently run. Dockside attendants will find space and tend lines in the busy summer months. Call 250-956-3881 or VHF Channel 66A prior to arrival – this will enable the staff to designate moorage effectively. No reservations available. BBX internet service.

FUEL   PORT MCNEILL MARINE AND AVIATION FUELS is open year-round; call on Channel 66A. Ice, propane and marine supplies are available at the head of the dock.

BOAT LAUNCH   Municipal.

CAUTIONARY NOTE: *The anchorage is well sheltered from the W. Ensure that your anchor is well set, as dead kelp is layered over the mud. Although open to the SE (and winds from that quarter can rip through the anchorage), seas appear to disperse in the bay. Dreamspeaker, along with many other boats, survived a night of gale-force winds; confidence in your boat's ground tackle and anchor set are essential.*

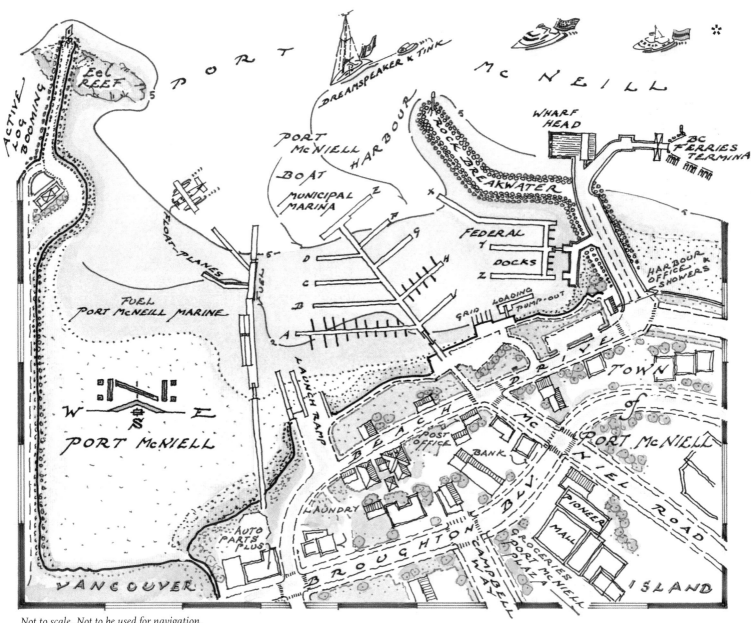

Not to scale. Not to be used for navigation.

8.2 SOINTULA HARBOUR, MALCOLM ISLAND

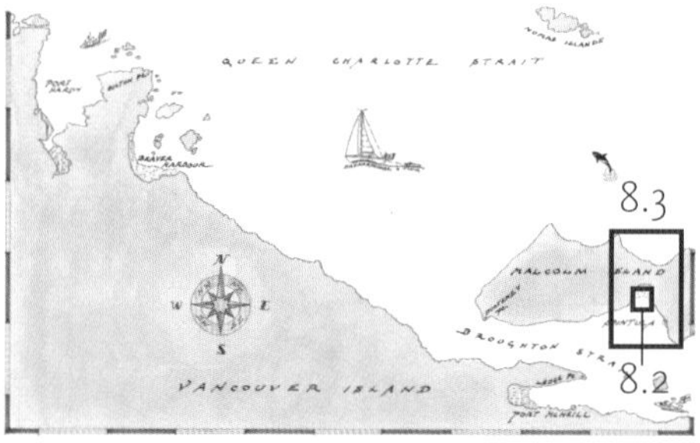

✲50°38.34'N 127°01.99'W

CHARTS 3546.

APPROACH To the W of Dickenson Point. Stay clear of the ferry route. The public wharf in Rough Bay lies NW of Sointula and the ferry terminal.

PUBLIC WHARF N of the village of Sointula. Managed by the Malcolm Island Lions Harbour Authority. Don't expect dockside attendants; this is an efficient but laid-back facility. Call 250-973-6544.

Note: You can also visit Sointula by ferry from Port McNeill.

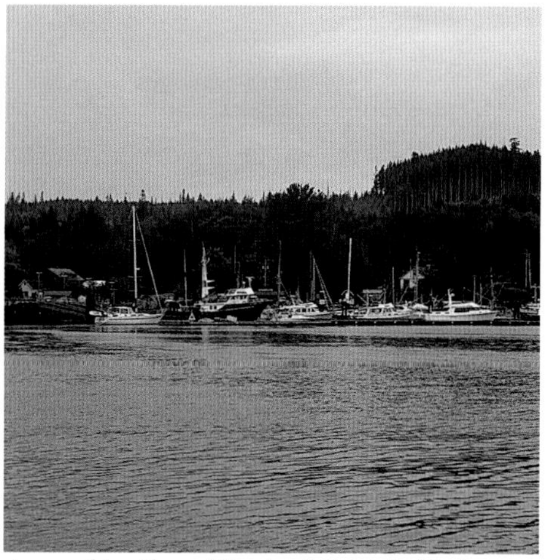

Approaching the public wharf, Sointula Harbour

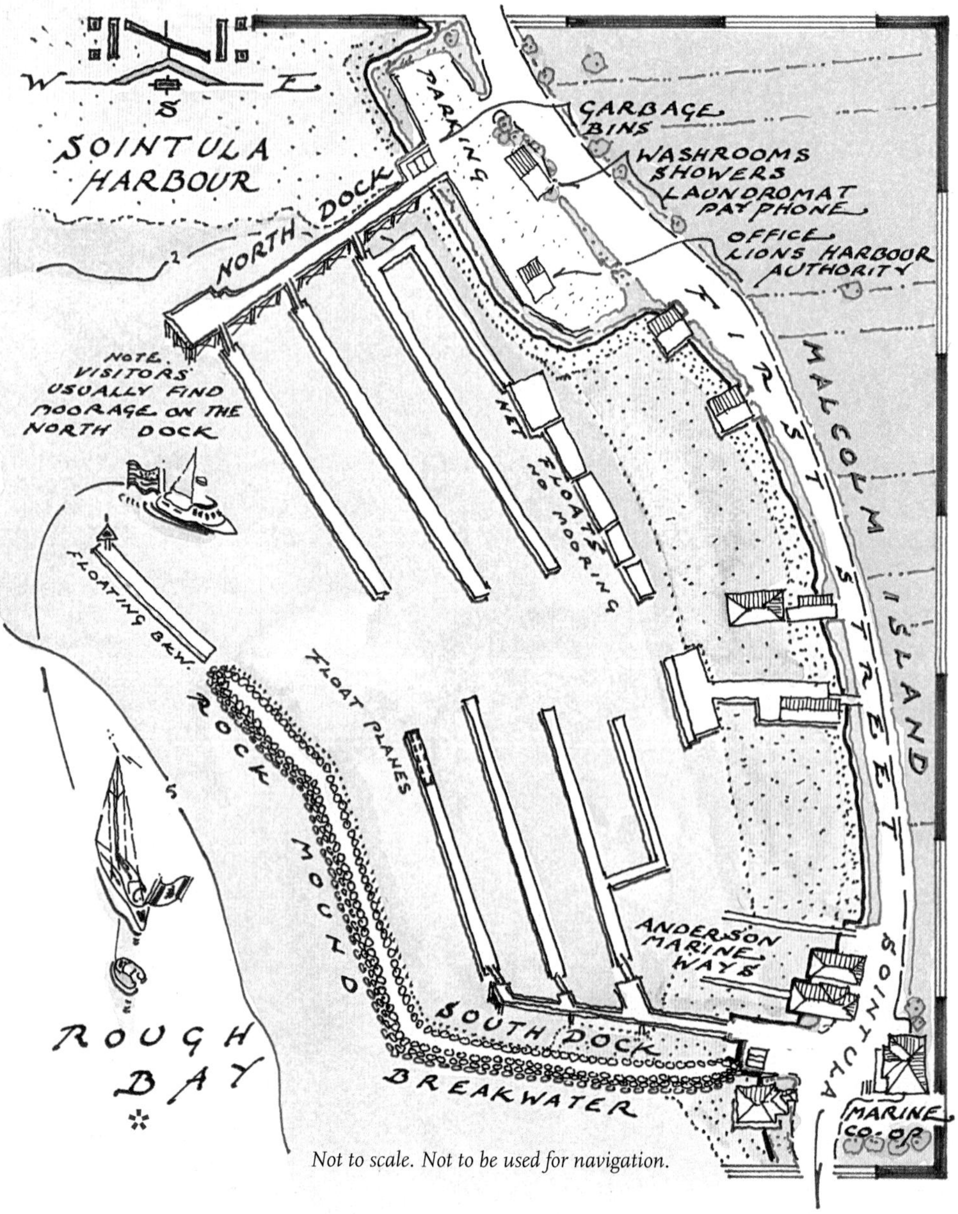

Not to scale. Not to be used for navigation.

"Sointula was established by a group of Finnish utopians led by journalist and idealist Matti Kurikka" (Liv Kennedy – *Coastal Villages,* see p. 188). A thriving community where co-operative movement is still strong, the island's population retains much of its founding philosophy. Clean shower and laundry facilities welcome boaters at the public wharf; they are well used by locals so it's first-come, first-served. Power, water and ice are available. It's a pleasant 2 km (1.2 mile) walk into the Village of Sointula; browse in the MARINE CO-OP, stock up at COAST SELECT SMOKEHOUSE and pop into the enticing arts and crafts studios and the museum.

At THE WILD ISLAND DELI AND CAFÉ, relax over lunch, or prepare a picnic from the bakery and deli. To provision, go no farther than the historic, well-stocked MARINE CO-OP. The liquor store is downstairs; upstairs carries a selection of hardware, toys and clothing. Open 9:30-5:30 Monday–Saturday. An eclectic mix of local art, gifts and books can be found in CHOYCES. Look for Paula Wild's insightful *Sointula – Island Utopia* (see p. 188).

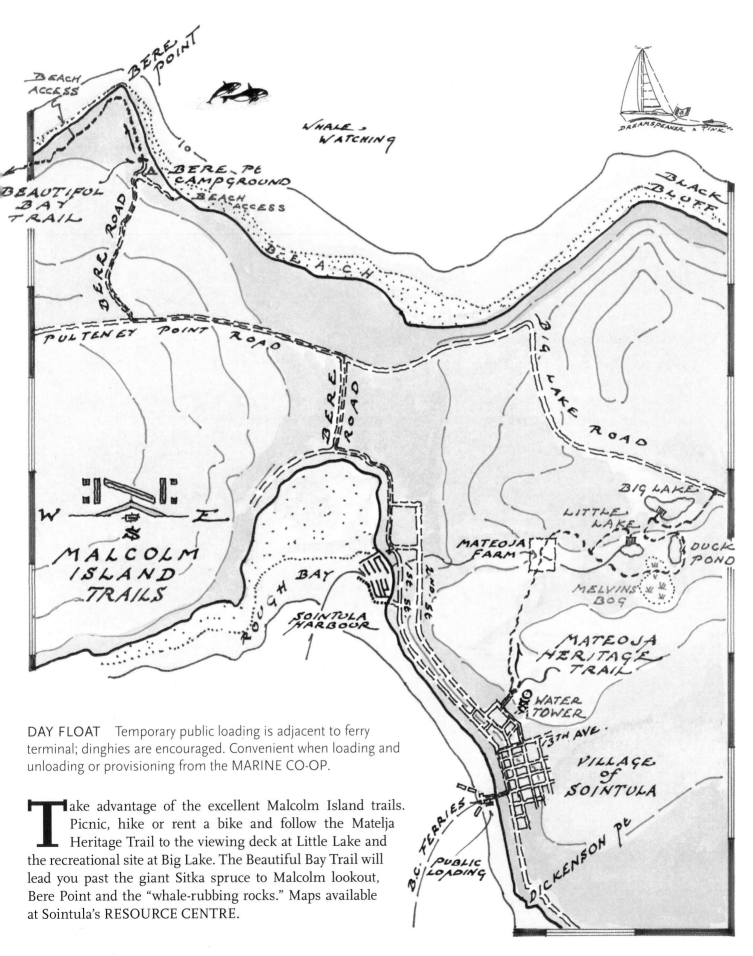

DAY FLOAT Temporary public loading is adjacent to ferry terminal; dinghies are encouraged. Convenient when loading and unloading or provisioning from the MARINE CO-OP.

Take advantage of the excellent Malcolm Island trails. Picnic, hike or rent a bike and follow the Matelja Heritage Trail to the viewing deck at Little Lake and the recreational site at Big Lake. The Beautiful Bay Trail will lead you past the giant Sitka spruce to Malcolm lookout, Bere Point and the "whale-rubbing rocks." Maps available at Sointula's RESOURCE CENTRE.

8.4 BEAVER HARBOUR, VANCOUVER ISLAND

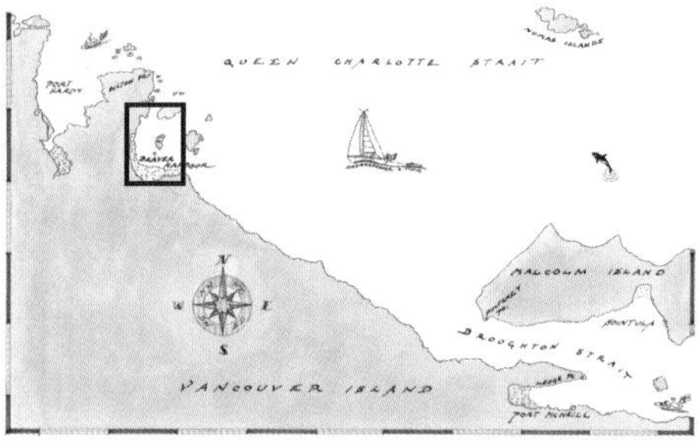

✲50°42.40'N 127°23.07'W

CHARTS 3548.

APPROACH From the E, between Thomas Point and Deer Island. An alternative approach may be made via Daedalus Passage.

ANCHOR There are a number of anchor spots off the shell beaches and the Vancouver Island shoreline. Well protected from the W and moderately sheltered from the E, anchor in depths of 4-10 m (13-32 ft) with holding good in mud.

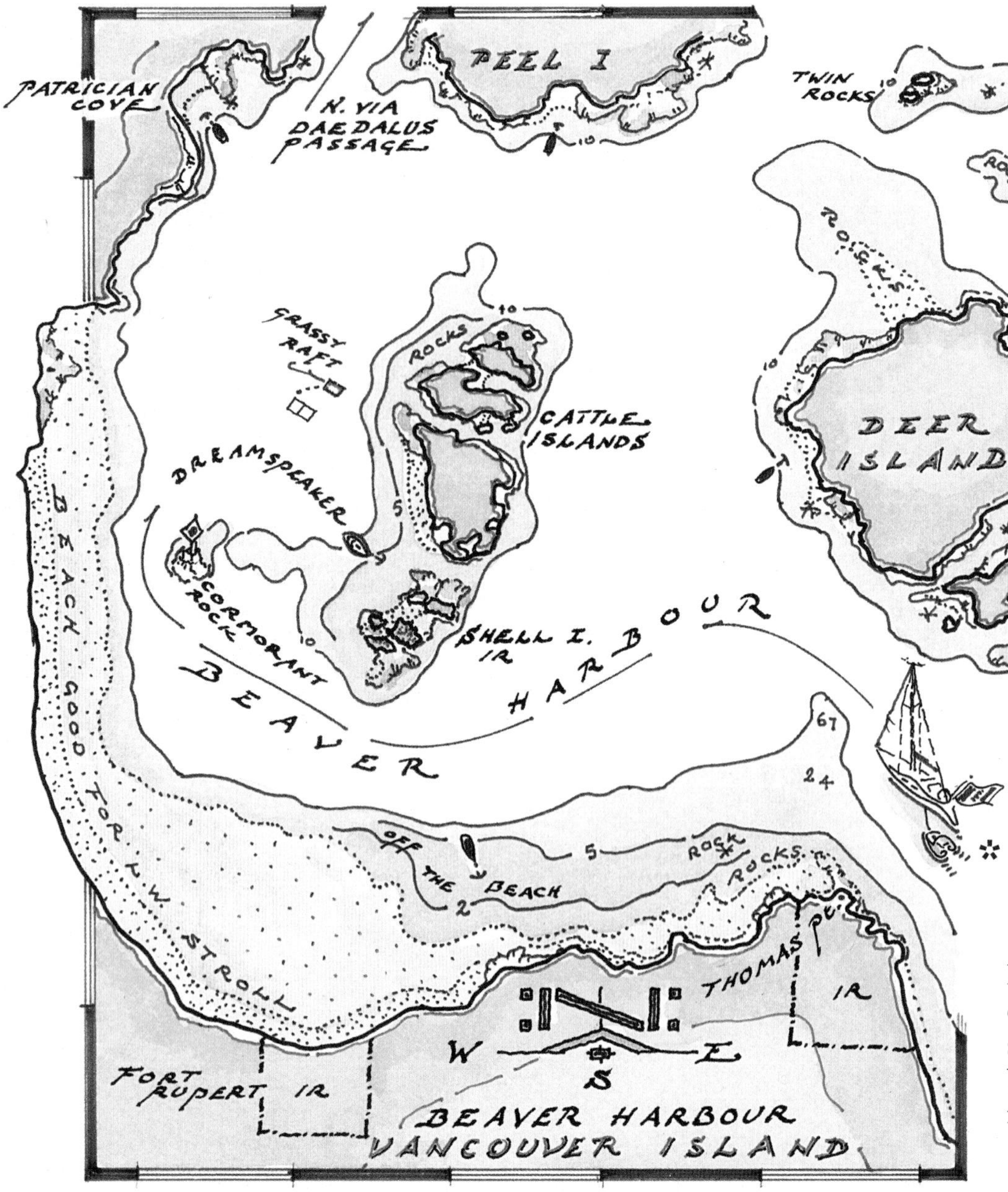

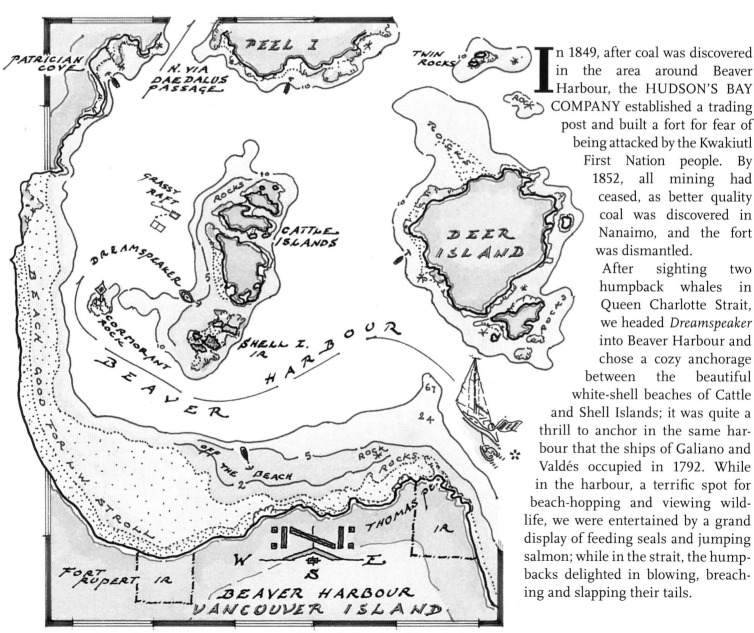

Not to scale. Not to be used for navigation.

In 1849, after coal was discovered in the area around Beaver Harbour, the HUDSON'S BAY COMPANY established a trading post and built a fort for fear of being attacked by the Kwakiutl First Nation people. By 1852, all mining had ceased, as better quality coal was discovered in Nanaimo, and the fort was dismantled.

After sighting two humpback whales in Queen Charlotte Strait, we headed *Dreamspeaker* into Beaver Harbour and chose a cozy anchorage between the beautiful white-shell beaches of Cattle and Shell Islands; it was quite a thrill to anchor in the same harbour that the ships of Galiano and Valdés occupied in 1792. While in the harbour, a terrific spot for beach-hopping and viewing wildlife, we were entertained by a grand display of feeding seals and jumping salmon; while in the strait, the humpbacks delighted in blowing, breaching and slapping their tails.

A tranquil evening in Beaver Harbour

8.5 PORT HARDY, VANCOUVER ISLAND

✻50°43.80'N 127°28.68'W

Seagate Wharf from Carrot Park

Downtown Port Hardy

Chainsaw-carved signs are a local specialty

A comprehensive service centre for boaters and fishermen, Port Hardy was our last big commercial stop before crossing Queen Charlotte Strait to Blunder Harbour. Nearby Bear Cove is the southern terminal for the Vancouver Island–Prince Rupert ferry and an airport nearby. Port Hardy is also a popular rendezvous stop for visitors and crew.

The small public wharf at the end of Granville Street is the most convenient spot to tie up and walk the half-block to GLEN-WAY FOODS, a well-stocked and locally run grocery store that will deliver to the dock. The area around Market, Rupert and Granville Streets has every type of shop or service a boater might need; pop into the VISITOR INFO CENTRE on Market and pick up a downtown map, which will direct you to the post office, hospital, pharmacy, gift stores, art galleries (some of the best First Nations' art is produced on northern Vancouver Island), museum, hardware and marine stores, a GOVERNMENT LIQUOUR STORE and even a traditional barber shop.

Restaurants in the area are highly recommended for their choice of fresh fish and seafood and will often turn your catch into a gourmet meal. Alternatively, pick up a live crab at HARDY BOYS SMOKED FISH and let the chef at MALONE'S OCEANSIDE BISTRO cook it to perfection for you. To end the evening, enjoy a leisurely stroll along the waterfront sea walk, which is amber-lit at night and connects to the green lawns of CARROT PARK and the notorious "Welcome to Port Hardy" chainsaw-carved sign.

The more protected "Inner Basin" offers moorage at the public wharf and THE QUARTERDECK INN AND MARINA RESORT, which provides all the necessities – fuel, clean shower and laundry facilities, a well-stocked marine store, and the kid-friendly I.V.'S QUARTERDECK PUB. To visit the downtown shops and restaurants from here, take an invigorating walk along Hardy Bay Road, and then treat yourself to a taxi ride home. For a different view of Port Hardy, take a stroll from the marina along the scenic WALKWAY AND NATURE TRAIL (info at the resort).

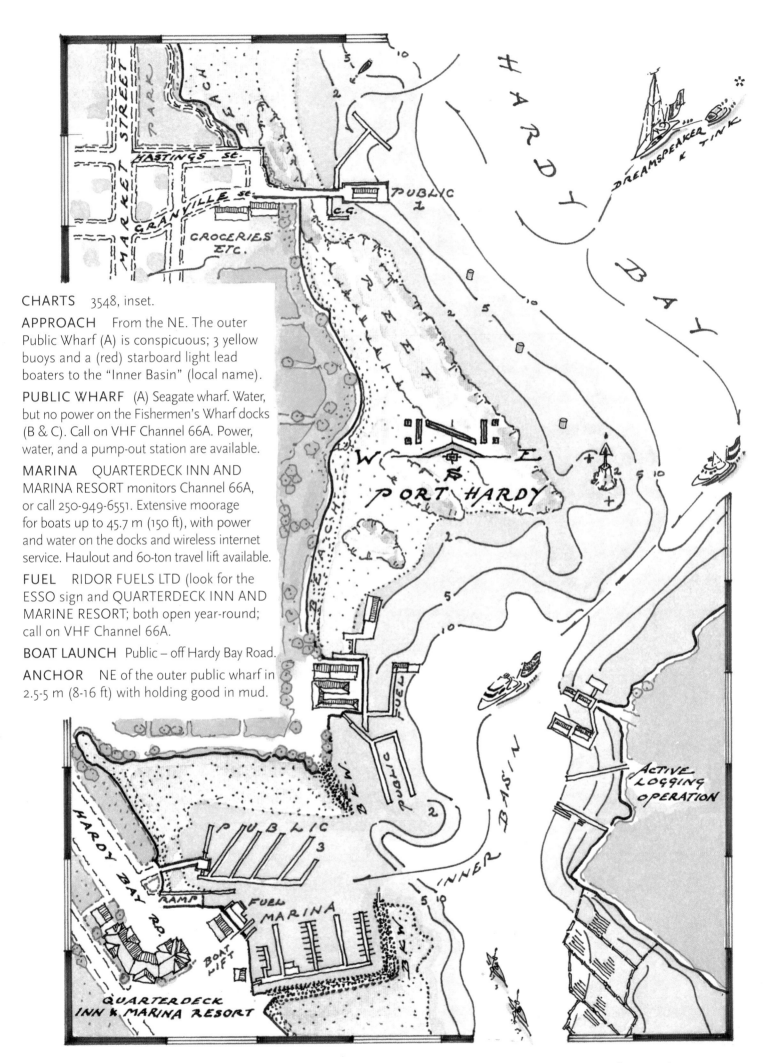

CHARTS 3548, inset.

APPROACH From the NE. The outer Public Wharf (A) is conspicuous; 3 yellow buoys and a (red) starboard light lead boaters to the "Inner Basin" (local name).

PUBLIC WHARF (A) Seagate wharf. Water, but no power on the Fishermen's Wharf docks (B & C). Call on VHF Channel 66A. Power, water, and a pump-out station are available.

MARINA QUARTERDECK INN AND MARINA RESORT monitors Channel 66A, or call 250-949-6551. Extensive moorage for boats up to 45.7 m (150 ft), with power and water on the docks and wireless internet service. Haulout and 60-ton travel lift available.

FUEL RIDOR FUELS LTD (look for the ESSO sign and QUARTERDECK INN AND MARINE RESORT; both open year-round; call on VHF Channel 66A.

BOAT LAUNCH Public – off Hardy Bay Road.

ANCHOR NE of the outer public wharf in 2.5-5 m (8-16 ft) with holding good in mud.

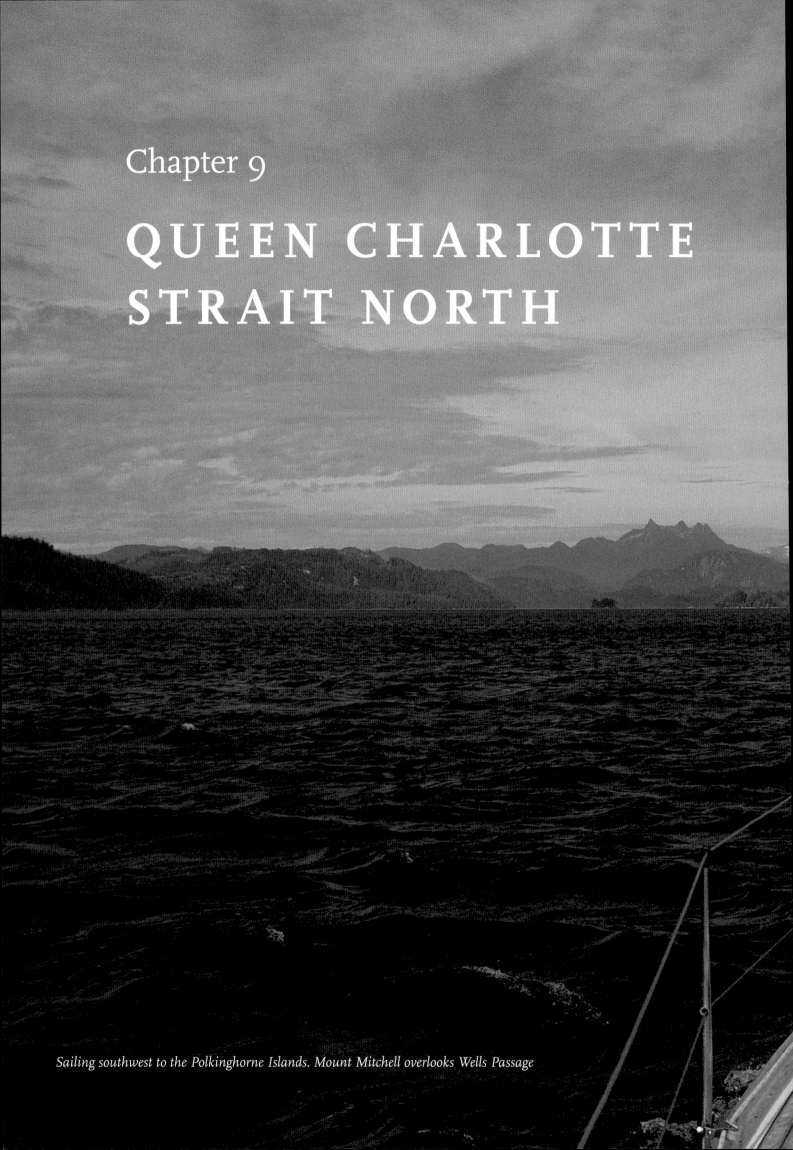

Chapter 9
QUEEN CHARLOTTE STRAIT NORTH

Sailing southwest to the Polkinghorne Islands. Mount Mitchell overlooks Wells Passage

New adventures around every corner

Chapter 9
QUEEN CHARLOTTE STRAIT NORTH

TIDES – *Volume 6,*
Canadian Tide and Current Tables
Reference Port – Alert Bay
Secondary Port – Raynor Group

WEATHER
Weather Station – WX1 162.55 MHZ
Area – Queen Charlotte Strait
Reporting Stations – Alert Bay, Herbert Island

CURRENTS
Secondary Station – Browning Island, NW of Blunden Harbour. This station will give a good indication of the strength of current flooding or ebbing along the Northern Queen Charlotte Strait shore.

CAUTIONARY NOTES: *Explore the destinations in this chapter with great caution, as there are shallows and rocks just waiting for a fresh keel. Best to run aground at dead slow on a rising tide, when patience will be the requirement for a safe recovery.*

Port Hardy to Blunden Harbour on the coastal mainland is 15 nautical miles northeast across Queen Charlotte Strait. A boater's haven, this sheltered anchorage is protected by a barrier of islands and islets. Here, you will find an inviting, white-shell beach backed by a deep midden and a colourful fisherman's cabin; the small anchorage near the entrance to Bradley Lagoon allowed us a day of exploration and sweet tranquility.

When unpleasant wind and sea conditions prevail in Queen Charlotte Strait, nip into the sheltered passage between the Raynor Group of islands and the Coastal Mainland to explore the choice of one-boat anchorages and mini shell beaches. Alternatively, visit the unexpected and beautifully rugged anchorage that lies further south, in sheltered Lewis Cove. With a wonderful view out to Queen Charlotte Strait, laze in the cockpit and watch the distant cruise liners heading north and south. If time and weather permit, don't miss a stopover in the charming Polkinghorne Islands near the entrance to Wells Passage in Queen Charlotte Strait; they offer an inviting cluster of rocks, islets and white-shell beaches to explore and a well-protected anchorage to overnight in.

Southeast of Wells Passage on Dickson Island, and often popular with club flotillas and boat rendezvous, "Deep Cove" offers a fair-sized anchorage with good protection from westerly winds. Less crowded and more scenic options are the sheltered anchorages in Carter Passage, where you can sit back, relax and immerse yourself in the area's beauty and tranquility. Commodious and peaceful anchorage is also possible in Tracey Harbour, Broughton Island, where we found protection from all winds and experienced one of the most brilliant scarlet sunsets.

FEATURED DESTINATIONS

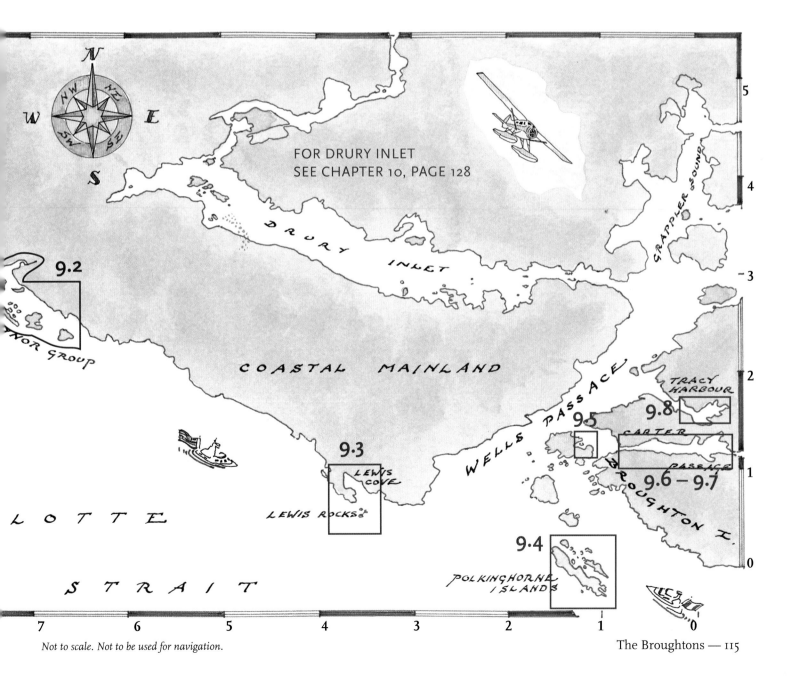

Not to scale. Not to be used for navigation.

9.I BLUNDEN HARBOUR

✿50°53.89'N 127°16.18'W

CHARTS   3548.

APPROACH   From the SE. Enter between Barren Rock and Shelf Head. A course mid-channel is clear and free of obstructions.

ANCHOR   The outer harbour, W of the Augustine Islands, is commodious and protected from all quarters. Take your pick in depths of 5-7.5 m (16-24 ft) where the holding is good in mud.

"Kingfishers Pool" (named by us) in the upper reaches of Blunden Harbour is totally protected, with anchorage for 1 to 2 boats. Swing to the current in depths of 2-3 m (6-9 ft) with good holding in mud.

Note: Entrance into Bradley Lagoon is possible only at HW and best explored by dinghy and outboard with reserve fuel.

A barrier of islands and islets, with plenty of room to swing, protects the sheltered anchorage of Blunden Harbour, a boater's haven. Investigating in *Tink,* we found beautifully marbled granite and sandstone shorelines and boulders resembling petrified chocolate-chip cookie dough.

The wide, inviting shell beach is backed by a midden and massive nurse logs from the now abandoned village. Follow the salmonberry and salal bordering the beach to a colourful fisherman's cabin with a rope swing and picnic table.

The silence and tranquility in the small anchorage near the entrance to Bradley Lagoon is often interrupted by the piercing screech of the resident kingfishers, hence our name for it.

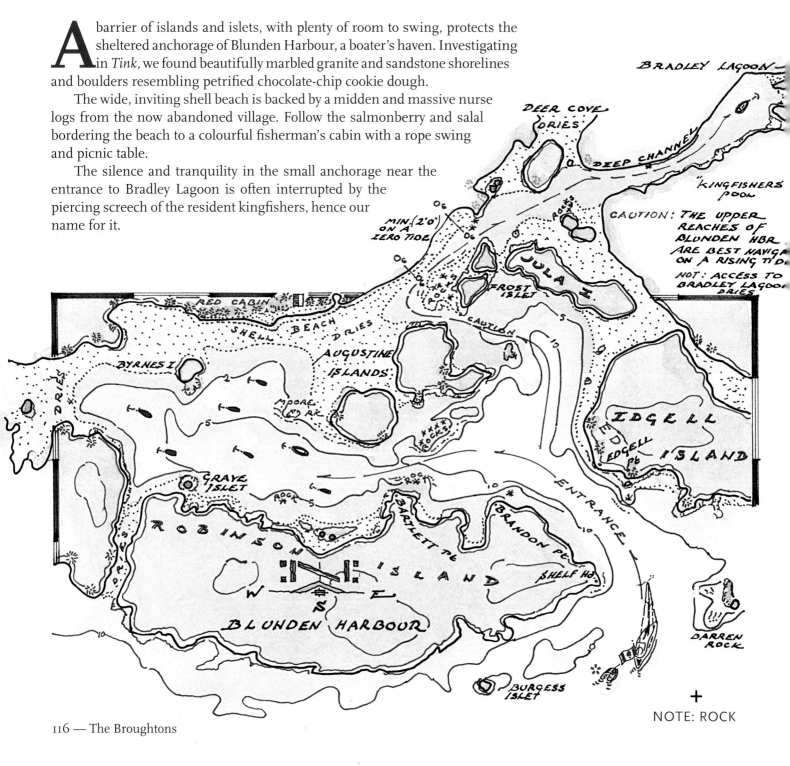

Stairs from the shell beach lead to a colourful cabin

CHARTS 3548.

APPROACH From the N; follow the route as indicated, and navigate with care as there are many unmarked rocks, although kelp is a good indicator of their position. Alternate approach from the S; there is deep water between the rocks and the SW island that forms the entrance to the inside passage, which is also deep and clear of obstructions.

ANCHOR Temporary, as indicated, in 5-10 m (16-32 ft). Holding varies.

✳50°53.82'N 127°15.30'W

When unpleasant wind and sea conditions prevail in Queen Charlotte Strait, nip into the sheltered passage between the Raynor Group of islands and the Coastal Mainland; explore the choice of one-boat anchorages and mini shell beaches from Cohoe Bay to Akam Point. Drop a picnic hook and beachcomb or enjoy an expansive view out to the strait while tucked into one of the delightful picnic stops.

Not to scale. Not to be used for navigation.

9.3 LEWIS COVE

✤ 50°49.03'N 127°03.32'W

CHARTS   3547.

APPROACH   From the SW between a large marked rock and the peninsula, or from the SE with a straight run in. Best approached at LW.

ANCHOR   Along the western shore or as indicated. Good protection from westerly wind although open to the SE. Holding good in shell and mud in depths of 5-10 m (16-32 ft).

One of the tide-trimmed, rocky islets

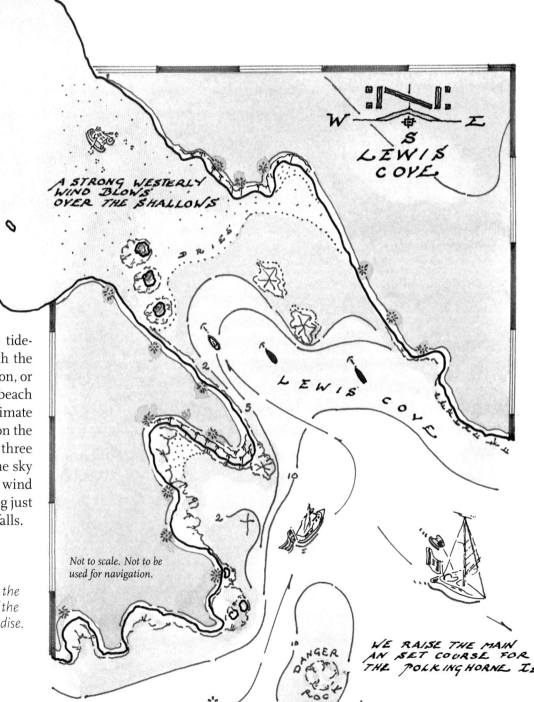

A beautifully rugged and unexpected anchorage lies north of Lewis Rocks in sheltered Lewis Cove. With a wonderful view out to Queen Charlotte Strait, laze in the cockpit and watch the distant cruise liners heading north and south, or dinghy over to the three lovely islets topped with tide-trimmed salal bushes. Feast with the birds on ripe salal berries in season, or explore the shallows and sandy beach beyond the rocks. For the ultimate birdwatching experience, stand on the highest point of the first islet (all three dry at low water) and watch as the sky fills with gulls gliding on the wind currents before diving and fishing just beyond the shallows as the tide falls.

CAUTIONARY NOTE: *Kelp indicates the outward reach of Lewis Rocks, S of the peninsula; these are a birder's paradise.*

CHARTS   3547.

APPROACH

(A) From the SE; the run in is clear.

(B) On a rising tide and with extreme caution, from the E. A shallow bar runs a short distance south of the rock.

(C) From the N, at the entrance, run in close to the E side. Look out for patches of kelp in the channel because a reef extends out from the western shore.

ANCHOR

(1) SE of the islet and rock crescent, with the best protection from strong westerly winds. Holding good in sand/shell/kelp in depths of 7-10 m (22-32 ft). Open to the SE.

(2) On a rising tide, in the small pool surrounded by rocks; navigate with caution. Good protection from strong westerly winds in depths of 3-5 m (9-16 ft). Open to the SE.

(3) In the channel as indicated. Better protection in a southeasterly. Holding good in depths of 2-5 m (6-16 ft). A strong 20+ knot westerly wind was blowing across the entrance when *Dreamspeaker* was at anchor, and a light swell did enter the channel.

❁ (A) 50°47.40'N 126°54.62'W
❁ (B) 50°47.91'N 126°54.94'W
❁ (C) 50°48.33'N 126°56.72'W

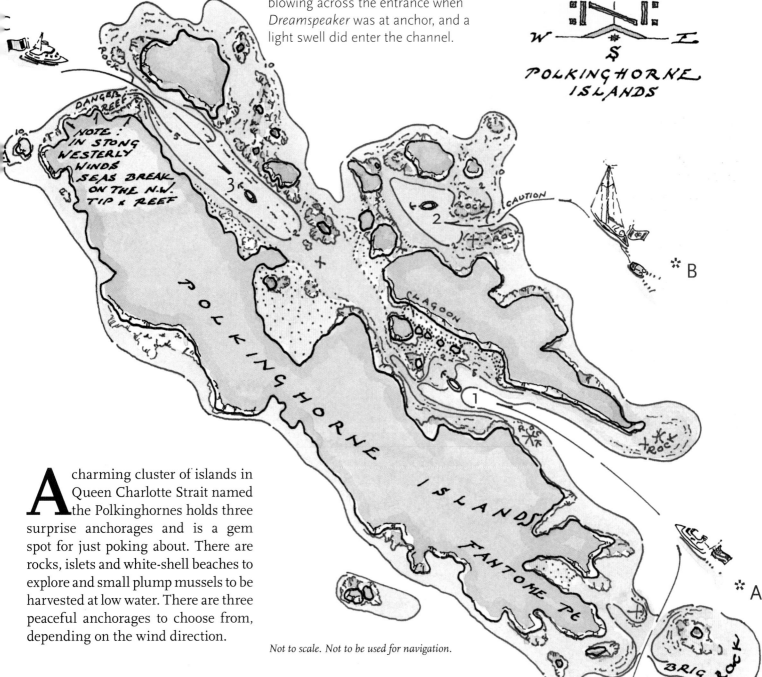

A charming cluster of islands in Queen Charlotte Strait named the Polkinghornes holds three surprise anchorages and is a gem spot for just poking about. There are rocks, islets and white-shell beaches to explore and small plump mussels to be harvested at low water. There are three peaceful anchorages to choose from, depending on the wind direction.

Not to scale. Not to be used for navigation.

9.5 "DEEP COVE," DICKSON ISLAND

❋50°50.35'N 126°55.38'W

CHARTS   3547.

APPROACH   From the NE. A rocky shallow area 2.1 m (6.8 ft) extends out from the N shore.

ANCHOR   "Deep Cove" (named by us) is a fair-sized anchorage with good protection from westerly winds. The cove is deep, 10+ m (32+ ft), and convenient rope loops secured on shore make stern-tying a possible option if crowded. Holding and bottom condition not recorded.

Not to scale. Not to be used for navigation.

Often popular with club flotillas and boat rendezvous, "Deep Cove" was busy with boaters manoeuvring, anchoring or taking stern lines ashore as we dropped anchor close to the cove entrance. With depth sounder in hand, we took *Tink* on an exploratory row, stopping off to enjoy a picnic lunch on the rocks overlooking the anchorage. Encouraged by an afternoon westerly wind, we left our temporary anchorage to enjoy a fine sail to Tracey Harbour.

Seawind illuminated in Napier Bay, Tracey Harbour

9.6 ENTRANCE TO CARTER PASSAGE, BROUGHTON ISLAND

✳50°50.19'N 126°54.83'W

CHARTS 3547.

APPROACH With caution, as large rocks are centrally located prior to the entrance. Best approached at LW or HW slack, the pass and centre channel are clear and, although rocks on the S shore are well marked by kelp, favour the N shore.

CAUTIONARY NOTE: *The pass at the eastern end, beyond the anchorage, dries at 3.7 m (12 ft). Do not attempt transit to Greenway Sound.*

From a distance, the narrows into Carter Passage look a little daunting; however, once inside, they are much wider than thy appear, with equally navigable depths.

Bow-watch at the entrance to Carter Passage

NOTE: CHART 3547 INDICATES A MINIMUM DEPTH OF 3M (9.8 FE) AND TIDAL RAPIDS OF 7 KNOTS ON THE EBB & FLOOD. NARROWS TO 15 M (50 ft) NORTH OF ROCKS ON THE SOUTH SIDE

Seals laze on rocks awash in Wells Passage

ANCHORAGES IN CARTER 9.7
PASSAGE, BROUGHTON ISLAND

ANCHOR   At the E end of the pass where depths are more suitable in 8-10 m (26-32 ft) and holding is good in mud. The anchorages in Carter Passage are well protected from all directions, although westerly winds do funnel through, keeping boats steady.

A commodious, peaceful and highly scenic anchorage, there are two small coves and one large bay to give boaters their choices of where to drop the hook – then sit back, relax and immerse yourself in the area's beauty and tranquility.

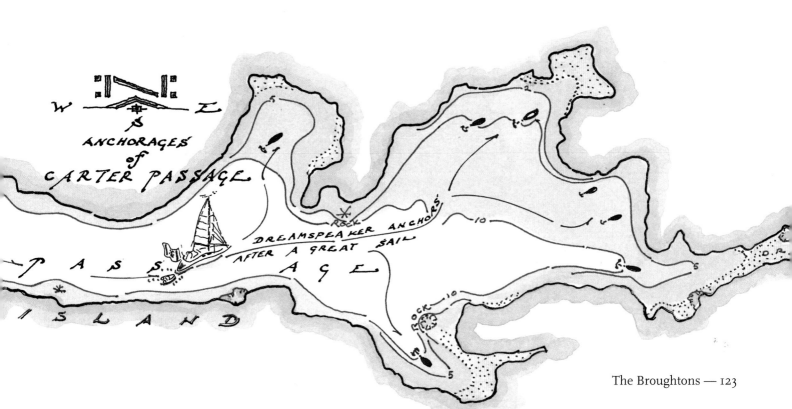

Looking west – Tracey Harbour aglow

NAPIER BAY, TRACEY HARBOUR, BROUGHTON ISLAND 9.8

CHARTS 3547.

APPROACH The centre channel in Tracey Harbour is clear of obstructions. When approaching the anchored log breakwater off Carter Point, take the northern route into Napier Bay or the southern route to "Little Napier Bay" (named by us).

ANCHOR In Napier Bay where you will find protection from all winds in depths of 5-12 m (16-39 ft) with holding good in mud. Be aware of the submerged pipeline near the head of the bay. "Little Napier Bay" is big enough for only 2-3 boats with depths of 5-10 m (16-32 ft). Holding is good in mud.

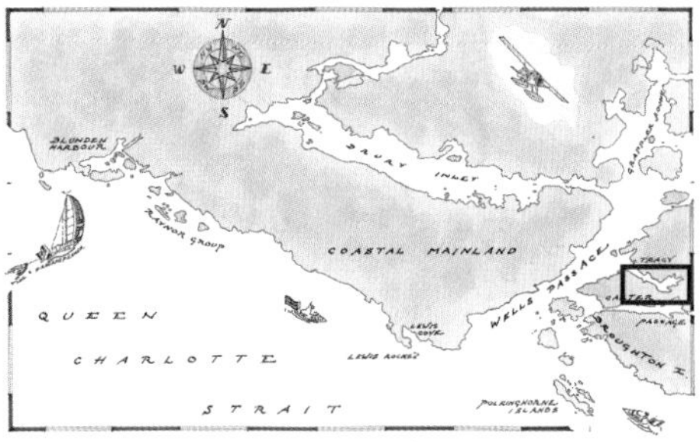

⁂50°50.90'N 126°51.83'W

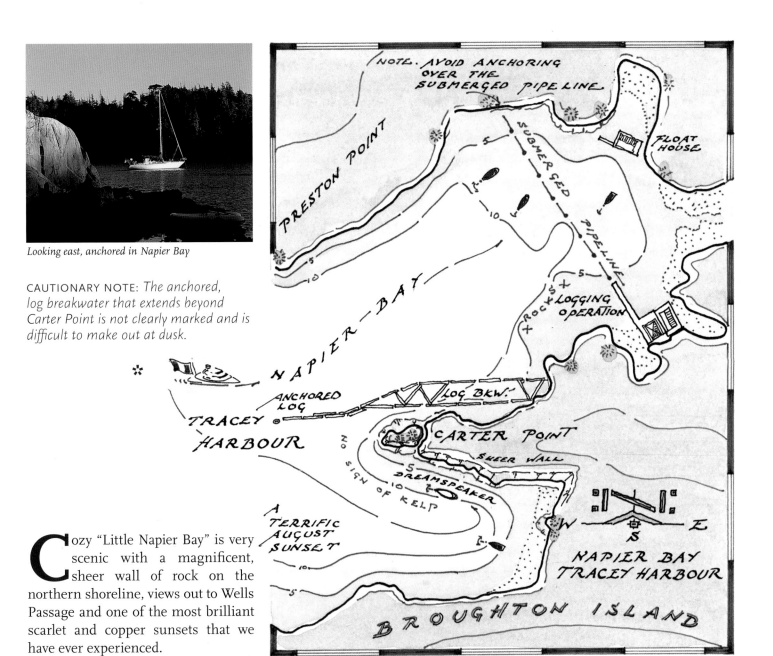

Looking east, anchored in Napier Bay

CAUTIONARY NOTE: *The anchored, log breakwater that extends beyond Carter Point is not clearly marked and is difficult to make out at dusk.*

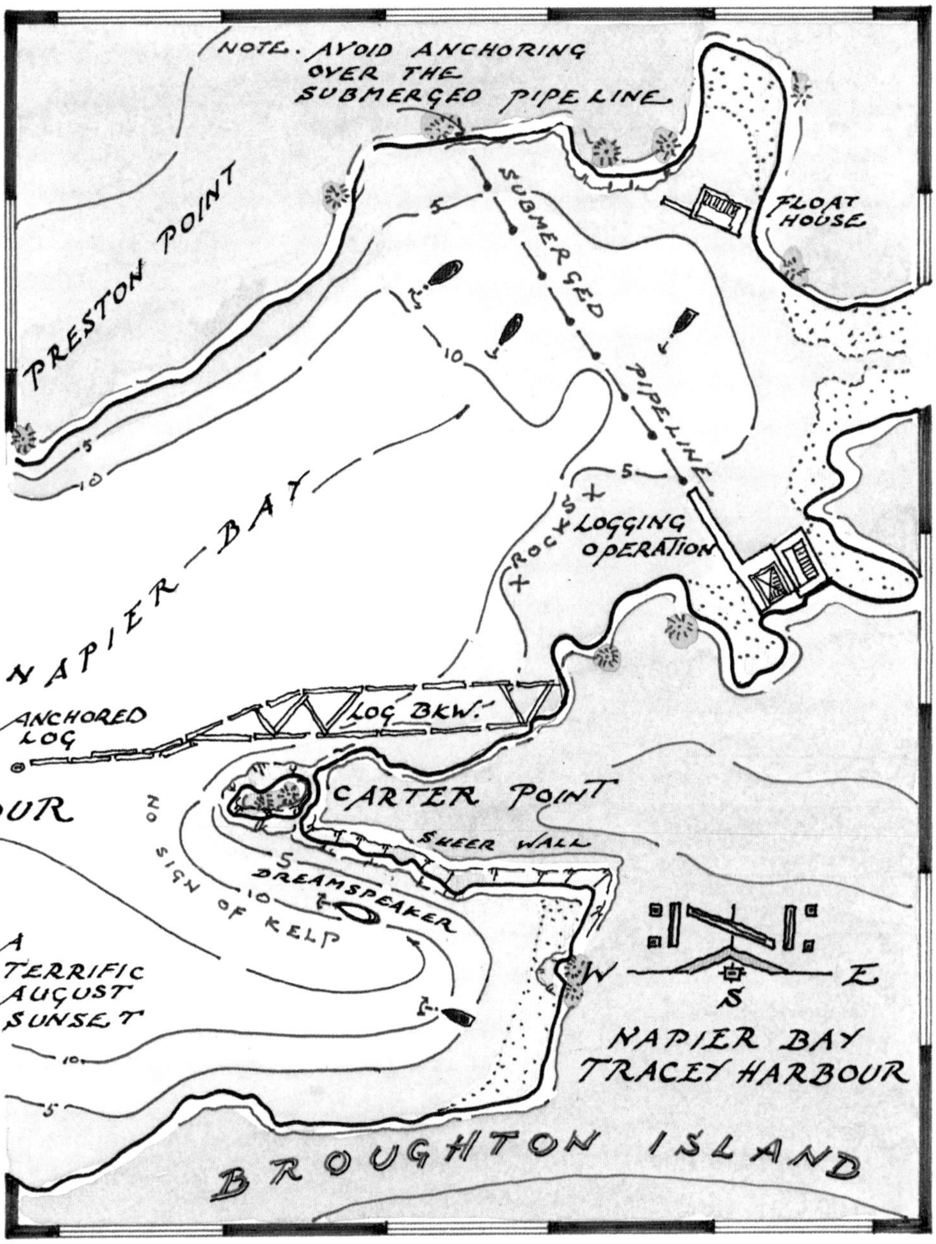

Cozy "Little Napier Bay" is very scenic with a magnificent, sheer wall of rock on the northern shoreline, views out to Wells Passage and one of the most brilliant scarlet and copper sunsets that we have ever experienced.

Drury Inlet – a quiet sense of mystery

Chapter 10
DRURY INLET

Chapter 10
DRURY INLET

TIDES – *Volume 6,*
Canadian Tide and Current Tables
Reference Port – Alert Bay
Secondary Ports – Stuart Narrows,
Jennis Bay

CURRENTS
Reference Station – Stuart Narrows on
Alert Bay
Reference port (tide) – Alert Bay

WEATHER
Weather Station – WX1 162.55 MHZ
Area – Queen Charlotte Strait
Reporting Stations – Alert Bay

Anne investigates Sutherland Bay.

CAUTIONARY NOTES: *Currents are strong in Stuart Narrows at the entrance to Drury Inlet – up to 6 knots on the flood tide and 7 knots on the ebb. Note the position of "Centre Reef" in the narrows, as it can come as a surprise with all the deep water around. Be aware of strong and turbulent currents, especially around Dove Island and off Charters Point at the entrance to Actress Passage – best transited at slack water or with the tide in your favour.*

Drury Inlet, with its quiet sense of mystery, is certainly the place to explore when planning a few days away from the more crowded anchorages. Although the current runs swiftly in Stuart Narrows, with a small amount of turbulence at the entrance, it is still best to run into the inlet with the flood, and out with the ebb tide. Although there are anchorages in Davis and Richmond Bay on the southern shoreline, they both become uncomfortable at its head when a strong westerly picks up in the inlet.

Jennis Bay is a well-protected anchorage. A private lodge and float lie north of the entrance. On our visit a generator was popping away. To find placid waters, head up to the delightful Muirhead Islands where you will find a snug and protected anchorage with a collection of islets, rocks and pocket shell beaches worth exploring by dinghy and kayak.

Sutherland Bay at the head of the inlet offers peace and quiet, a lovely view to Mount Ellis and an abundance of wildlife. The bay has excellent anchorage for large and small boats, with plenty of room to swing. *Dreamspeaker*'s crew did not venture past Skeen Point into Actaeon Sound because of the iffy weather forecast. "Bond Basin" provides a calm, sheltered anchorage between Actress Passage and Actaeon Sound and a staging point for those travelling farther north to explore Bond Lagoon and Actaeon Sound.

18

FEATURED DESTINATIONS

CHARTS   3547, insert Stuart Narrows.

APPROACH   Best at LW slack; the flooding current will assist one into the inlet.

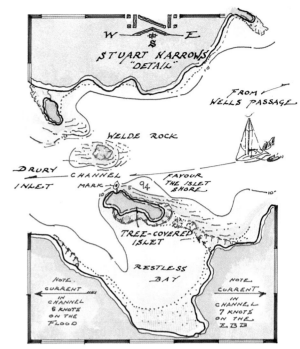

ENTRANCE TO DRURY INLET

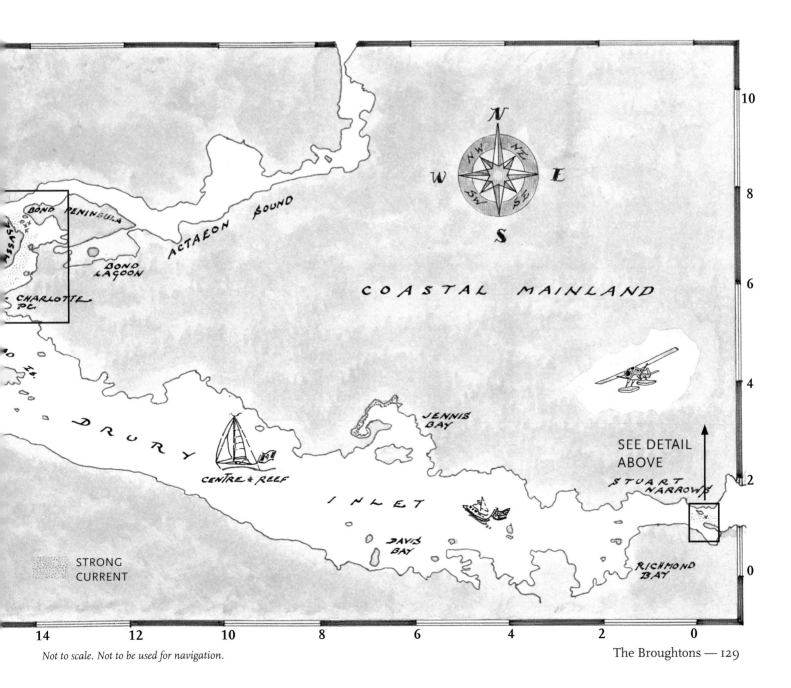

STRONG CURRENT

Not to scale. Not to be used for navigation.

Harmony in the Muirhead Islands

MUIRHEAD ISLANDS 10.1

CHARTS 3547.

APPROACH From the E at LW. Clear the rocks to the S, prior to heading N into the small cove formed by the Muirhead Islands to the E and N and the rocks and islets to the W.

ANCHOR Ample room for 2-3 boats with a stern line ashore. Well sheltered from prevailing E and W winds, with holding good in gravel/mud/shell.

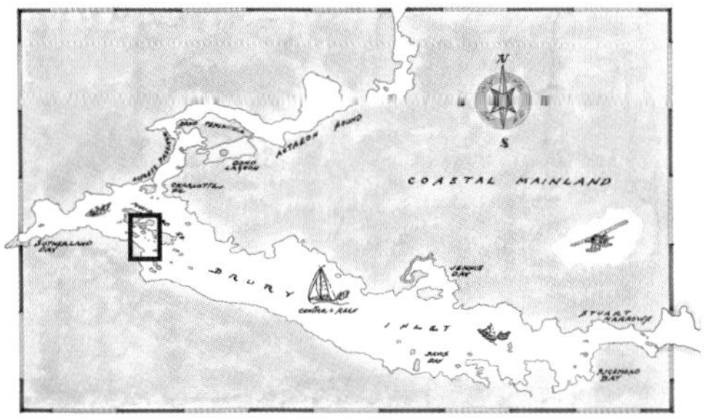

✲50°55.15'N 127°08.59'W

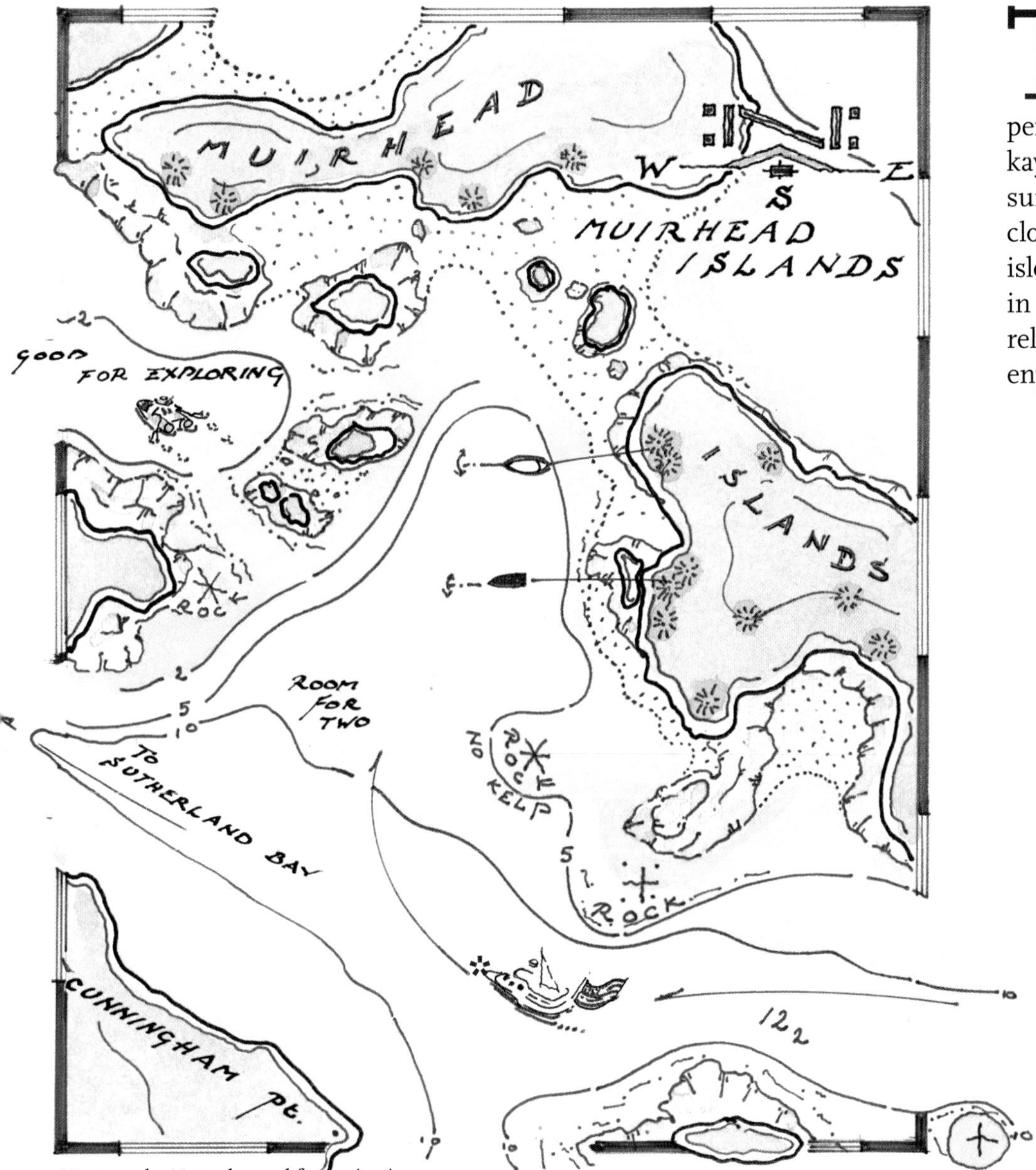

Not to scale. Not to be used for navigation.

This delightful cluster of islands, islets and rocks forms a snug and protected anchorage, perfect for exploring by dinghy and kayak. Low water exposes pockets of sun-bleached shell fragments, and a closer inspection of the islands and islets reveals ripe, plump salal berries in season. After a day's adventuring, relax in the cockpit with a cool drink, enjoying the sunset and serenity.

10.2 SUTHERLAND BAY

✻50°55.58'N 127°10.70'W

CHARTS   3547.

APPROACH   Sutherland Bay lies at the head of Drury Inlet. The bay is free of obstructions.

ANCHOR   In depths of 2-5 m (6-16 ft) with good holding in mud. The anchorage is quite commodious with protection from westerly winds.

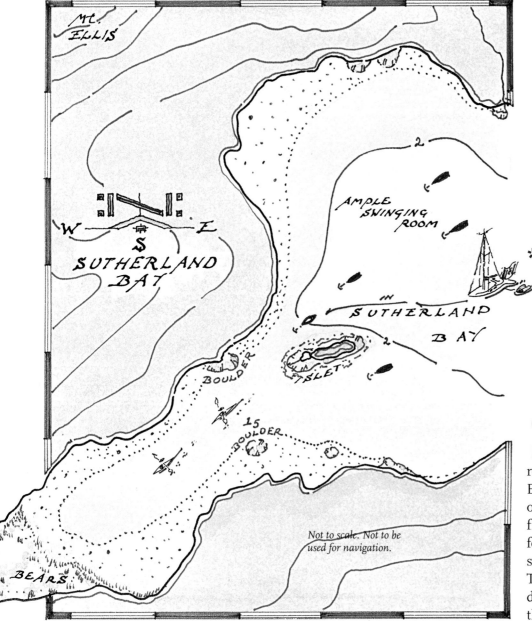

Not to scale. Not to be used for navigation.

Sutherland Bay offers peace and quiet and excellent anchorage for larger boats, with plenty of room to swing and a view to Mount Ellis. Explore the shoreline by dinghy or kayak and observe the wildlife – from a charming family of mergansers feeding in the shallows, to curious seals popping up beside your craft. The trails to Bradley Lagoon should definitely be left to the bears that use them!

"BOND BASIN," ACTRESS PASSAGE 10.3

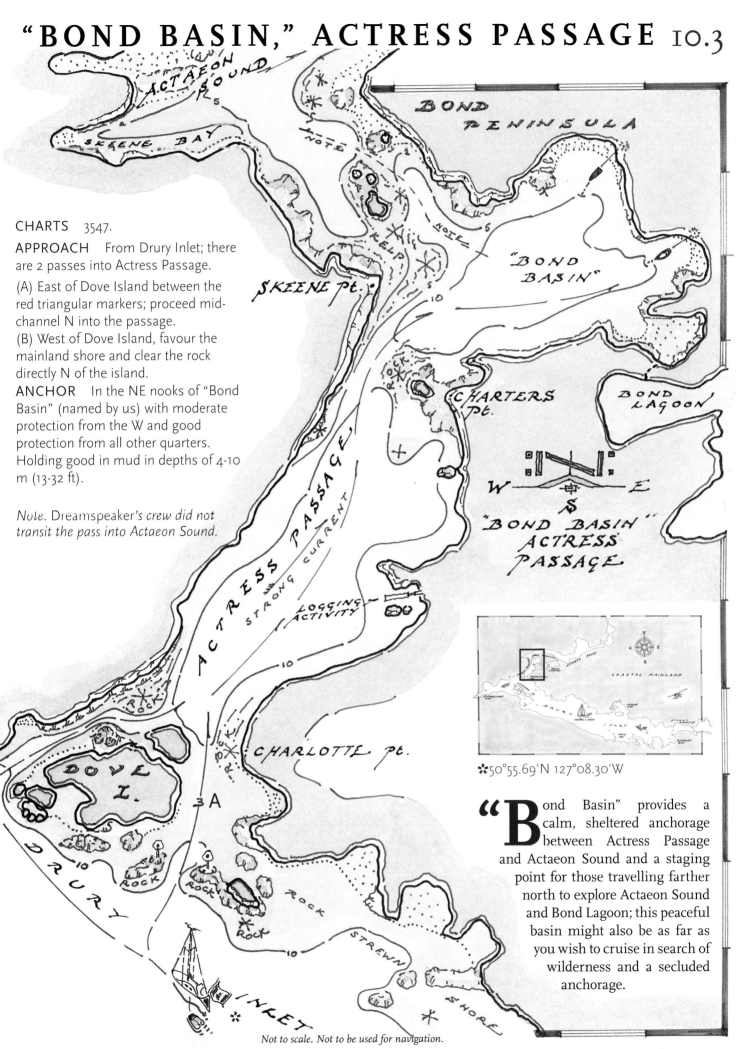

CHARTS 3547.

APPROACH From Drury Inlet; there are 2 passes into Actress Passage.

(A) East of Dove Island between the red triangular markers; proceed mid-channel N into the passage.

(B) West of Dove Island, favour the mainland shore and clear the rock directly N of the island.

ANCHOR In the NE nooks of "Bond Basin" (named by us) with moderate protection from the W and good protection from all other quarters. Holding good in mud in depths of 4-10 m (13-32 ft).

Note: Dreamspeaker's crew did not transit the pass into Actaeon Sound.

⚓ 50°55.69'N 127°08.30'W

"Bond Basin" provides a calm, sheltered anchorage between Actress Passage and Actaeon Sound and a staging point for those travelling farther north to explore Actaeon Sound and Bond Lagoon; this peaceful basin might also be as far as you wish to cruise in search of wilderness and a secluded anchorage.

Not to scale. Not to be used for navigation.

The arrival of a Canadian Naval vessel in Sullivan Bay

Chapter 11

GRAPPLER AND
MACKENZIE SOUND

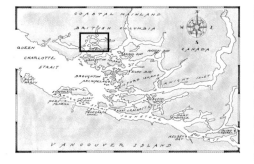

Stairs to a heavenly fresh water dip, Turnbull Cove.

Chapter 11
GRAPPLER AND MACKENZIE SOUND

TIDES – *Volume 6,*
Canadian Tide and Current Tables
Reference Port – Alert Bay
Secondary Ports – Sullivan Bay, Jessie
Point (entrance to Kenneth Passage)

CURRENTS
No specific reference or secondary
stations cover this chapter. Slack water,
in the passages off both Watson Point
and Jessie Point are similar to slack at
Roaringhole Rapids (see note chart
3547).

WEATHER
Weather Station – WX1 162.55 MHZ
Area – Queen Charlotte Strait
Reporting Station – Alert Bay

CAUTIONARY NOTES: *Currents run swiftly through all the channels and passages, creating a certain amount of current in all the destinations covered in this chapter. Do not be tempted to take the "short-cut" through Hopetown passage into Mackenzie sound at HW and note the position of the rock off Watson Point in Grappler Sound as this one was a near miss for Dreamspeaker's keel! Because of Roaringhole Rapids and the lack of suitable anchorage depths, an excursion into Nepah Lagoon is not recommended.*

The community of Sullivan Bay is conveniently situated on northern Broughton Island and historic Sullivan Bay Marine Resort is relaxed, friendly and full of character. The floating village is an eclectic mix of colourful float homes from the early 1940s and offers the cruising boater facilities to fuel, provision, shower, throw in a load or two of laundry and rendezvous with friends; it's the perfect spot to begin your cruise into the scenic waters of Grappler and Mackenzie Sound – the start of the coastal mainland's labyrinth of passages and channels.

Hopetown Passage north of Sullivan Bay offers a small, peaceful anchorage; swing to the current and savour the magnificent views, with mighty Mount Stephens standing guard. Note that the narrow, boulder-strewn pass into Mackenzie Sound has a very strong current and can only be navigated by shoal draft boats at HW. The comfortably large anchorage in Claydon Bay is backed by Mount Emily. Explore Embley Lagoon and navigate the tidal falls into Overflow Basin by dingy.

Surrounded by a rocky shoreline and steep forested sides, harbour-sized Turnbull Cove offers good anchorage and an invigorating hike to lovely Huaskin Lake where you can take a fresh-water swim.

En route from Steamboat to Nimmo Bay, look out for the spectacular cliff face at Anne Point; an inconspicuous nook east of Turner Island also reveals a cozy one-boat anchorage. The prettiest spot to anchor in Burly Bay is tucked in behind Blair Islet.

In settled weather westerly winds tend to die off at the end of the day, making the anchorage at the head of Mackenzie Sound a peaceful spot to drop the hook for the night.

The morning mirror calm of Nimmo Bay is an experience not to be missed.

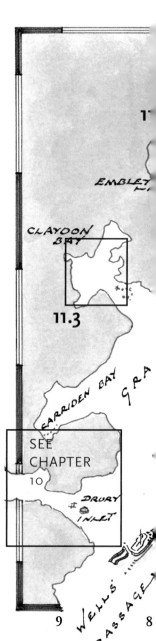

FEATURED DESTINATIONS

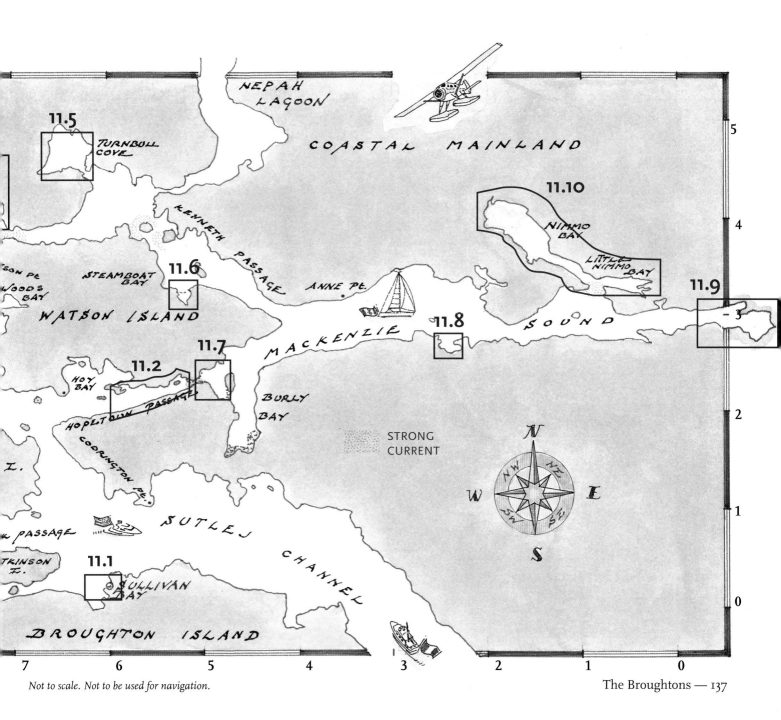

Not to scale. Not to be used for navigation.

11.1 SULLIVAN BAY, BROUGHTON ISLAND

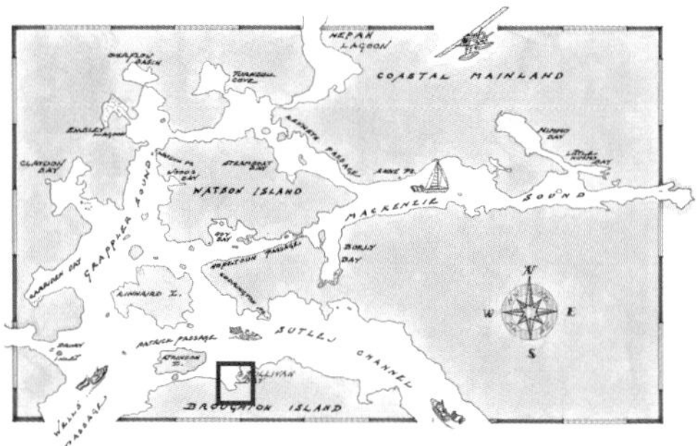

⁂50°53.29'N 126°49.81'W

CAUTIONARY NOTE: *Do not underestimate the force of the cross current at the docks. Come to a full stop prior to making the run in and assess the current's direction and strength.*

"The International Airport," fuel tanks and fuel dock

The store is a focal point

The 'Town Hall Restaurant' serves tasty, hearty meals

Historic SULLIVAN BAY MARINE RESORT is relaxed, friendly and full of character. The unique floating village is an eclectic mix of wooden structures and float homes brought into the bay during the early 1940s and it still keeps its fun, quirky personality today. Almost everything that stands still is painted with vibrant collages and the charming gardens and planters along the boardwalk overflow with flowers; gardening-deprived guests are encouraged to contribute to their care during the summer months.

The resort has a post office and an excellent store with fresh produce brought in every 2-3 days in high season. The GOVERNMENT LIQUOR STORE outlet is well stocked but requires that purchases be paid for only in cash – for everything else you can use your credit card. Clean but cozy showers offer hot water, although the laundry facilities supply only cold. Prepay both at the store before using. Garbage disposal is self-service with no fee when using the recycling bins; a large tin drum is provided for burnable products. The village smokehouse is available by reservation.

The TOWN HALL floating restaurant is licenced and open for breakfast, lunch and supper. This cozy spot makes a welcome addition to the village amenities, with a Saturday evening menu that might include prime rib and Yorkshire pudding or steak and lobster specials. On display are historic photographs of Sullivan Bay between the mid-'40s and late '50s, when it was one of the main float and biplane fuelling stops on the coast. Queen Charlotte Airlines, the third largest airline in Canada, owned by entrepreneur Jim Spilsbury, was one of their major customers, and his fascinating and entertaining book *Spilsbury's Coast* is a must read for any boater cruising this coast (see *Selected Readings*, page 188).

Float plane services to and from the resort can be found on Sullivan Bay's website (www.sullivanbay.com), as well as information on summer events and the famous July 4th Fireworks Parade and potluck dinner.

CHARTS 3547.

APPROACH The floating village with its colourful roofs is conspicuous as you enter Sullivan Bay. The run in is free of obstructions.

MARINA Sullivan Bay Marine Resort offers extensive visitor moorage with power, wireless internet service via BBX, and unlimited water. They monitor Channel 66A and a dock attendant nearly always is on call.

Contact them by satellite phone 403-997-0111, messages at 250-286-4877 or email palyn@telus.net.

FUEL At the resort fuel float, where propane also is available.

CAUTIONARY NOTE: *Do not underestimate the force of the cross current at the docks. Come to a full stop prior to making the run in and assess the current's direction and strength.*

The float home that sports both flags!

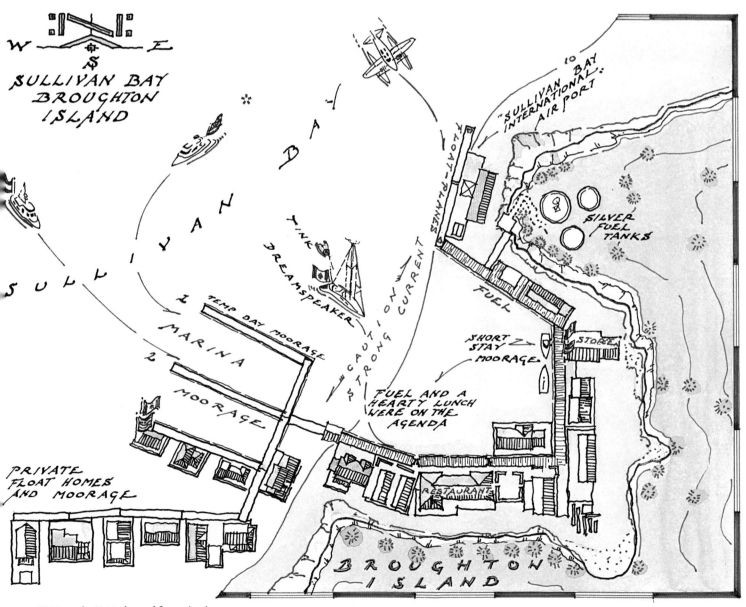

Not to scale. Not to be used for navigation.

II.2 HOPETOWN PASSAGE, HOY BAY

✻50°55.06'N 126°49.28'W

CHARTS 3547.

APPROACH   From the W, along the steep southern shoreline of Hopetown Passage which lies S of the First Nations Community.

ANCHOR   As indicated in (1) which has less current or (2) in settled· weather, between the kelp. Swing to the current in depths of 2.5-4 m (8-13 ft), with fair holding in gravel and rock.

Note: Anchorage (2) is only for boaters who feel comfortable anchoring in the current, between kelp.

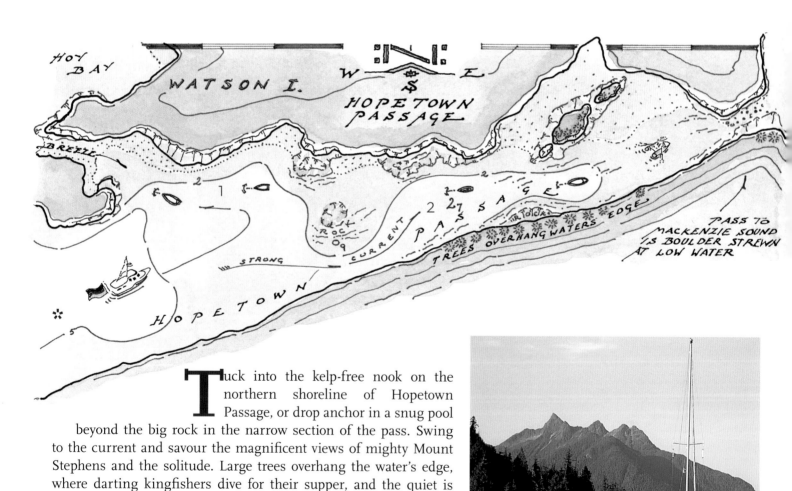

Tuck into the kelp-free nook on the northern shoreline of Hopetown Passage, or drop anchor in a snug pool beyond the big rock in the narrow section of the pass. Swing to the current and savour the magnificent views of mighty Mount Stephens and the solitude. Large trees overhang the water's edge, where darting kingfishers dive for their supper, and the quiet is occasionally disturbed by the soft splash of leaping salmon.

Mighty Mount Stephens

CHARTS 3547.

APPROACH From the SE out of Grappler Sound. Favour the W shore, as rocks lie to the NE. If anchoring NE of the islet, favour the W shore.

ANCHOR Good protection from westerly winds can be found in the N basin and from SE winds in the S basin. Holding good in mud in depths of 3-6 m (9-19 ft).

✱50°55.56'N 127°53.12'W

In both of the finger-like coves, ruins of trestle structures that once formed logging jetties add a little history to Claydon Bay. The comfortably large anchorage, backed by Mount Emily, is a very pleasant spot to spend the day or to overnight. Explore the grassy islet or visit the ruins and beachcomb at leisure while graceful sandpipers feed on the rising tide.

Ruins of the trestle structures

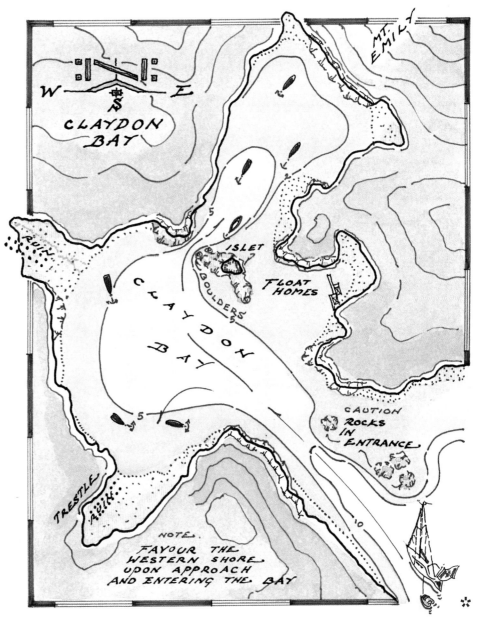

�֎50°56.41'N 126°51.85'W

CHARTS   3547.

APPROACH   From the S. Clear the rock off Watson Point and keep in mind the strong currents.

ANCHOR   (1) North of the islet on the E shore, with a stern line ashore. (2) East of the gap to Overflow Basin with a taut stern line ashore. (3) Drop anchor along the 10 m (32 ft) sounding on the W shore. A lovely anchorage in settled weather with holding good in mud, in depths of 6-10m (19-32 ft).

Note: It is necessary to have a reliable outboard and dinghy if you plan to navigate the tidal falls into Overflow Basin before or after high water slack. The gap dries at LW.

A large section of Embley Lagoon dries at LW, although the entrance is shallow but navigable by dinghy.

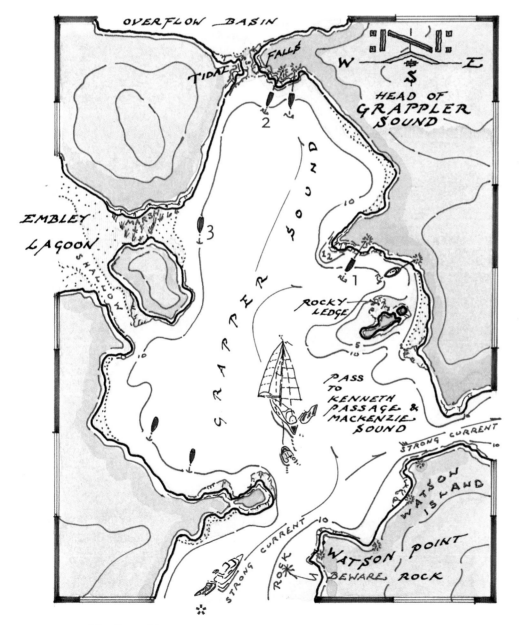

A lucky boat anchored adjacent to the tidal falls

Each of the three anchorages at the head of Grappler Sound has its own personality; the cozy nook north of the small islet keeps the light longest, while anchoring close to the tidal falls at the entrance to Overflow Basin is a dramatic and much coveted overnight spot. Anchoring off the western shoreline will include a fine view into peaceful Embley Lagoon, where the marsh is home to a large family of flighty mergansers.

Tink took us on a thrilling and fun trip through the tidal falls. Once inside, the basin was sunny and tranquil; it was a thrilling experience being flushed out with the ebb, before it became too strong.

CHARTS 3547.

APPROACH From the head of Grappler Sound. The entrance is lined with kelp, although the centre channel gives a clear run in.

ANCHOR No need to crowd your neighbours in this commodious and protected anchorage. Take a stern line or swing in depths of 5-10 m (16-32 ft), as easterly winds tend to swirl around. Holding good in mud.

Note: Westerly winds will funnel through the gap in the SW corner.

✳50°57.26'N 126°49.57'W

Shoreline access to base of the steep trail

Harbour-sized Turnbull Cove is surrounded by a rocky shoreline and steep forested sides and offers good anchorage and a hike to Huaskin Lake, which was once home to a large logging camp. The trail is maintained by the Ministry of Forests, allowing your crew with the opportunity to hike, take a fresh-water swim from the wooden raft and enjoy a picnic lunch at the table provided.

Pull your dinghy up to the rock-strewn beach and walk to the base of the steep trail; help yourself to one of the many recycled walking sticks, which are a great help during the often slippery upward climb. The descent to the lake is via dozens of stairs cut into a secured, sturdy log covered with a non-slip surface – a thoughtful addition, indeed.

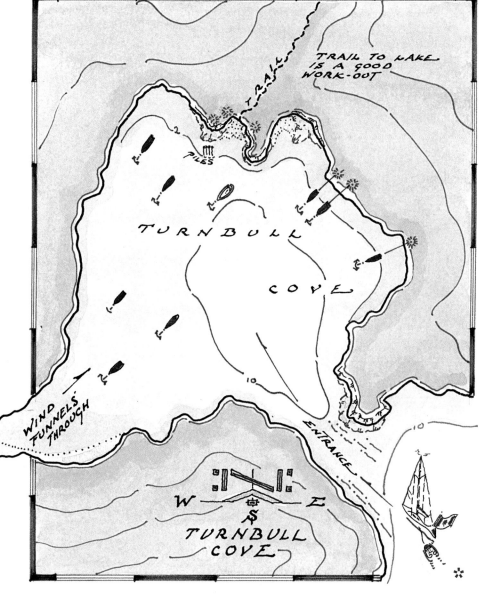

Dreamspeaker glides past Anne Point

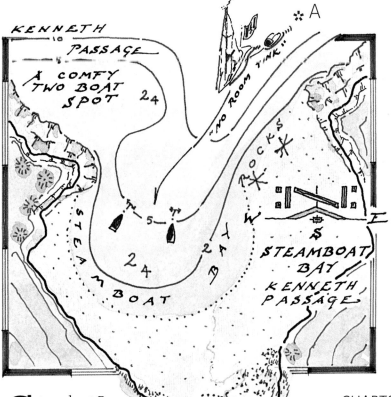

❈(A) 50°56.26'N 126°48.21'W
❈(B) 50°55.84'N 126°43.89'W

Two lucky boats in Steamboat Bay

Steamboat Bay is a little gem of an anchorage, sadly no advance booking was available, so we moved on.

CHARTS   3547, inset Kenneth Passage.
APPROACH   From the N, at LW kelp marks the rocks to the E.
ANCHOR   2 boats comfortably in depths of 4-8 m (13-26 ft).

11.7   "ANNE COVE"

Midway between Steamboat Bay and the head of Mackenzie Sound, an inconspicuous nook east of Turner Island revealed a pocket paradise, which we named "Anne Cove." The small beach is backed by a stream and a patch of crisp sea asparagus. The lone tree on "Crab-Apple Islet," also named by us, provided a hatful of the tart fruit for crab-apple jelly and a spot of shade for our picnic.

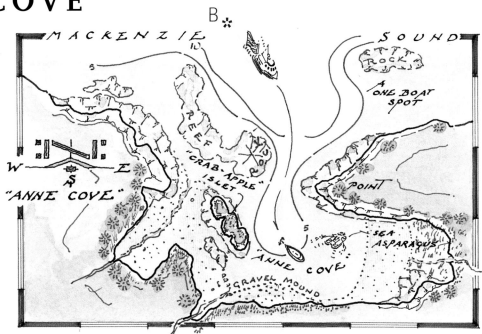

CHARTS   3547.
APPROACH   As indicated. Mid-channel between Turner Island and the S shore of Mackenzie Sound. Best approached at LW when rocks are visible.

ANCHOR   A one-boat anchorage in depths of 4-6 m (13-19 ft), well sheltered from westerly and easterly winds. Holding good in mud and shell.

II.8 "BLAIR COVE," BURLY BAY

✱50°55.45'N 126°47.45'W

CHARTS 3547.

APPROACH From the NE. The run in is free of obstructions.

ANCHOR As indicated, in depths of 4-8 m (13-26 ft). Holding good in mud and gravel.

Note: Do not attempt to pass through to Hopetown Passage or between Blair Islet and the mainland, as both are boulder-strewn.

Company in lovely "Blair Cove"

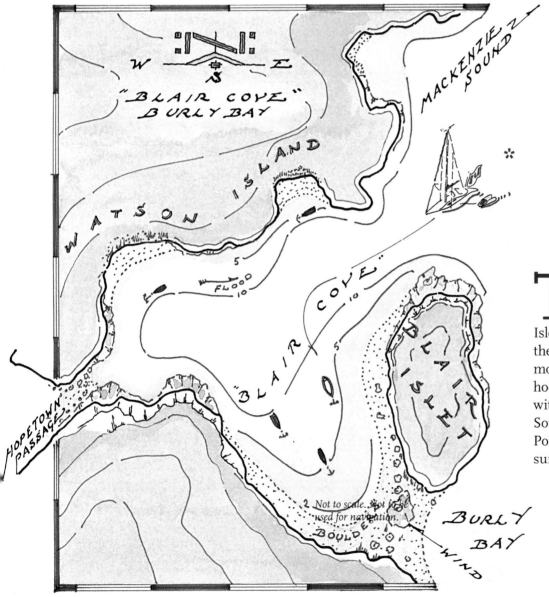

The prettiest spot to anchor in Burly Bay is "Blair Cove" (named by us), tucked in behind Blair Islet, with a dramatic outlook through the gap to the Matthew Range of mountains. Alternatively, drop your hook along the northwest shoreline with a clear view into Mackenzie Sound, and take in the beauty of Anne Point and the sheer rock face aglow at sunset.

MV Sir James Douglas

CHARTS 3547.

APPROACH From the W. Logging operations were evident on both the N and S shore. The entrance lies mid-channel between remnants of a log breakwater.

ANCHOR Although the anchorage is open to the W, reasonable protection in a strong westerly can be found into the N or S corners. Holding is good in mud and gravel, in depths of 4-6 m (13-19 ft).

✿50°55.98'N 126°39.07'W

In settled weather, westerly winds tend to die off at the end of the day, making the anchorage at the head of Mackenzie Sound a peaceful spot to drop the hook for the night. The stream that flows from Mackenzie Lake into the basin has created a small beach for exploring at low water.

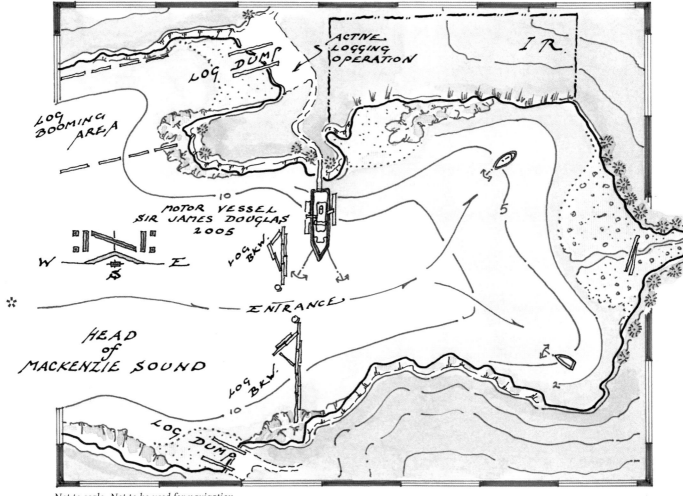

Not to scale. Not to be used for navigation.

II.10 LITTLE NIMMO BAY AND NIMMO BAY

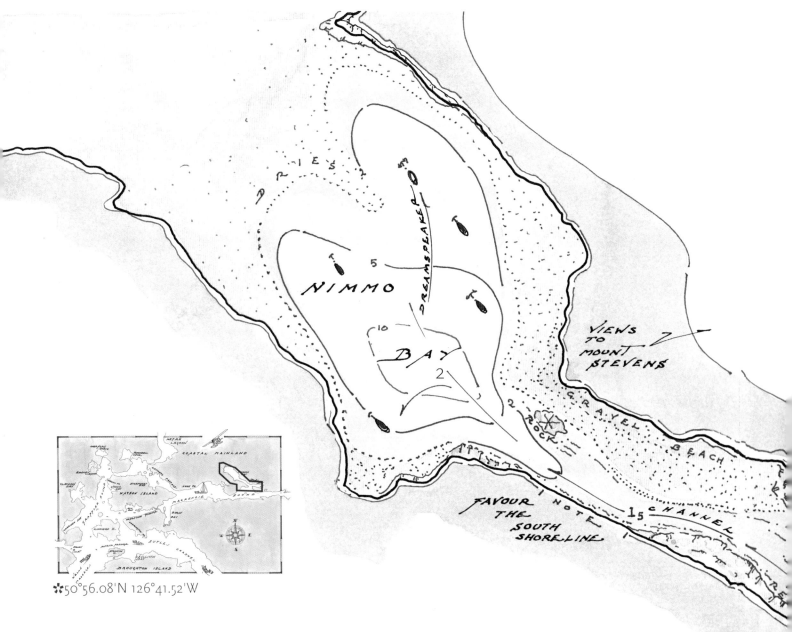

Map labels: PRIORIES, DREAMSPEAKER, NIMMO, BAY, VIEWS TO MOUNT STEVENS, GRAVEL BEACH, ROCK, FAVOUR THE SOUTH SHORELINE, NOTE, CHANNEL

✷ 50°56.08'N 126°41.52'W

Having negotiated the entrance into the Little Nimmo Bay, we anchored south of the lodge. The disturbance of the generator and helicopters from the resort sent us scurrying to the anchorage west of the entrance for the night. The following morning on a rising tide, dead slow, we crept west along the channel into Nimmo Bay, which is a glorious spot to anchor – tranquility at its best. We discourage an excursion ashore, as the shoreline is home to bear.

If space is available, the NIMMO BAY RESORT is happy to offer boaters day adventures by helicopter, transient moorage or dinner by invitation. Call ahead on 250-949-2549 and standby on VHF Channel 21A. Visit their web site www.nimmobay.com for tour information.

The resort's red-roofed cabins indicate the entrance MA

Glassy calm in Nimmo Bay

CHARTS   3547.

APPROACH   (A) From the S. The resort's colourful cabins are conspicuous on approach. The entrance to Little Nimmo Bay is best navigated on a rising tide. The clear channel is W of centre and best transited when the rocks on the western shore are still visible. Beware of the nugget of rock E of centre and the reef that extends N off Nimmo Point. Note that the consensus of local knowledge is that the charted least depth of 30 cm (1 ft) lies E of the entrance channel. (B) Nimmo Bay, on a rising tide. Leave the rock in centre channel to the N and take a curve around the edge of the reef extending out from the southern shore; favour the S shore upon entering the bay. Note that it is easy to run aground on the gravel that extends off the N shore.

ANCHOR   (1) E or W of the entrance in depths of 4-8 m (13-26 ft), with holding good in mud. (2) Drop your hook in Nimmo Bay, as indicated. Holding good in mud. Watch your depth sounder as the head dries extensively.

Note: The water was glassy calm when Dreamspeaker *was anchored in Nimmo Bay, although a moderate westerly was blowing in Mackenzie Sound. Local knowledge reports that Little Nimmo Bay has good protection from westerly winds, while Nimmo Bay has reasonable protection.*

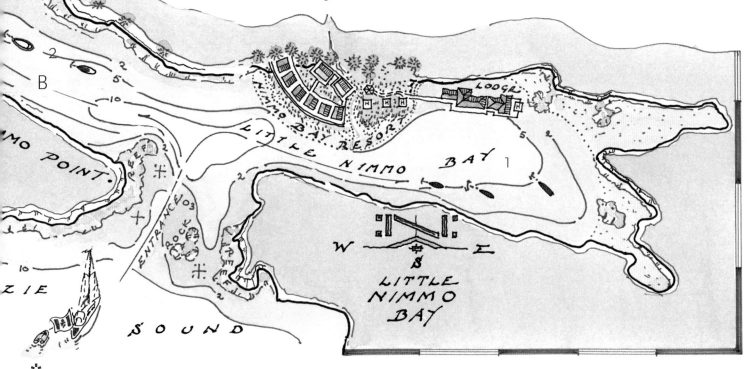

Chapter 12

BROUGHTON ISLAND, GREENWAY SOUND TO CULLEN HARBOUR

Greenway Sound Marine Resort accommodates yachts both large and small

Illusive winds in Fife Sound

Chapter 12

BROUGHTON ISLAND, GREENWAY SOUND TO CULLEN HARBOUR

TIDES – *Volume 6,*
Canadian Tide and Current Tables
Reference Port – Alert Bay
Secondary Port – Sunday Harbour

CURRENTS
No specific reference or secondary stations cover this chapter; however currents run swiftly through the channels and passages, creating a certain amount of current in most anchorages.

WEATHER
Weather Station – WX1 162.55 MHZ
Area – Queen Charlotte Strait
Reporting Station – Alert Bay

CAUTIONARY NOTES: *Beware – A rock in "Laura Cove" is situated between the islet and Trivett Island. At the entrance to Booker Lagoon, Booker Passage has a reef that extends out from Long Island. Look out for the stone man on the reef tip.*

12.3

Greenway Sound off Sutlej Channel runs east then south and almost cuts Broughton Island in two; although it is deep, it has few anchorages from which to choose. At the entrance to the sound, tucked behind Cecil Island, are two nooks that provide comfortable day and overnight anchorage. When the sun sets, the westerly winds in Greenway Sound die off and the northeast outflow winds take over, making this a protected, cozy corner.

GREENWAY SOUND MARINE RESORT has well-maintained docks, a small store for provisioning, delicious milkshakes and moorage fees that include garbage disposal. The abundant supply of water for showers and laundry make this tidy, well-kept marina an inviting destination for all cruising boaters. Nearby BROUGHTON LAKES MARINE PARK offers a maintained trail and traditional log road that allows boaters to stretch their sea legs with a scenic walk.

Behind Broughton Point, at the east end of Carter Passage you will find a small anchorage that affords good protection for the night. Tucked into the head of Berry Cove, it's possible to ignore the nearby fish farm in Cypress Harbour and enjoy a picnic lunch in the cockpit. For a peaceful overnight anchorage, pop into sheltered Stopford Bay and sleep soundly in its all-round protection.

One of the more popular anchorages on the eastern shore of Broughton Island is in Laura Bay, off Penphrase Passage. Locally named "Laura Cove," this anchorage is an unexpected little gem tucked behind a grassy islet off Trivett Island. Enjoy a stunning view of Wishart Peninsula and Kingcome Inlet.

In Fife Sound, west of Pearse Peninsula, a fringe of islands and islets protect roomy Cullen Harbour from westerly winds. The anchorage provides a convenient staging point for boaters cruising east or west through the Broughtons and access via Booker Passage, to explore Booker Lagoon.

8

FEATURED DESTINATIONS

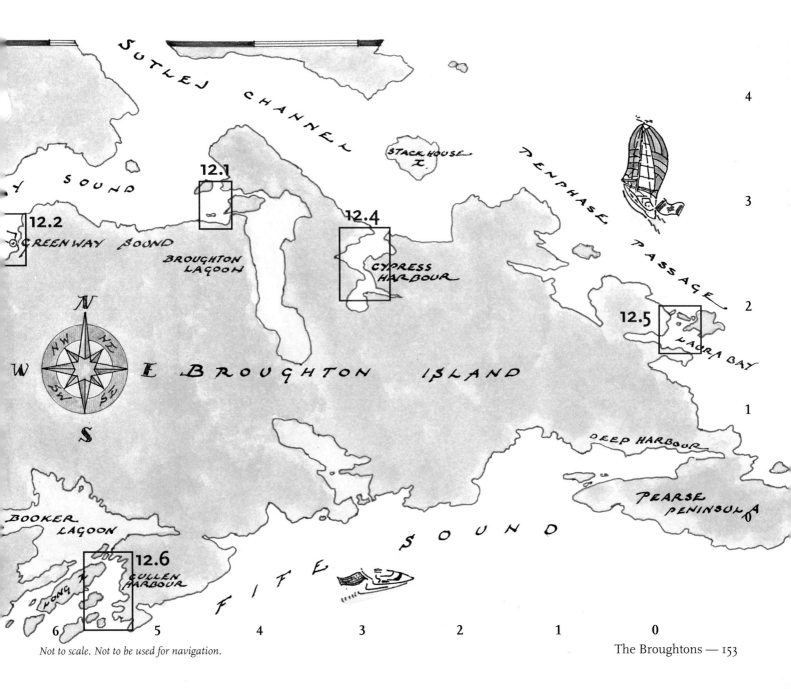

Not to scale. Not to be used for navigation.

12.1 ENTRANCE TO BROUGHTON LAGOON, GREENWAY SOUND

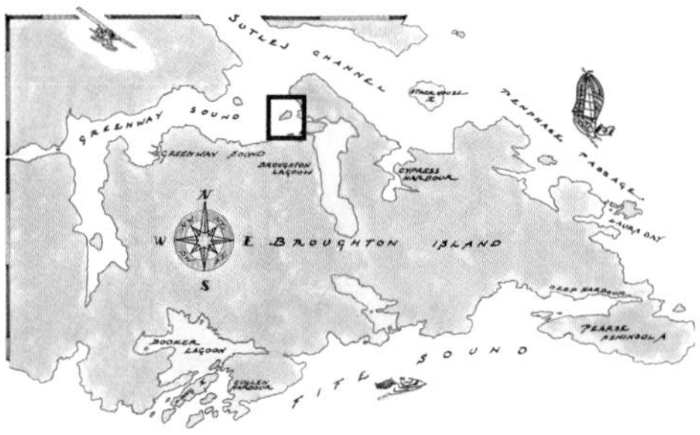

✲50°50.71'N 126°43.00'W

CHARTS 3547.

APPROACH From the W out of Greenway Sound. A large fish farm on the NW side of Cecil Island is highly conspicuous.

ANCHOR

(1) In the current, just outside the tidal rapids; room for 1-2 boats and protected from westerly winds.

(2) Behind "Lion Islet" (named by us), pass to port or starboard. There is room for 2-4 boats, and although a little bumpy during a westerly, things calm down when the evening outflow winds begin.

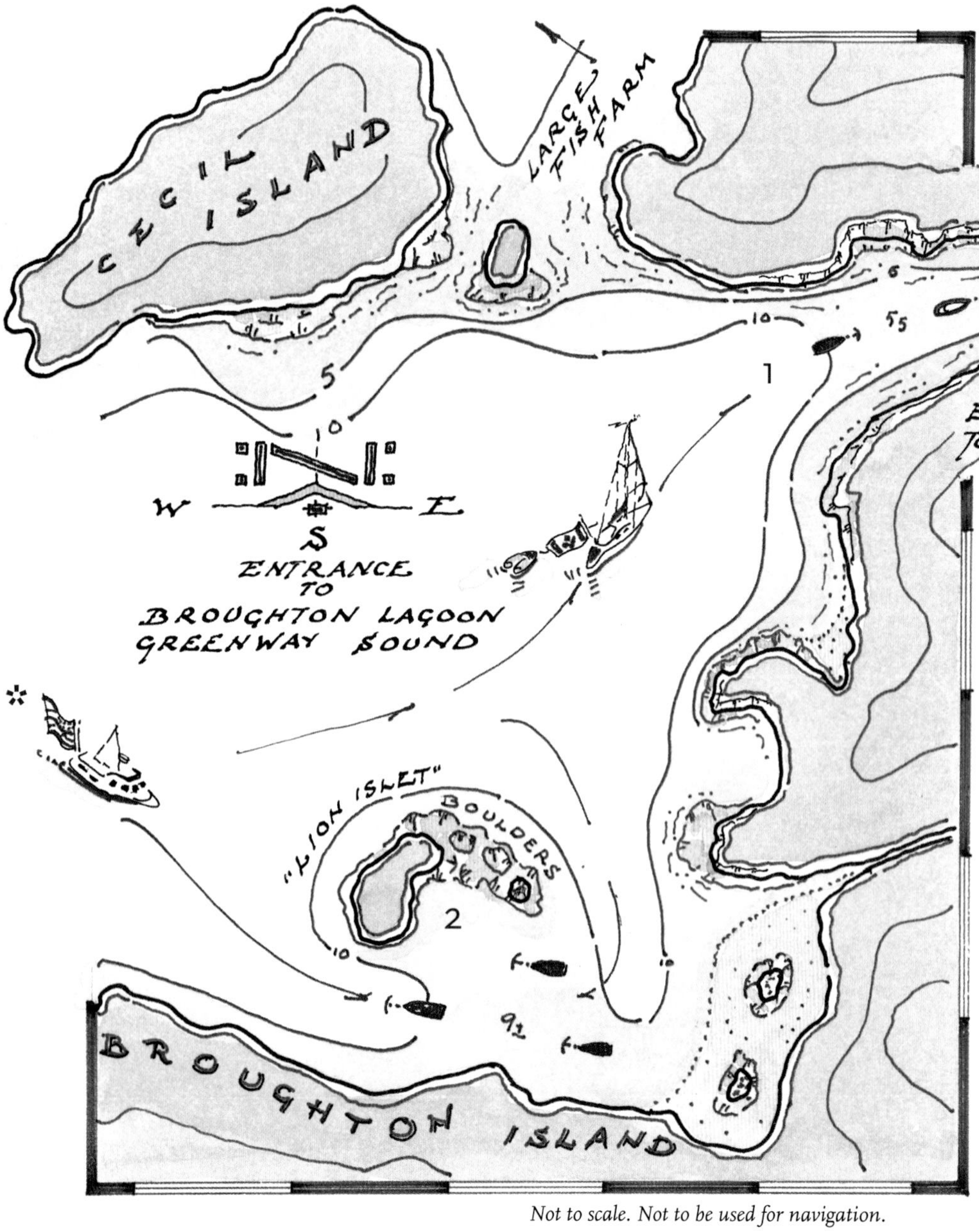

Not to scale. Not to be used for navigation.

Greenway Sound is deep with few anchorages from which to choose. At the entrance to the sound, tucked behind Cecil Island, two convenient nooks provide comfortable day and overnight stops; when the sun sets, the westerly winds in Greenway Sound die off and the NE outflow winds take over, making this a protected and cozy corner.

Exploring lake-like Broughton Lagoon is best done at high water slack with a reliable outboard and reserve fuel.

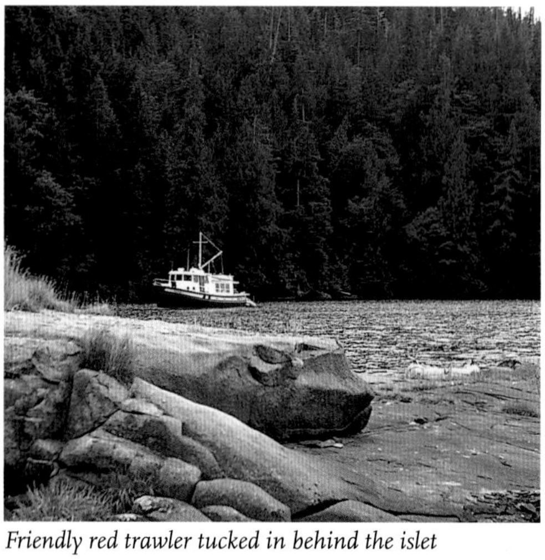

Friendly red trawler tucked in behind the islet

GREENWAY SOUND MARINE RESORT 12.2

CHARTS 3547.

APPROACH From the NW out of Greenway Sound. The run in is clear of obstructions.

MARINA Moorage is by reservation, with a 3 p.m. check-in/out time. Greenway Sound Marine Resort monitors VHF Channel 66A or call 250-974-7044. The marina can accommodate boats 6.5-26 m (20-80 ft), provides 24-hour shore power (15, 30 and 50 amp) and unlimited good water. Float plane services can be arranged.

Note: Please check the resort web site for marina and restaurant updates and news from the owners at www. greenwaysound.com.

✷50°50.48'N 126°46.57'W

Wide carpeted docks for exercise, moorage fees that include garbage disposal and an abundant supply of water for showers and laundry make this tidy, well-kept marina an inviting destination for all cruising boaters.

The well-stocked store carries dry and canned goods, frozen food and vegetables, and fruit and dairy products that are flown in for freshness. Their eight flavours of hard ice cream make delicious milk shakes and floats and, when topped with an espresso coffee, a sinful dessert; ice, hardware, books, gifts and video rentals also are available.

Nearby BROUGHTON LAKES MARINE PARK has a dinghy dock, maintained trails and a traditional log road that allows boaters to stretch their sea legs with a scenic walk. Allow a few hours to hike through the forests of Mount Ick to Beaver Dam Lake and Broughton Lake Viewpoint; take a refreshing dip in the tannic waters of Broughton Lake, picnic on the grassy shore and enjoy the stillness of nature at its best. A map is available from the marina office.

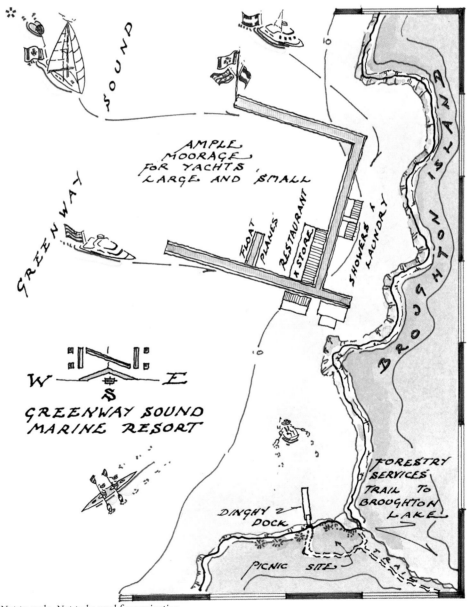

Not to scale. Not to be used for navigation.

12.3 BROUGHTON POINT, GREENWAY SOUND

✱50°50.31'N 126°48.70'W

CHARTS   3547.

APPROACH   From the E; the cut to Carter Passage lies S of Broughton Point; a clear view W opens up. Keep S of the islet on approach. The E entrance to Carter Passage dries and is strewn with boulders.

ANCHOR   In a pool NW of the islet or in the channel, as indicated. There is room for 2-3 boats to swing to the current in depths of 4-10 m (13-32 ft). Holding is good in mud and gravel. Protected from northeast outflow winds by the point and islet.

Typical rainforest shoreline

After a glorious day's sail exploring every nook and cranny in Greenway Sound, we tucked *Dreamspeaker* behind Broughton Point at the east end of Carter Passage and dropped our hook for the night. This anchorage affords good protection, as westerly winds do not funnel this far into the channel. The odd sports fishing boat zooming by might be the only disturbance. We experienced a tranquil evening and glassy smooth waters in the morning.

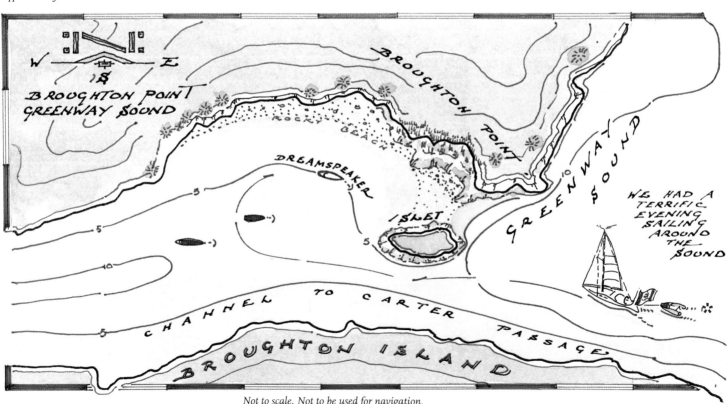

Not to scale. Not to be used for navigation.

CHARTS   3547.

APPROACH   From Sharp Passage; enter between Fox Rock and Donald Head. The fish farm in Miller Bay is mighty conspicuous. The run in to Berry Cove and the channel to Stopford Bay are clear.

ANCHOR   In Berry Cove, which is open to the NE and outflow winds in 4-8 m (13-26 ft) with good holding in gravel and mud. For all-round protection, anchor in Stopford Bay, the harbour's inner basin, in depths of 2-5 m (6-16 ft) with holding good in mud.

Note: Miller Bay is in the lee of the fish farm, which operates 24 hours a day.

✳50°50.53'N 126°39.62'W

Tucked into the head of Berry Cove, it's possible to ignore the nearby fish farm and enjoy a picnic lunch in the cockpit. For a peaceful overnight anchorage, drop anchor in sheltered Stopford Bay, explore the shoreline by dinghy or kayak and sleep soundly in its all-round protection. Be aware of the possibility of logging debris on the bottom of the bay.

Rock bluffs backing Berry Cove

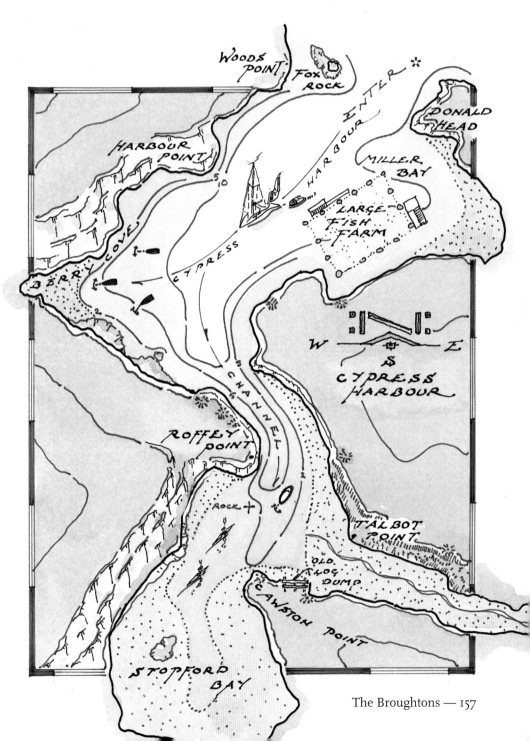

A beach fire completes the day in Laura Cove

CHARTS   3515.

APPROACH   From the E, along the S shore of Trivett Island. Enter the cove leaving the islet to the E.

ANCHOR   In popular "Laura Cove" as indicated in 2-4 m (6-13 ft) with stern line ashore.

Note: A rock lies between the islet and Trivett Island.

✲50°49.20'N 126°33.79'W

O ne of the more popular anchorages on the eastern shore of Broughton Island is in Laura Bay; locally named "Laura Cove" is an unexpected little gem tucked behind a grassy islet off Trivett Island. To accommodate as many boats as possible during the busy summer season, it is best to take a stern line ashore; beach your dingy on the isthmus that connects Broughton and Trivett Island to enjoy a stunning view over Penphrase Passage, across to Wishart Peninsula and north to Kingcome Inlet.

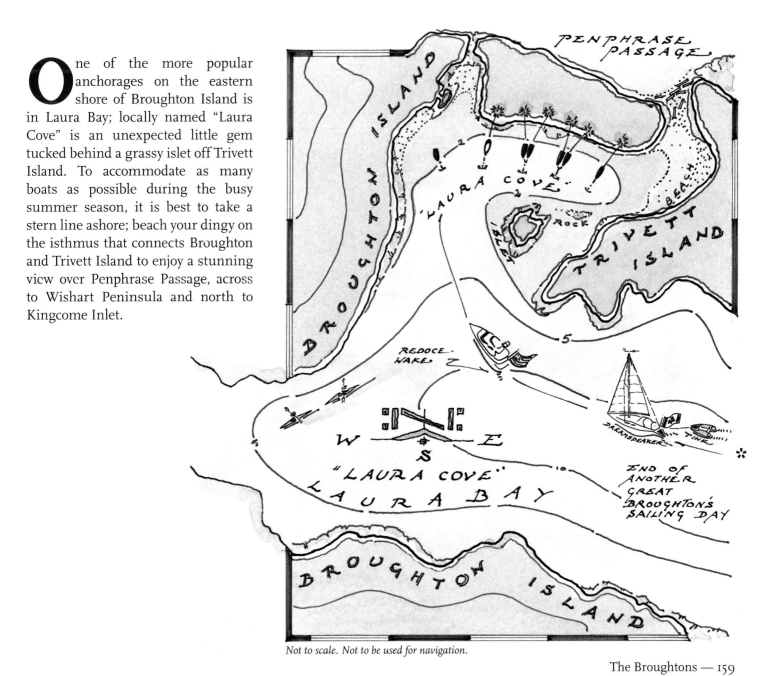

Not to scale. Not to be used for navigation.

12.6 CULLEN HARBOUR, BOOKER PASSAGE

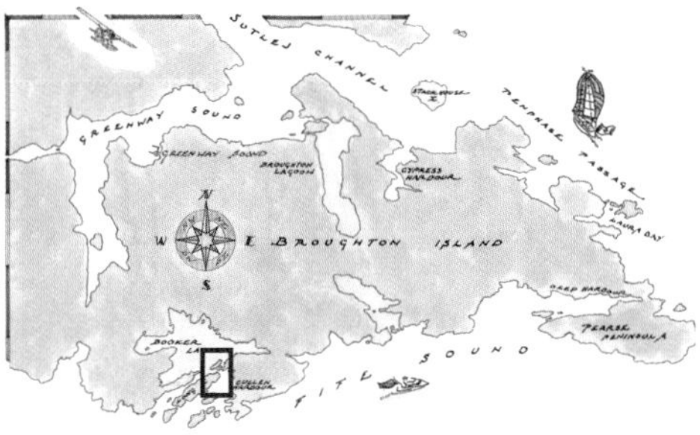

✲50°45.88'N 126°44.49'W

CHARTS 3547.

APPROACH From the S, favour the Nelly Islet shore. The centre channel of Cullen Harbour is clear. Booker Passage is deep but best transited at LW slack. Kelp fringes the channel with a minimum charted depth of 6.4 m (21 ft).

ANCHOR In commodious Cullen Harbour with good protection from all prevailing winds. *Dreamspeaker* held well on a rocky/gravel bottom in 4-8 m (13-26 ft).

Note: If transiting Booker Passage to Booker Lagoon, look out for the stone man "Inukshuk" on the tip of the reef that extends out from Long Island.

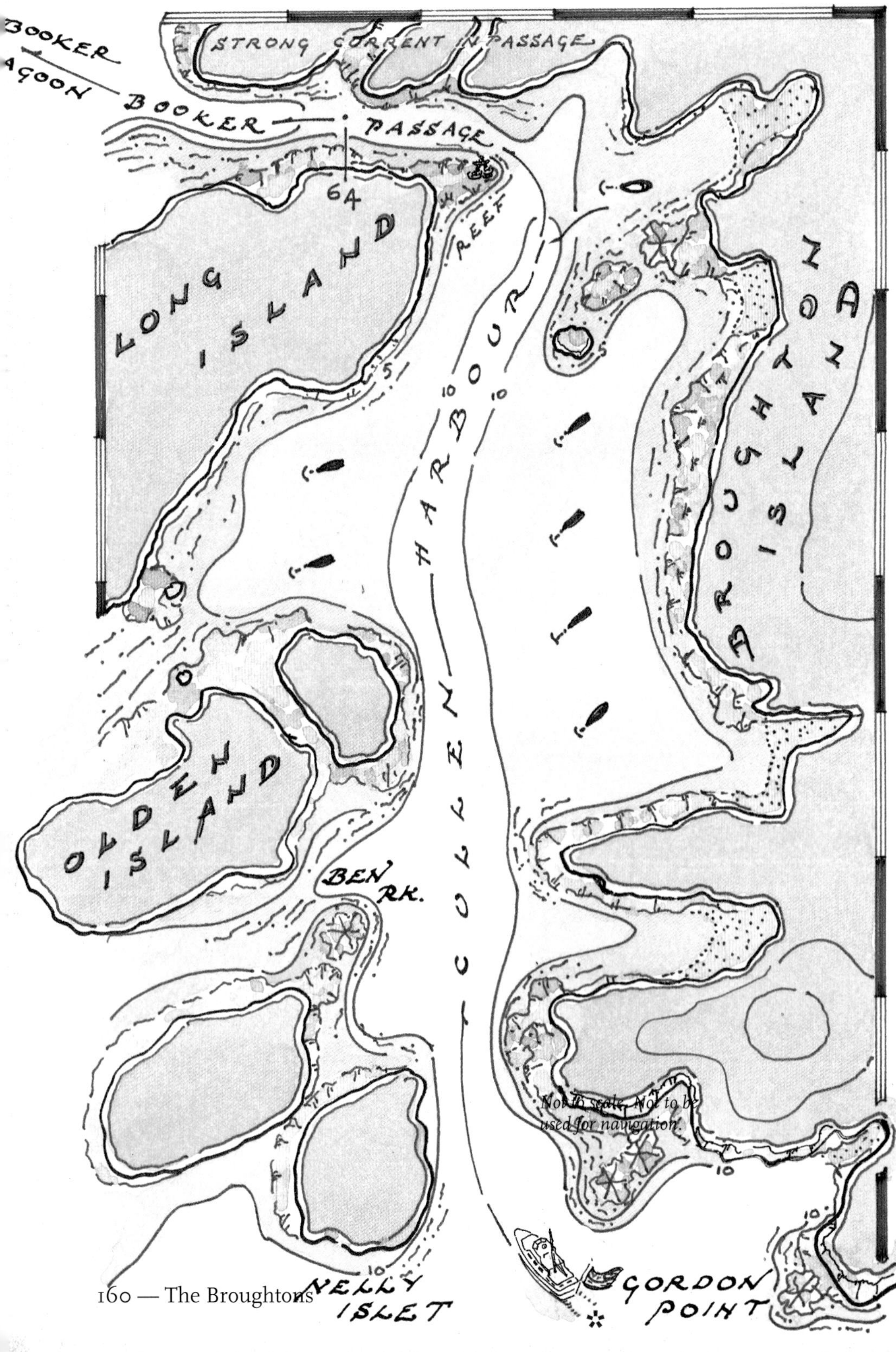

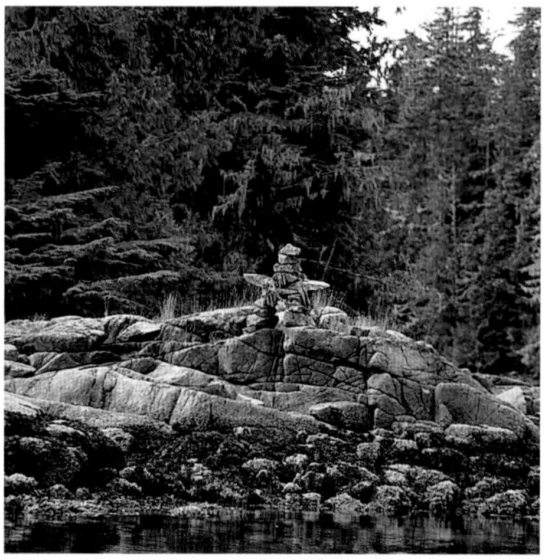

"Stone Man" marks the tip of the reef

The fringe of islands and islets protects roomy Cullen Harbour from the westerly winds in Queen Charlotte Strait and provides a convenient staging point for boaters cruising east or west through the Broughtons.

Access to extensive Booker Lagoon, which for some is great exploration territory, is via Booker Passage. We entered at low water slack and popped out before the flood got too strong, then dropped anchor in the harbour's very northern nook, with a lovely view into the passage, marked to the west by a navigational stone symbol or "inukshuk."

SHAWL BAY, TRIBUNE CHANNEL TO KWATSI BAY AND BOND SOUND

Photo opportunity at "Lacy Falls," Tribune Channel

Chapter 13
SHAWL BAY, TRIBUNE CHANNEL TO KWATSI BAY AND BOND SOUND

Anne discovers the waterfall at Kwatsi Bay

TIDES – *Volume 6,*
Canadian Tide and Current Tables
Reference Port – Alert Bay

CURRENTS

No specific reference or secondary stations cover this chapter; however, currents run swiftly through the channels and passages creating a certain amount of current in most anchorages.

WEATHER

Weather Station – WX1 162.55 MHZ
Area – Queen Charlotte Strait
Reporting Station – Alert Bay

CAUTIONARY NOTES: *The pass between Shawl and Moore Bay should only be navigated on a rising tide when it is half tide or above. The Burdwood Group of Islands are better protected from westerly winds with little protection from the east.*

Because there are no really suitable anchorages in Wakeman Sound and Kingcome Inlet, Moore Bay offers a good base for day trips up the inlets and channels or to use as a staging point.

Shawl Bay has always been a meeting place for loggers and fishermen; today cruising boaters meet at Shawl Bay Marina to rendezvous with friends, share potluck and indulge in the complementary pancake breakfasts. Don't forget to stock up on freshly baked bread and sticky buns before leaving. Fed by the glacial waters of Kingcome River, the converging waters at the junction of Wakeman Sound and Kingcome Inlet take on a milky-green hue. A short detour south will take you into Belleisle Sound. Backed by lofty Mount Mathison and the conical-shaped mounds of Craig Hills, this is one of the most spectacular settings to drop your anchor.

Stunning Simoom Sound is dominated by the mask-like, black granite face of Bald Mountain and although the sound appears calm, strong winds can find their way in.

The Burdwoods are a group of low-lying islands, islets and rocks in the west end of Tribune Channel and were home to the Kwakiutl people around eight thousand years ago. They offer a myriad of pocket shell beaches and are pure heaven for kayaking parties and the boat-bound crew.

Kwatsi Bay Marina, tucked into the northwest portion of this bay off Tribune Channel, welcomes visitors to share in their peaceful wilderness setting during the spring and summer months. Wide docks and shaded lounging areas invite fun, laid-back interaction with visiting boaters.

The Ahta River, at the head of magnificent Bond Sound, has its headwaters in British Columbia's Coast range and is the only major watershed south of Cape Caution that still remains un-logged.

BROUGHTON
ISLAND

18

FEATURED DESTINATIONS

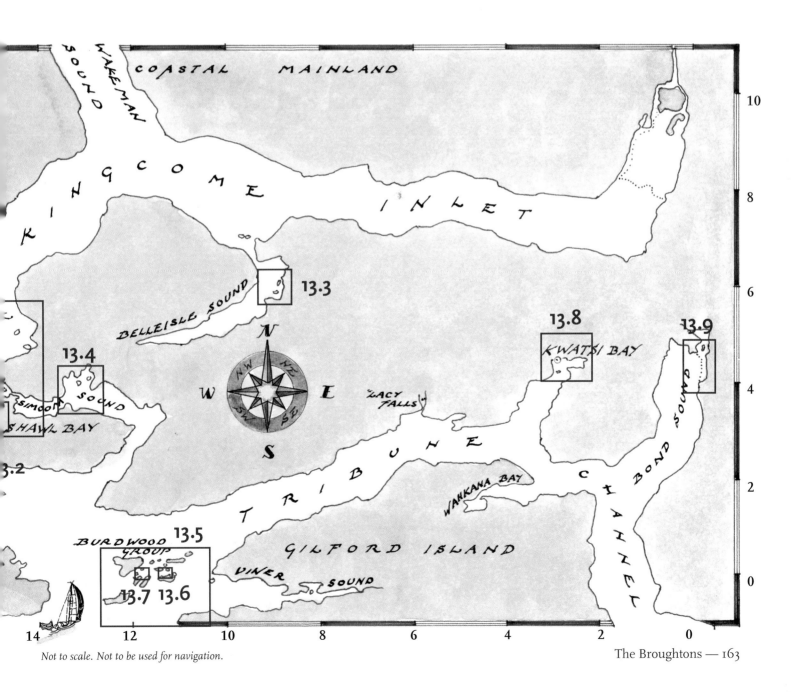

Not to scale. Not to be used for navigation.

✿ (A) 50°50.96'N 126°35.45'W
✿ (B) 50°52.84'N 126°33.36'W

CHARTS   3515 Knight Inlet

APPROACH   (A) Shawl Bay from Penphrase Passage. The approach to the marina is deep and without obstructions. The pass between Gregory Island and the mainland is used frequently by small craft. The chart indicates a minimum depth of 0.6 m (2 ft) – favour the mainland shore after half-tide plus. (B) Moore Bay from Kingcome Inlet. Beware of the 3 major rocks that straddle the entrance.

ANCHOR   There is no suitable anchorage in Shawl Bay; however, there are 3 Forestry Service Buoys and numerous spots indicated in Moore Bay, in which to anchor in depths of 6-12 m (19-39 ft). Holding and protection vary.

Note: Thief Rock is visible only by the debris flooding around its peak and the foraging birds at HW. The "Hard to Miss" rocks (named by us) barely dries at HW.

Because there really are no suitable anchorages in Wakeman Sound and Kingcome Inlet, Moore Bay offers a good base for day trips up the inlets and channels, or to use as a staging point prior to embarking on the next leg of your cruise.

Dreamspeaker found a cozy spot to anchor below the steep cliffs, tucked in behind the "Hard to Miss" rocks. The Forestry Service dinghy dock at the head of the bay provides a chance to stretch your legs, dip your toes in the icy stream and picnic beneath Mount Plumridge. Four campsites are also available.

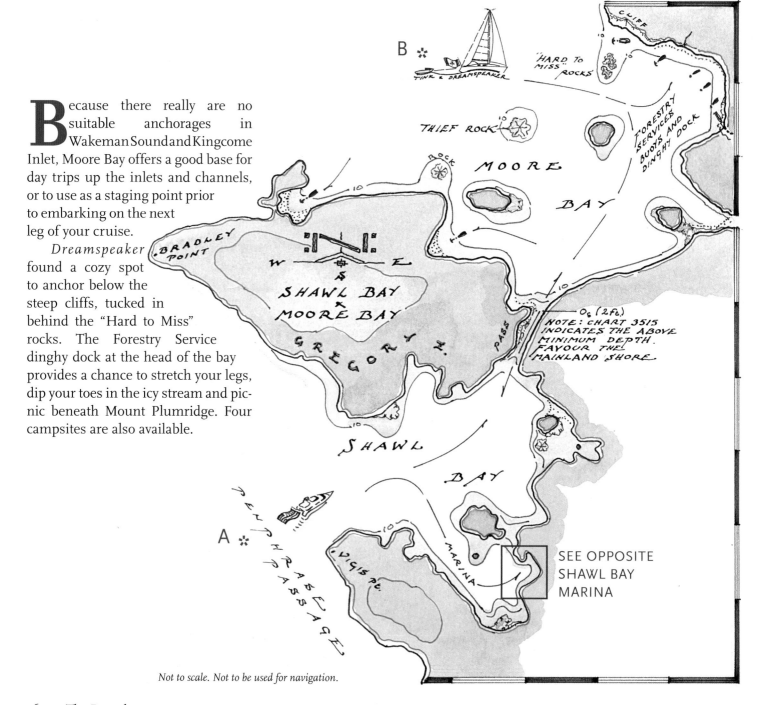

SEE OPPOSITE
SHAWL BAY
MARINA

Not to scale. Not to be used for navigation.

SHAWL BAY MARINA

CHARTS 3515, inset Knight Inlet.

APPROACH The marina is tucked into the NE corner of the southern portion of the bay.

MARINA Shawl Bay Marina monitors VHF Channel 66A or call 250-483-4169. For updated information, visit www.shawlbay.com or email shawlbaymarina@direcway.com. Water and 15/30 amp power are available on the docks. Payment by cash only – no credit cards. Floatplane and taxi service to Port McNeill are also available

Note: Marina owners, the Browns, offer complimentary evening coffee and dessert to add to the Shawl Bay experience.

The blue roof of the picnic tent is conspicuous

The original docks in Shawl Bay were owned by the Viner Logging Company and became an historic meeting place for loggers and fishermen. Today, boaters meet up at the friendly, family-owned marina to rendezvous with friends, share potluck suppers under the picnic tent and indulge in the all-you-can-fit-in, complimentary pancake breakfasts (served from 8-9 a.m. daily).

Relaxed and informal, floating SHAWL BAY MARINA is owned by Lorne and Shawn Brown. It is a fun place to socialize while catching up on laundry and boat tasks. The small store carries some fresh produce, milk, tinned goods, gifts and books. There can be a line out the door when Lorne's freshly-baked bread and sticky buns are delivered hot from the oven. Aunty Jo, who says she has "lived at Shawl Bay forever," will process your moorage fees and store account and is well versed in coastal pioneering stories, local gossip, and loves visiting with people, especially during Happy Hour.

The marina is dog friendly and welcomes boat-bound hounds to stretch their legs and visit the doggy-dedicated pocket lawn – please note that your pooch should remain on board during *human* meal times on the picnic dock.

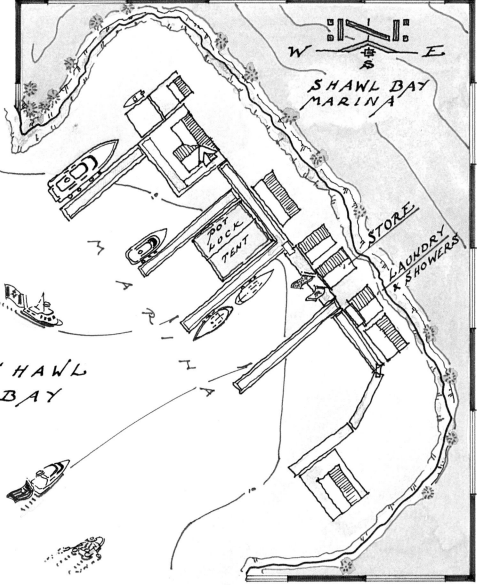

Not to scale. Not to be used for navigation.

13.3 BELLEISLE SOUND, KINGCOME INLET

✳ 50°54.57'N 126°25.63'W

CHARTS 3515, inset Knight Inlet.

APPROACH From Kingcome Inlet, between Edmond Islet and the mainland. The entrance channel and run into Belleisle Sound and anchorage is deep and without obstruction.

ANCHOR Anchorage for a few boats S of "Belle Island" (our name), off the creek's gravel shelf. Alternatively, in the 1-2 boat basin SW of "Belle Islet." Good protection from the E and SW in depths of 4-10 m (13-32 ft); the holding varies.

Note: The anchorage is open to outflow winds from Wakeman Sound.

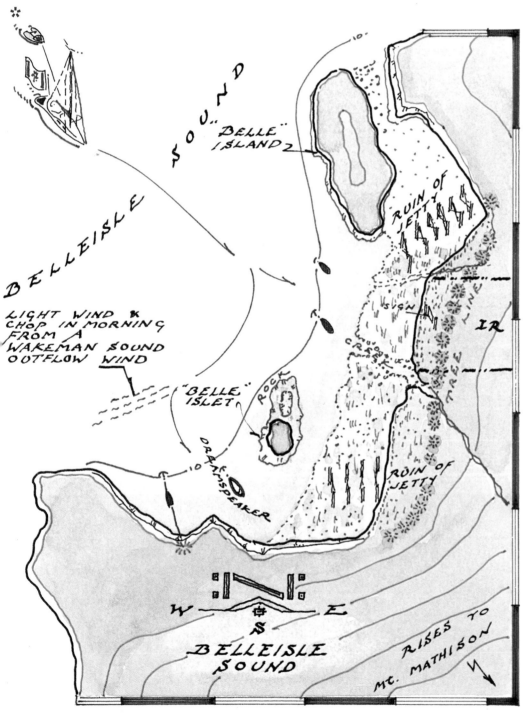

Ruins of 1960s' logging operations

Fed by the glacial waters of Kingcome River six miles up the inlet, the converging waters at the junction of Wakeman Sound and Kingcome Inlet take on a mystic, milky-green hue. Taking refuge from the fog and rain, we slipped through the narrow, steep-sided entrance into Belleisle Sound, a mist-shrouded hideaway that turned out to be one of the most spectacular anchorages in the area.

Backed by mighty Mount Mathison, with Mount Prescott to the west and the conical-shaped mounds of Craig Hills to the north, we anchored in a spot behind "Belle Islet" and were lulled to sleep by the soothing sound of a small waterfall that had built at the mouth of the creek. For the true story of "Dad McKay," who lived in a big hollow cedar stump in Belleisle Sound, read Bill Proctors' *Full Moon Flood Tide*.

The steep rock buffs dive deep into Tribune Channel

13.4 SIMOOM SOUND

CHARTS 3515, inset Simoom Sound.
APPROACH The entrance to Simoom Sound is deep and without obstructions. Bald Mountain dominates the N shore. The approach waypoint is off Hannant Point. The recommended anchorages are to the N and E.

ANCHOR As indicated in McIntosh Bay, which appears a little gloomy, and the coves to the E, behind Hannant Point. The islets and rock clusters have deep water all around, and the challenge is to find good anchoring depths and avoid the unmarked rocks.

✽50°51.44'N 126°30.64'W

Stunning Simoom Sound with its big features and fantastic scenery is dominated by the mask-like, black granite face of Bald Mountain and, although the sound appears calm, strong winds will sometimes find their way in and ruffle its waters.

Cruising through the peaceful waters of the sound to-day, its hard to imagine that between the early 1900s and the late 1930s (when the whole camp moved to little Simoom Sound) this was a well-populated area with scheduled visits from the Union Steamships. Boat Day was a big event and the freight/passenger boat visited once a week heading north and returned two days later on its southbound journey. A store, post office, blacksmith (to take care of the logging horses) and small school provided everything that the loggers and their families needed in the wilderness.

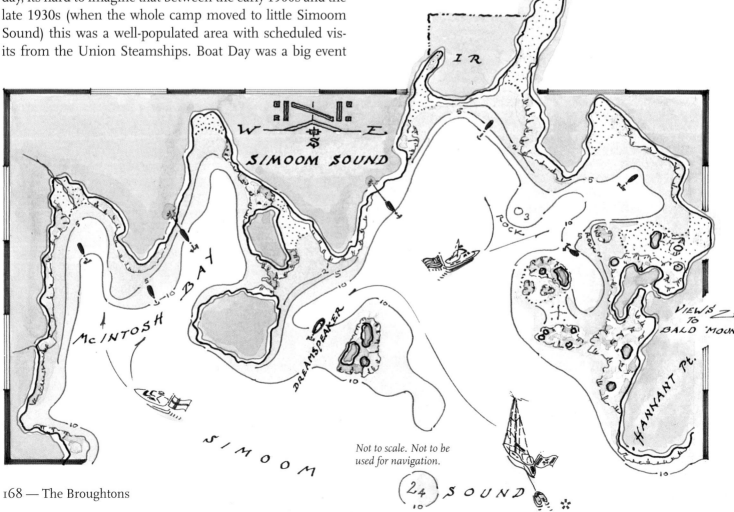

Not to scale. Not to be used for navigation.

Mirror-calm in Simoom Sound

East of "Twin Rocks" in the Burdwood Group

13.5 THE BURDWOOD GROUP

✤(A) 50°47.43'N 126° 30.17'W
✤(B) 50°47.70'N 126° 27.26'W

CHARTS   3515, with caution.

APPROACH   (A) At LW from Raleigh Passage – favour the W shore at the entrance between the 2 islets. (B) From Hornet Passage – note the islet omitted on chart 3515. The position as indicated is courtesy of a CHS aerial photograph. The channel lies between the 2 islets.

ANCHOR   The main anchorage in a typical southwesterly wind is N of the uncharted islet; however, in an easterly wind it is untenable. We did explore two 1-boat spots, "Twin Beaches" and "Twin Islets" (named by us) that provided shelter during an easterly wind.

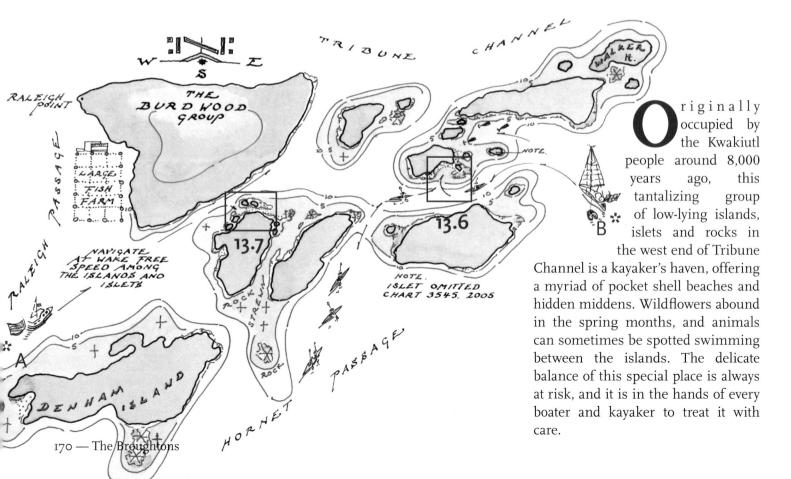

Originally occupied by the Kwakiutl people around 8,000 years ago, this tantalizing group of low-lying islands, islets and rocks in the west end of Tribune Channel is a kayaker's haven, offering a myriad of pocket shell beaches and hidden middens. Wildflowers abound in the spring months, and animals can sometimes be spotted swimming between the islands. The delicate balance of this special place is always at risk, and it is in the hands of every boater and kayaker to treat it with care.

ANCHOR   To the W of the rock and shell cluster with a stern line or anchor ashore. The pool formed by the beach and rocky outcrop gives adequate protection from the E.

The most popular camping spot in the group, "Twin Beaches" has a glorious white-shell beach for swimming and is the sight of one of the six or seven First Nations villages in the Burdwood Group. Just across the channel from the west-facing beach is the site of a unique and significant monument to the area's ancient aboriginal history. Ably described in Bill Proctor's *Full Moon Flood Tide* (see page 188), it is well worth locating the trail that leads to where a large, culturally modified red cedar stands proudly in the dense forest.

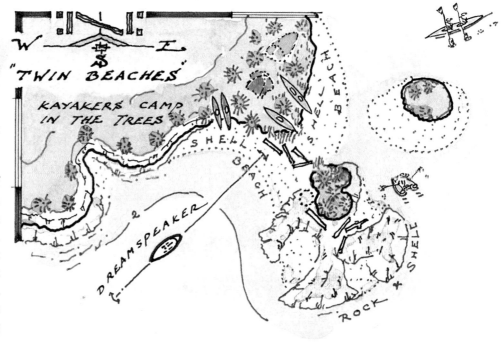

13.7 "TWIN ROCKS,"
BURDWOOD GROUP

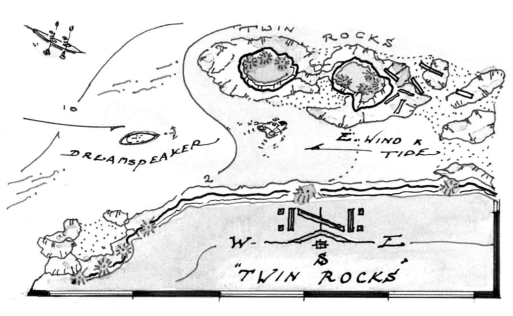

ANCHOR   Approach from the W between the 2 kelp patches. Anchor as indicated because then the tide and E wind will keep you steady. In a SW wind take a stern line to the outer rock to keep the boat from swinging.

"Twin Rocks" (named by us) is scattered with mini shell beaches, sun-bleached driftwood, grassy knolls, mussel-encrusted rocks and tidal pools; pure heaven for the boat-bound brood and the kid at heart.

13.8 KWATSI BAY, TRIBUNE CHANNEL

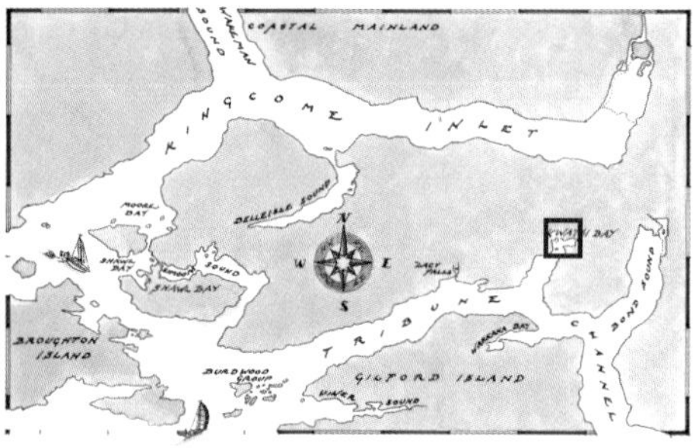

✲50°51.69'N 126°14.98'W

CHARTS 3515.

APPROACH From Tribune Channel, Kwatsi Bay is deep without obstructions. The run into the inner cove should be made to the east of the islet that lies off the W shore.

ANCHOR As indicated; this is deepwater, stern-to anchoring alternative with swinging room on the 10 m (32 ft) contour in the far E corner.

MARINA KWATSI BAY MARINA monitors Channel 66A or leave cellular messages (250-949-1384). Shower and laundry(?) facilities and treated water are available on the dock.

Kwatsi Bay Marina, tucked into the northwest portion of this dramatic bay, is a successful, family-run business. Max, Anka, and their children welcome visitors to share in their peaceful wilderness setting during the spring and summer months. The bay itself is a deep bowl created by the surrounding, steep-sided mountains interspersed with mini-waterfalls and magnificent views out to the south; you will often be rewarded with a visit from whales.

Wide docks and shaded lounging areas invite interaction with boaters and the Kwatsi Bay family, as this is their home. The daily five o'clock Happy Hour will often turn into a jovial potluck supper – just whip up your tried and true boat recipe, pop a beverage in the cooler, and don't forget your favourite silly joke.

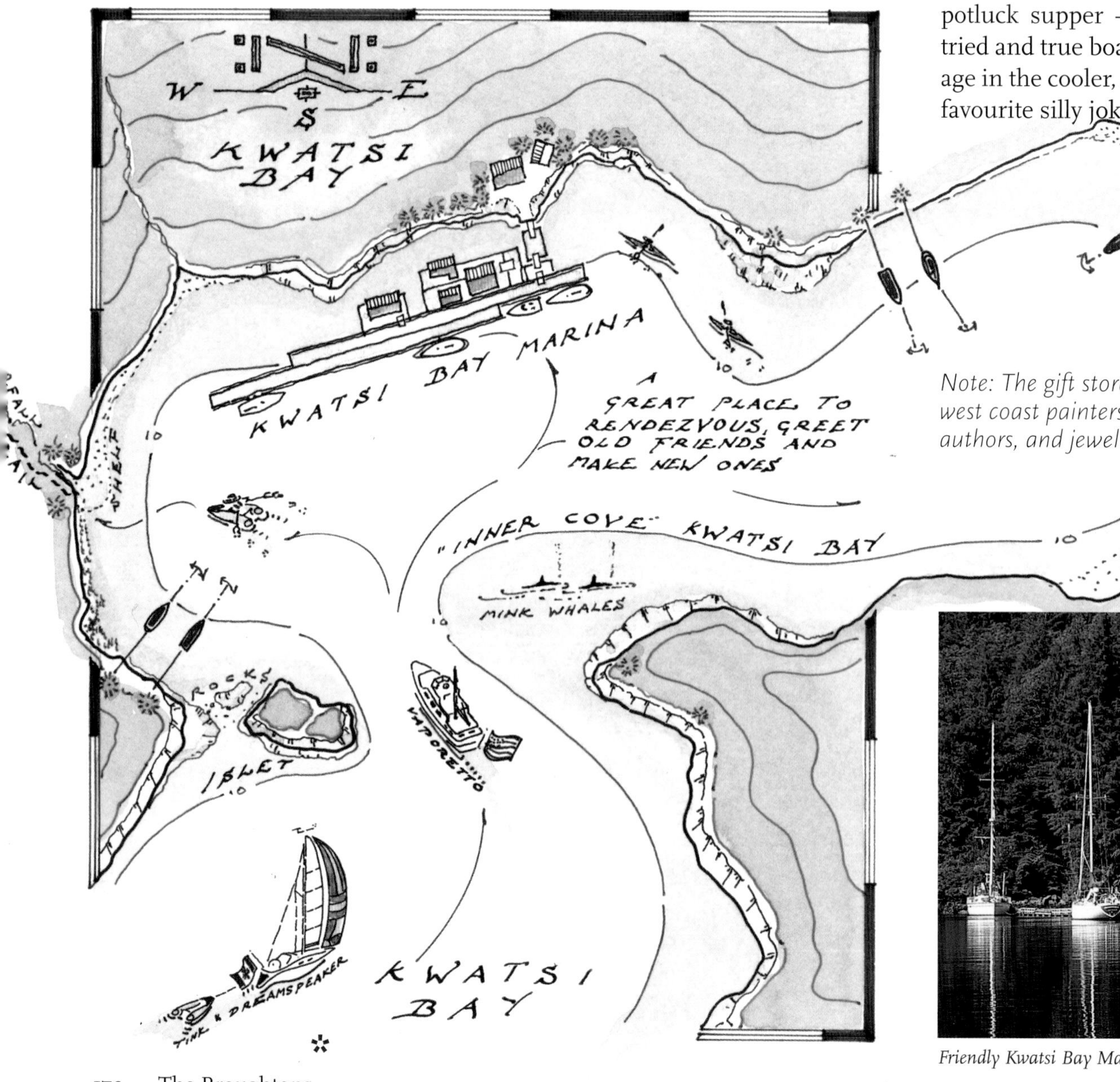

Note: The gift store carries works by west coast painters, carvers, potters, authors, and jewellery designers.

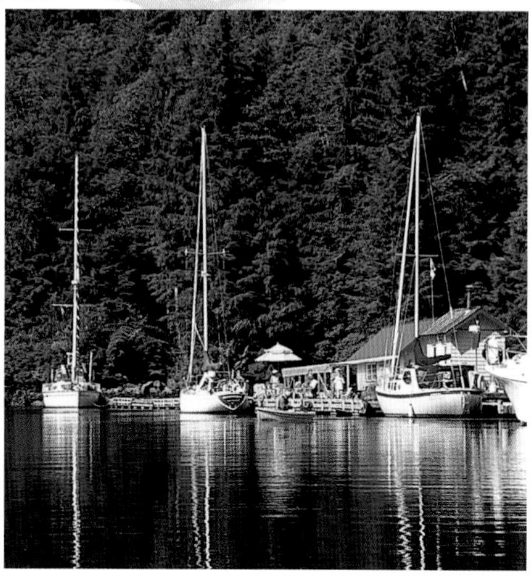

Friendly Kwatsi Bay Marina

50°51.64'N 126°10.46'W

CHARTS 3515.

APPROACH Without obstruction. The head of Bond Sound is deep with no protected anchorage.

ANCHOR Temporary. (1) As per *Shaunsea*, tucked in close behind a small outcrop of rocks which they suggest may give some protection from the S. (B) *Dreamspeaker* explored a rocky promontory in the N, off the Ahta River delta. Reasonable protection from an outflow wind, but no protection from the SW.

Idyllic sand shell beach, Bond Sound

A lovely strip of fine sand beach is etched with sun-bleached shell fragments, where Bond Sound meets the Ahta River mouth. From here you can beach your dinghy and climb along the seaweed-covered rocks to view the abundant wildlife in the shallows of the river delta.

With its headwaters in British Columbia's Coast range, the healthy, nine-mile long Ahta River is the only major watershed south of Cape Caution that still remains un-logged. The surrounding old-growth forest provides habitat for endangered species, a safe nesting environment for bald eagles, certain owl species and a huge variety of wildlife.

The Ahta River Valley is reputed to be one of the most beautiful settings you could ever wish to visit and encompasses an unspoilt and diverse ecosystem. The area is prime grizzly bear habitat and is also home to otter, beaver and many species of wildfowl and songbirds.

Note: Be aware of the extremely steep drop-off in both anchorages – a stern line ashore is highly recommended if you plan to overnight or leave your boat at any time.

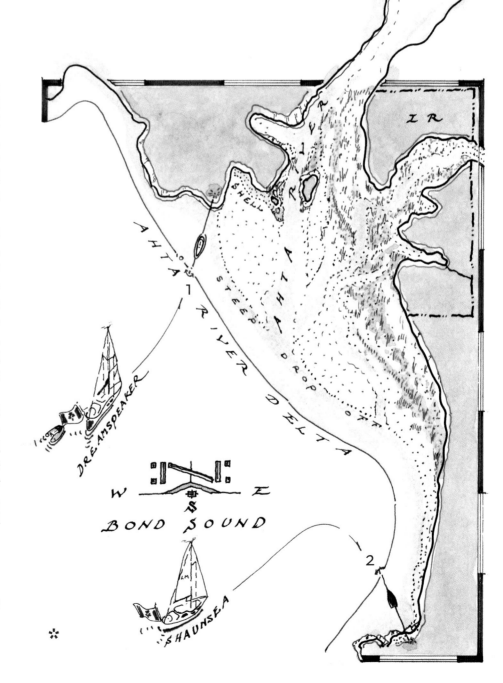

Dwarfed by the Coastal Mountain Range, a tug and boom head west in Knight Inlet

Chapter 14

KNIGHT INLET, LAGOON COVE TO CHATHAM CHANNEL

An evening pot-luck feast at Lagoon Cove Marina

Chapter 14
KNIGHT INLET, LAGOON COVE TO CHATHAM CHANNEL

TIDES – *Volume 6,*
Canadian Tide and Current Tables
Reference Port – Alert Bay
Secondary Ports – Glendale Cove,
Lagoon Cove

CURRENTS
Reference Station – Seymour Narrows
Secondary Station – Chatham Channel

WEATHER
Weather Station – WX1 162.55 MHZ
Area – Queen Charlotte Strait,
Johnstone Strait
Reporting Station – Alert Bay

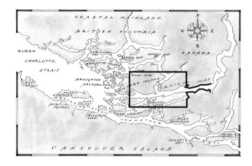

CAUTIONARY NOTES: *Knight Inlet may lure the cruising boater with its turquoise waters, however, it has a reputation equal to Johnstone Strait and not a place to be if bad weather is forecast.*

The waters in Chatham Channel may not be turbulent, however, 5 knots of current spells caution. If a log boom or other vessels are in the channel, do not be tempted to overtake – stay back and in line with the range markers.

There are few good anchorages in this part of Tribune Channel, which makes the protected anchorage off Kumlah Island a pleasant surprise.

Nearing Knight Inlet, the waters of Tribune Channel and Sargeaunt Passage take on a muted turquoise hue and we were enticed into the pass by a group of playful porpoises blowing at the entrance. Although Sargeaunt Passage is deep and steep-sided, it has the best anchorage in the area and provides a staging point for the trip up Knight Inlet to Glendale Cove.

The section of water east of Hoeya Head to Glendale Cove offers no shelter from easterly or westerly winds but with a strong westerly in your favour, you can enjoy an exhilarating sail up Knight Inlet into the cove and small anchorage.

With fuel, water and power available on the docks, a laid-back, friendly ambience and the Barbers' legendary 'happy hour bucket of prawns' put Lagoon Cove Marina on the Broughtons' social cruising chart. This industrious couple have been successful in making their hospitable marina into an extension of their own pleasant boating experiences; a kid-friendly place where cruising families and parties of boaters love to tie up for a day or two to hike the old logging roads, catch up with friends and make new acquaintances at happy hour.

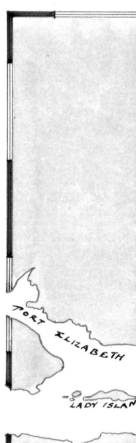

9

FEATURED DESTINATIONS

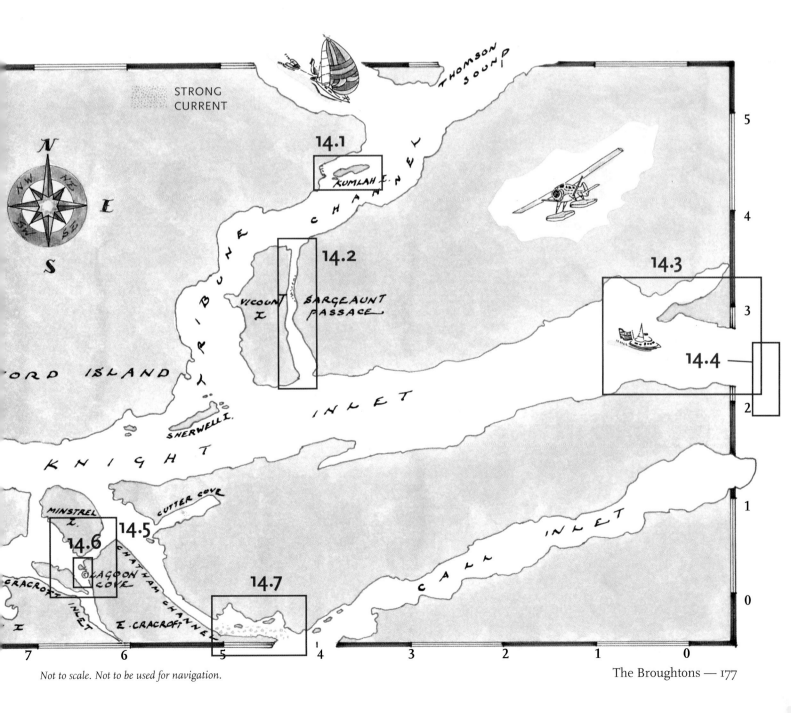

Not to scale. Not to be used for navigation.

14.1 KUMLAH ISLAND, TRIBUNE CHANNEL

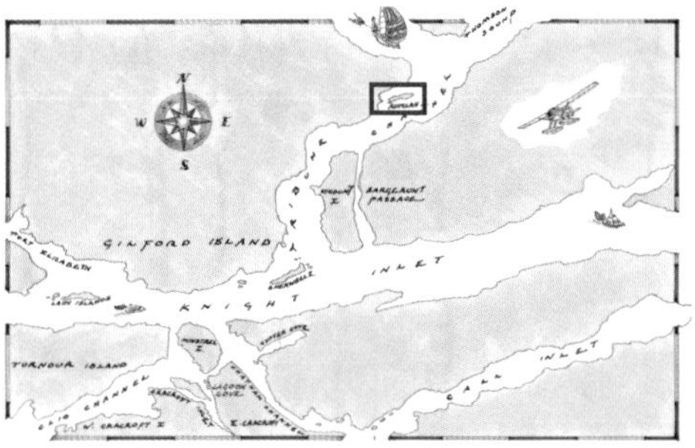

✲(A) 50°44.69'N 126°09.39'W
✲(B) 50°44.27'N 126°10.52'W

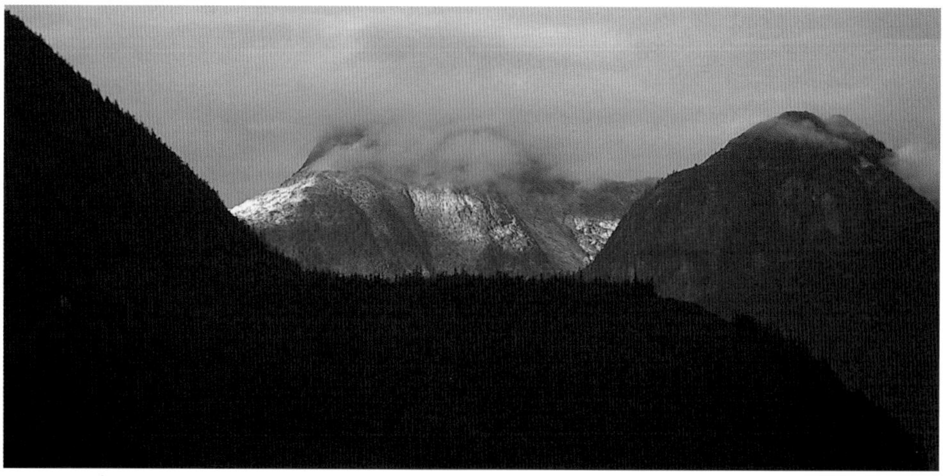
Views up Thompson Sound to snow-topped Mount Everard

CHARTS 3515.

APPROACH (A) From the E, the run in from Tribune Channel is free of obstructions. (B) From the S, favour the Kumlah Island shore to clear the reef off the tip of Gilford Island

ANCHOR In the centre channel within the 5 m contour; there is a charted minimum depth of 4.6 m (15 ft). The holding is good over a gravel rocky bottom, where your boat will swing to the current. An alternative anchorage can be found off the gravel beach, with a stern line ashore. A mussel-encrusted mooring buoy lies on the 10 m (32 ft) contour – use at your own discretion.

Note: The current flows in a clockwise direction around Kumlah Island, on both the flood and ebb tides.

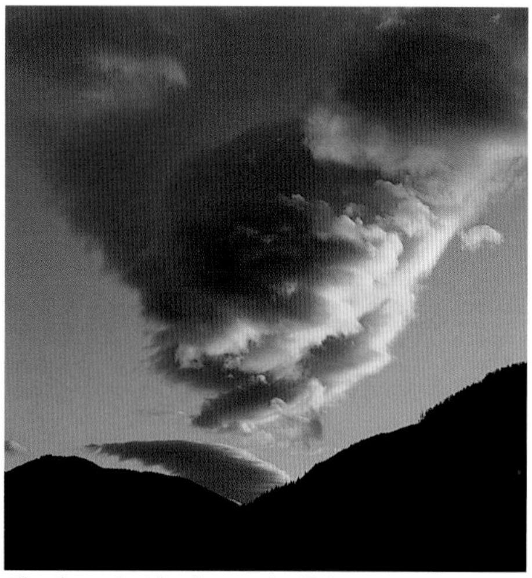
Clouds washed by the evening light

There are very few good anchorages in this part of Tribune Channel. Kumlah Island appears to be the meeting point of the current around Gilford Island and kept *Dreamspeaker* steady while at anchor. With remarkable views up Thompson Sound to snow-capped Mount Everard, this calm, sunny spot allowed us to dry out the boat and bedding after many days of rain.

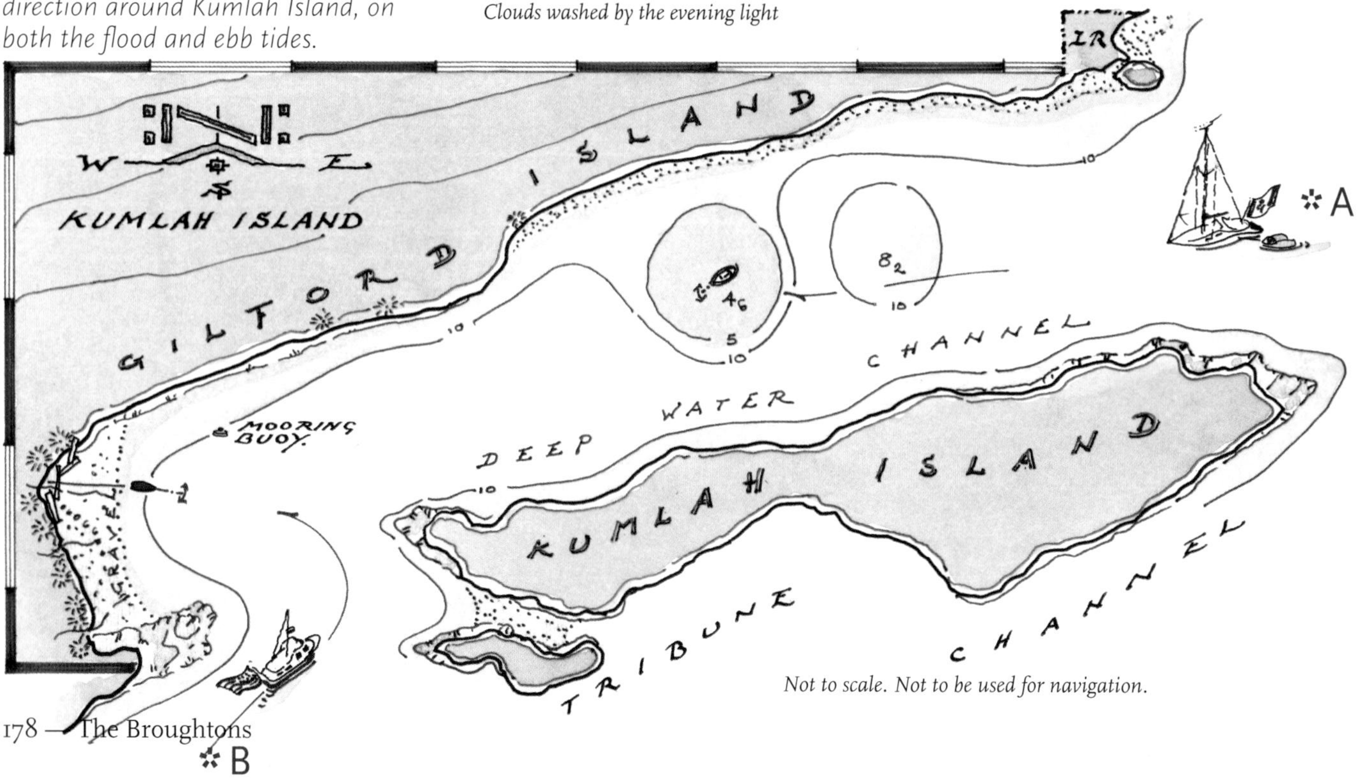

Not to scale. Not to be used for navigation.

SARGEAUNT PASSAGE 14.2

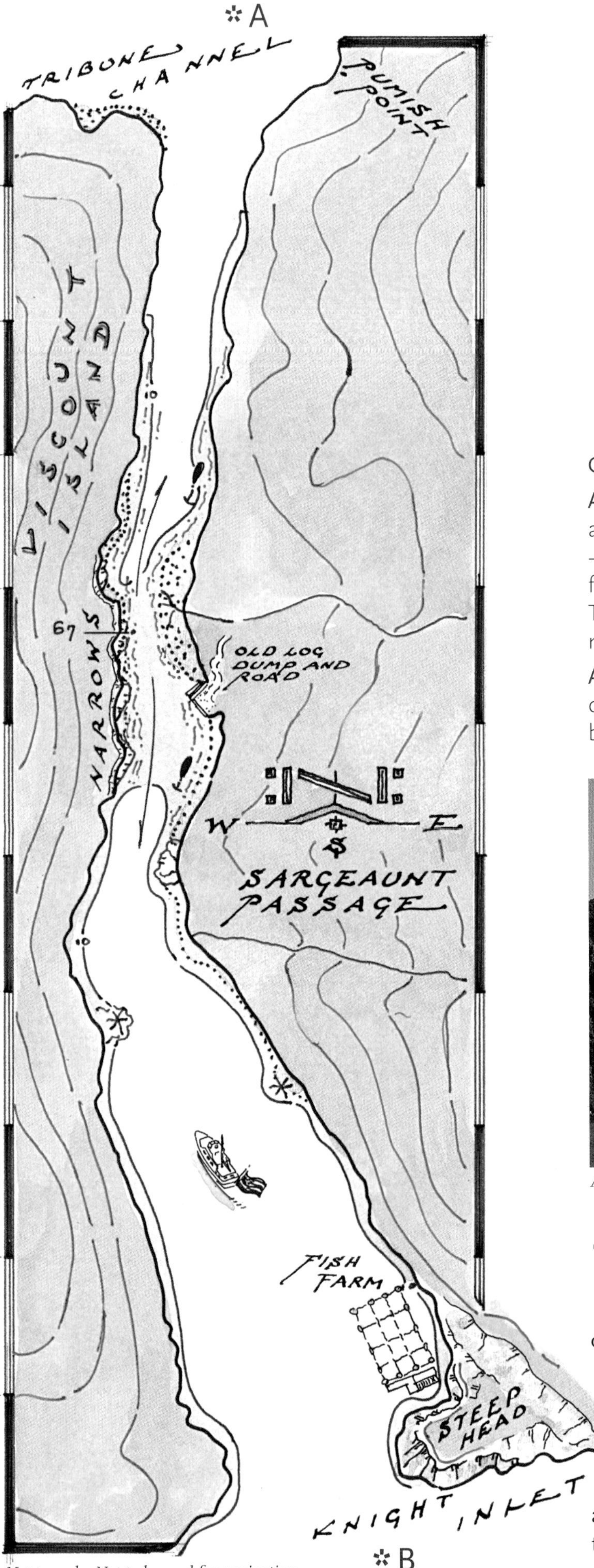

Not to scale. Not to be used for navigation.

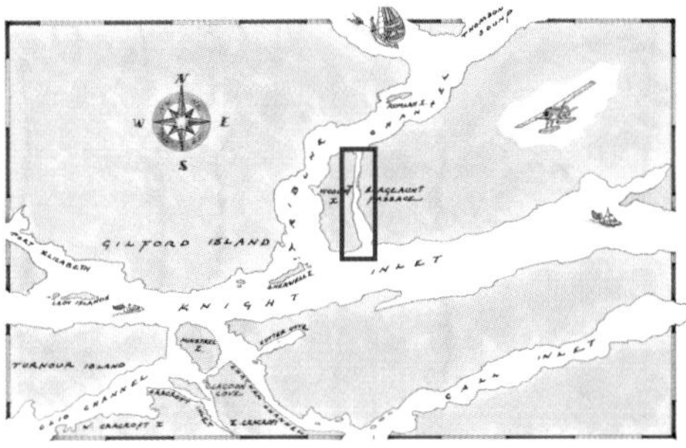

✲(A) 50°42.89'N 126°11.74'W
✲(B) 50°40.00'N 126°11.28'W

CHARTS 3515.

APPROACH The passage between Viscount Island and the mainland is narrow, kelp-fringed and steep-sided – favour the Viscount Island shore; this detour is used frequently by pleasure boats and small commercial craft. The passage is deep, with a minimum charted depth of 6.7 m (22 ft) at the narrows.

ANCHOR 2 small bights with good shelter and anchoring depths of 5-10 m (16-32 ft) can be found N and S of the gravel beach/delta that protrudes W, from the mainland shore.

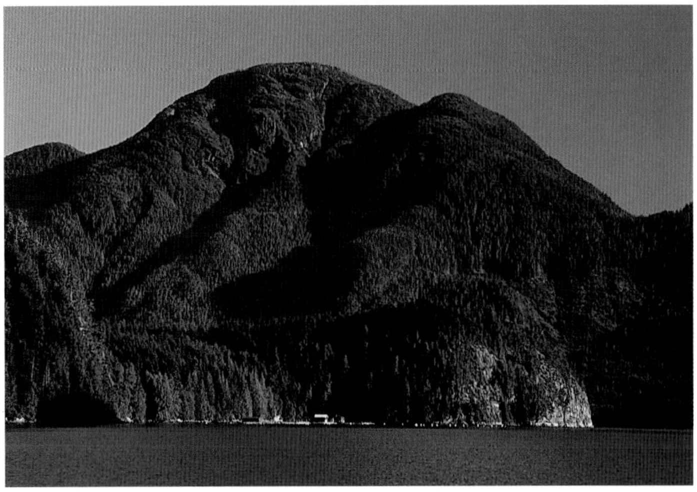

A fish-farming operation nestled under Steep Head

Nearing Knight Inlet, the waters of Tribune Channel and Sargeaunt Passage take on a muted, turquoise hue and we were enticed into the pass by a group of playful porpoises blowing at the entrance. Although Sargeaunt Passage is deep and steep-sided, it has the best anchorage in this area, providing a staging point for a trip up Knight Inlet to Glendale Cove. Once home to a large cannery in the early 1900s and logging operations until quite recently, all that remains is a float and logging road – if walking the pooch, let the bears know that you are around.

KNIGHT INLET, HOEYA HEAD TO GLENDALE COVE

CHARTS 3515.

APPROACH Although this portion of Knight Inlet is deep, straight and without obstruction, it is also notorious for dangerous sea conditions when the wind is against the current. Plan your trip with the wind and current in your favour.

Note: Shelter from the E can be found in Hoeya Sound, but the portion from E of Hoeya Head to Glendale Cove offers no shelter from either E or W winds.

❀(A) 50°40.47'N 126°01.51'W
❀(B) 50°41.42'N 125°44.10'W

With a strong westerly wind in our favour, we enjoyed an exhilarating sail up Knight Inlet, arriving in record time at Macdonald Point. The Lodge in Glendale Cove is private and has no facilities for visiting boats. If you wish to view bears feeding on the Glendale River estuary, please observe the international protocol and keep all human and wild animal stress levels to a minimum (see page 13).

Note: If a gale-force westerly or outflow wind is forecast, Glendale Cove is not the place to be! Knight Inlet can be as treacherous as Johnstone Strait in a wind-against-current situation.

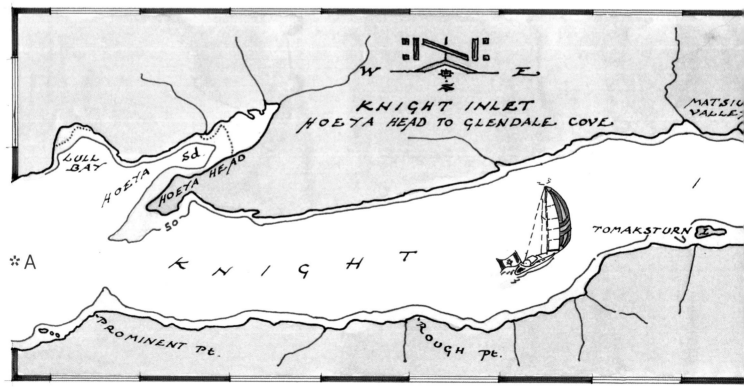

Not to scale. Not to be used for navigation.

GLENDALE COVE, KNIGHT INLET 14.4

CHARTS   3515.

APPROACH   From Knight Inlet, rounding Macdonald Point, head SE. Knight Inlet Lodge is highly conspicuous on the eastern shore.

ANCHOR   Glendale Cove is deep and shelves rapidly – the challenge is finding suitable anchoring depths. We anchored *Dreamspeaker* in the one-boat bight off the river's mouth, which shallows rapidly. There is moderate protection from the W and the anchorage is open to outflow winds. Holding is good in sand, on the 10 m (32 ft) contour.

Rounding Macdonald Point, Glendale Cove opens to the south

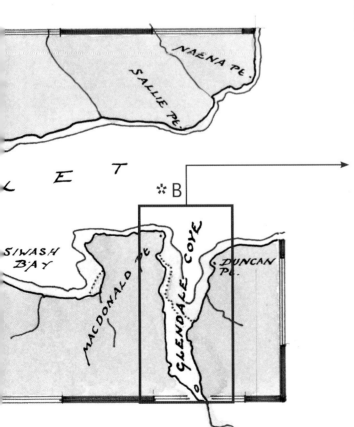

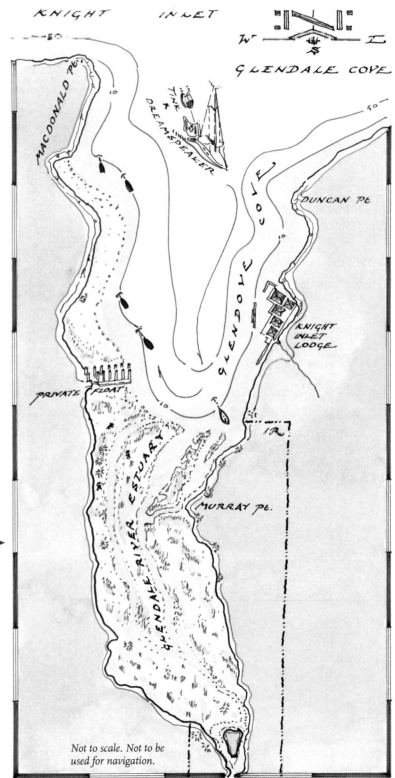

Not to scale. Not to be used for navigation.

14.5 THE BLOWHOLE TO LAGOON COVE

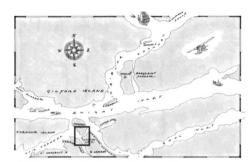

✤ (A) 50°36.80'N 126°18.15'W
✤ (B) 50°36.66'N 126°18.17'W
✤ (C) 50°36.23'N 126°19.49'W

CHART 3545.

APPROACH (A) Minstrel Island Public Wharf, from the E. In 2005 the resort was not in operation and the public wharf was unmanaged, but still available for moorage. (B) The Blowhole (a channel between Minstrel Island and East Cracroft Island). From the E out of Chatham Channel or from the W in Cleo Channel. The Blowhole is kelp-infested but regularly navigated by pleasure craft and small commercial vessels. Favour the Minstrel Island shore and stay N of the rock, as indicated. (C) Lagoon Cove,

East Cracroft Island. From the head of Cleo Channel between Perley and Farquharson Island. The run in is clear and free of obstructions.

ANCHOR In "Otters Cove" (our name), SE of The Blowhole. This anchorage provides moderate protection for 1-2 boats. Anchorage depths within Lagoon Cove are over 10 m (32 ft) plus and well protected. In settled weather moderate protection can be found at the head of the entrance to Cracroft Inlet in 6-8 m (19-26 ft). Both anchorages have good holding in mud.

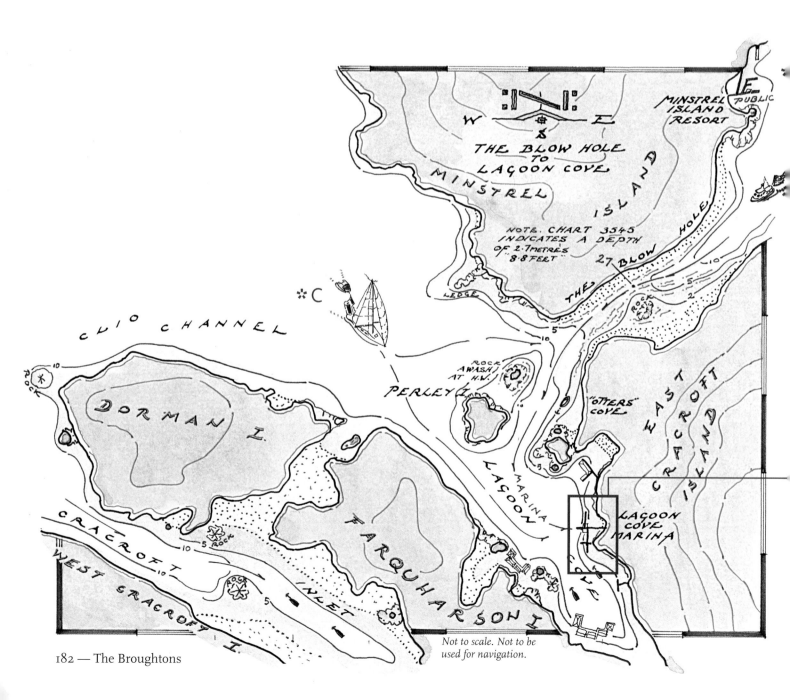

Not to scale. Not to be used for navigation.

Extensive moorage at Lagoon Cove Marina

CHART   3545.

APPROACH   The marina lies on the eastern shore. Groups of float homes are situated across from the marina and at the head of the cove.

MARINA   This well-maintained marina provides transient moorage, 15 and 30 amp power on the docks and a place to have fun. No reservation available, so plan to arrive early afternoon, as the marina fills up quickly. To ease moorage planning, call on VHF Channel 66A with your estimated arrival time. Access to the internet and a hot shower are possible when the generators are powered up.

FUEL DOCK   At the marina. Diesel and gas are available. Propane, ice, oil, charts and other small but important essentials can be obtained at the marina office.

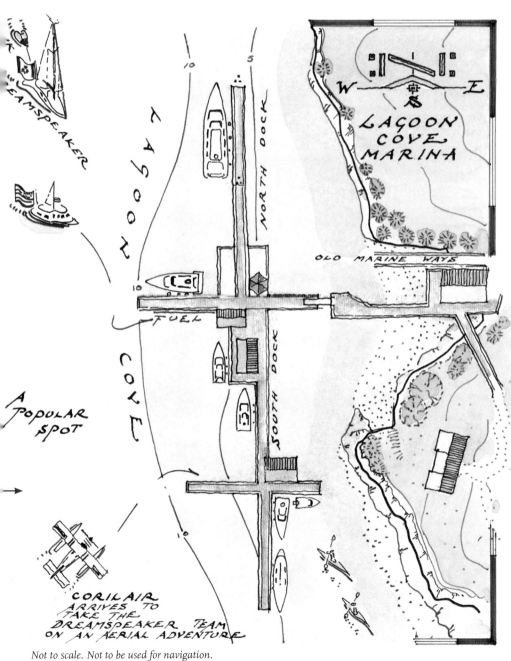

Not to scale. Not to be used for navigation.

The laid-back, friendly ambience, legendary *Happy Hour Bucket of Prawns* on the patio, have put Lagoon Cove Marina on The Broughtons' social cruising chart. Their cookbook is a must-have purchase if you plan to visit the other family marinas while cruising in the area (see page 188).

Bill and Jean have been successful in making their hospitable marina an extension of their own pleasant boating experiences – a kid-friendly place where they would love to tie up for a day or so, get off their boat and catch up with old friends or make new ones.

With the historic marina came an old marine ways, a workshop filled with marine artefacts and a small cottage surrounded by a variety of fruit trees and flowers. Many years of hard work, together with time and labour given by their loyal clients and friends, has made it possible for boating visitors to enjoy all the Barbers have to offer, including dog-friendly hiking trails through the forest. (Note that owners are responsible for their dogs at all times.)

Lagoon Cove Marina – Pop over to Vancouver Island or take a 'Broughtons' float plane adventure with friendly 'Corilair'

CHATHAM CHANNEL 14.7

CHART 3564 inset detail.

APPROACH (A) From the W aligning the boat to the easterly range (leading mark) off Ray Point. (B) From the E after rounding Root Point and off the port hand mark, aligning the boat to the westerly range (leading mark).

Note: Be aware that the E end of Chatham Channel is shallow and requires your boat to be kept on a straight and steady course. The strong, swift current of between 5-7 knots runs parallel to the East Cracroft shore on both the flood and the ebb tides. Although the channel is full of kelp the central pass is easily apparent.

⚜ (A) 50°35.00'N 126°14.73'W
⚜ (B) 50°34.73'N 126°12.31'W

Looking astern, west

COURTESY NOTE: *Do not overtake another boat while in the channel, whatever your speed; concentrate on lining up the markers. We ended our lovely Broughton cruise at Blind Channel Resort and found that Chatham Channel wasn't as restricted as it was rumoured.*

RANGE

ON

COURSE

IF

ALIGNED

Looking forward, east

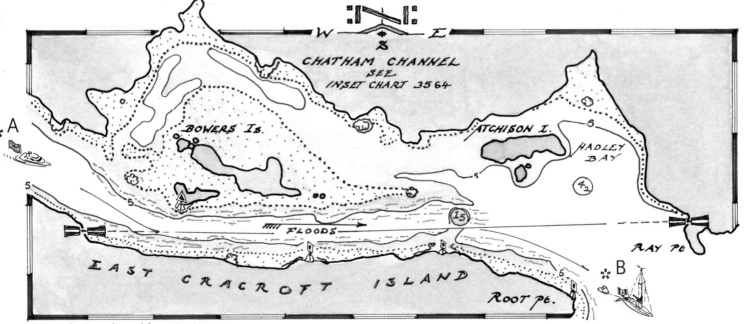

Not to scale. Not to be used for navigation.

Lone sailboat on the last of the evening wind approaches the entrance to Echo Bay

SELECTED READING
INDEX

SELECTED READING

Barber, Bill and Jean. *Lagoon Cove Marina. A Bit of History and a Book of Recipes.* Kearney, NE: Morris Press Cookbooks, 2004.

Baron, Nancy and John Acorn. *Birds of Coastal British Columbia.* Edmonton: Lone Pine Publishing, 1997.

BC Marine Parks Guide. 2nd Edition. Vancouver: OP Publishing, 2005.

Blanchet, M. Wylie. *The Curve of Time.* Sidney, BC: Gray's Publishing Ltd., 1977.

Campbell River Museum Society. *The Raincoast Kitchen. Coastal Cuisine with a Dash of History.* Madeira Park, BC: Harbour Publishing, 1997.

Chappell, John. *Cruising Beyond Desolation Sound. Channels and Anchorages from the Yuculta Rapids to Cape Caution.* Revised Edition: Surrey, BC. Naikoon Marine, 1987 (out of print 2006).

Clark, Lewis. *Wild Flowers of the Sea Coast in the Pacific Northwest.* Madeira Park, BC: Harbour Publishing, 2004.

Day, Beth. *Grizzlies in their Backyard.* Surrey, BC. Heritage House, 1994.

Douglass, Don and Reanne Hemingway-Douglass. *Exploring the South Coast of British Columbia. Gulf Islands and Desolation Sound to Port Hardy and Blunden Harbour.* Anacortes, WA: FineEdge.com. 2nd Edition, 1999.

Drushka, Ken. *Working in the Woods. A History of Logging on the West Coast.* Madeira Park, BC: Harbour Publishing, 1992.

Hadley, Michael. *God's Little Ships. A History of the Columbia Coast Mission.* Madeira Park, BC: Harbour Publishing, 1995.

Hale, Robert. *Waggoner Cruising Guide.* Bellevue, WA: Weatherly Press. Updated and Published Annually.

Harold, Hughina. *Totem Poles and Tea.* 2nd Edition. Surrey, BC: Heritage House, 2006.

Hoar, David and Noreen Rudd. *Cooks Afloat! Gourmet Cooking on the Move.* Madeira Park, BC: Harbour Publishing, 2001.

Hume, Stephen. *A Stain Upon the Sea: West Coast Salmon Farming.* Madeira Park, BC: Harbour Publishing, 2004.

Henry, Tom. *The Good Company. An Affectionate History of the Union Steamships.* Madeira Park, BC: Harbour Publishing, 1994.

Hill, Beth. *Guide to Indian Rock Carvings of the Pacific Northwest Coast.* Surrey, BC: Hancock House Publishers, 1984.

_____. *Upcoast Summers.* Ganges, BC. Nunaga Publishing, 1975.

Iglauer, Edith. *Fishing with John.* Madeira Park, BC: Harbour Publishing, 1992.

Kennedy, Liv. *Coastal Villages.* Madeira Park, BC: Harbour Publishing, 1991

Lowman Carey, Betty. *Bijaboji. North to Alaska by Oar.* Madeira Park, BC: Harbour Publishing, 2004.

McAllister, Ian and Karen. *The Great Bear Rainforest. Canada's Forgotten Coast.* Madeira Park, BC: Harbour Publishing, 1997.

McKerville, Hugh. *The Salmon People.* Sidney, BC: Gray's Publishing, 1967.

Morton, Alexandra. *Beyond the Whales. The Photographs and Passions of Alexandra Morton.* Victoria, BC: Touchwood Editions, 2004.

_____. *Listening to the Whales. What the Orcas Have Taught Us.* New York, NY, Ballantine Books, 2004.

Morton, Alexandra and Bill Proctor. *Heart of the Raincoast. A Life Story.* Victoria, BC: TouchWood Editions, 2005.

Pacific Yachting's *Marina Guide and Boater's Blue Pages: The Complete Guide to BC Marinas and Marine Services.* Magazine Supplement (January Issue), updated and published annually by *Pacific Yachting Magazine.*

Proctor, Bill and Yvonne Maximchuk. *Full Moon Flood Tide. Bill Proctor's Raincoast.* Madeira Park, BC: Harbour Publishing, 2003.

Spilsbury, Jim. *Spilsbury's Album. Photographs and Reminiscences of the BC Coast.* Madeira Park, BC: Harbour Publishing, 1990.

Thommasen, Harvey, and Kevin Huchings. *Birds of the Raincoast. Habits and Habitat.* Madeira Park, BC: Harbour Publishing, 2004.

Turner, Nancy J. *Food Plants of Coastal First Peoples.* Vancouver: UBC Press, 1995.

Vassilopoulos, Peter. *North of Desolation.* Sound Seagraphic Publications Limited, 2003.

Walbran, John T. *British Columbia Coast Names, 1592–1902.* Vancouver: Douglas & McIntyre, 1971.

Wastell Norris, Pat. *High Boats. A Century of Salmon Remembered.* Madeira Park, BC: Harbour Publishing, 2003.

White, Howard, and Jim Spilsbury. *Spilsbury's Coast. Pioneer Years in the Wet West.* Madeira Park, BC: Harbour Publishing, 1991.

_____. *The Accidental Airline.* Spilsbury's QCA. Madeira Park, BC: Harbour Publishing, 1994.

Wild, Paula. *Sointula. Island Utopia.* Madeira Park, BC: Harbour Publishing, 1995.

Williams, Judith. *Two Wolves at the Dawn of Time.* Kingcome Inlet Pictographs, 1893–1998. Vancouver BC: New Star Books, 2001.

_____. *Clam Gardens, Aboriginal Mariculture on Canada's West Coast.* Vancouver, BC: New Star Books, 2006.

Wood, Charles E. *Charlie's Charts – North to Alaska: Victoria BC to Glacier Bay, Alaska.* Surrey, BC: Charlie's Charts, 2003.

OTHER DREAMSPEAKER PRODUCTS

VOYAGE OF THE DREAMSPEAKER
Anne & Laurence Yeadon-Jones

Voyage of the Dreamspeaker is a personal record of three magical and balmy months from early July to late September when Anne and Laurence cruised the beautiful coast of BC aboard their sailboat Dreamspeaker, with Tink their faithful dingy in tow. Their voyage took them from the cosmopolitan city of Vancouver to the laid-back anchorages of Howe Sound, the delights of the Sunshine Coast, warm-water swimming in the lakes of Desolation Sound and the majesty of Toba Inlet. The authors had always dreamed of taking an unhurried journey with their Dreamspeaker guides in hand to revisit favourite haunts that they had discovered during their fifteen years of adventuring and recording. This personal cruising companion will also give readers a special insight into a number of new experiences that Anne has smoothly interwoven with stories and discoveries from earlier journeys among the islands and along a coastline that they have grown to love. This coast has won their hearts.

Voyage of the Dreamspeaker is published by Harbour Publishing at www.harbourpublishing.com and distributed in the US by Fine Edge www.fineedge.com. Personalized books and guides are also available from the authors' web site at www.dreamspeaker.ca.

A DREAMSPEAKER DESTINATIONS DVD
Anne & Laurence Yeadon-Jones

A Dreamspeaker Cruising Guide authors Anne and Laurence Yeadon-Jones have added A Dreamspeaker Destinations DVD titled COASTAL MAGIC to their series of colourful and informative guides.

With Anne and Laurence as your hosts, this scenic DVD takes you on a 5-day dream cruise from the city of Vancouver, up the Sunshine Coast to Jervis Inlet and magical Princess Louisa Marine Park, backed by the powerful beauty of Chatterbox Falls.

The 5-day cruising itinerary includes the author's favourite anchorages and marinas en route to Princess Louisa Inlet: Snug Cove on Bowen Island, colourful Gibsons Landing, Halfmoon Bay, Simson Marine Park and the white sand beaches of Buccaneer Bay, popular Smuggler Cove Marine Park, Secret Cove and historic Pender Harbour.

A Dreamspeaker Destinations DVD – COASTAL MAGIC – is available worldwide at www.dreamspeaker.ca

INDEX

THE DREAMSPEAKER SERIES

BY ANNE & LAURENCE YEADON-JONES

A COMPREHENSIVE SET OF CRUISING GUIDES TO THE COASTAL WATERS OF THE PACIFIC NORTHWEST

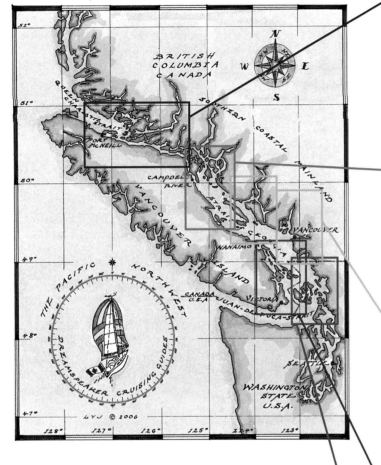

VOLUME 5
The Broughtons
– Vancouver Island, Kelsey Bay to Port Hardy
(available May 2006)

VOLUME 2
Desolation Sound & the Discovery Islands

VOLUME 3
Vancouver, Howe Sound & the Sunshine Coast
– Princess Louisa Inlet and Jedediah Island

Each volume is a colourful, illustrated cruising companion full of charts, data, tips and visitor information, and features more than 100 beautifully hand-drawn maps of public wharfs, marinas and small boat anchorages, including both popular and little-known highlights. You'll find everything from safe all-weather havens to secluded picnic spots and marine parks.

VOLUME 1
Gulf Islands & Vancouver Island
– Victoria & Sooke to Nanaimo

VOLUME 4
The San Juan Islands